PRAISE FOR
The Word According to Eve

"In a brilliant survey of the work of women scholars in biblical studies, Murphy provides one of the finest and most comprehensive introductions...A must read for anyone wishing to understand the goals and the results of contemporary feminist biblical criticism."

—*Publishers Weekly*

"A sharp, smart, eye-opening book, completely free from polemic ...a fascinating synthesis."

—Peter Kurth, *Salon*

"Were Elizabeth Cady Stanton alive now...she could not but rejoice at seeing women storm the bastion of biblical scholarship."

—John Updike, *The New Yorker*

"At the moment when *Time* magazine's cover asks, 'Is feminism dead?' comes this exceptional overview of feminist scholarship in biblical studies."

—*Library Journal*

"Readable, serious, humorous, thoroughly intelligent...Cullen Murphy stands shoulder to shoulder with the feminist biblical scholars he discusses, getting his facts and his nuances beautifully right."

—Alicia Ostriker, author of
Feminist Revision and the Bible

"Highly engaging and readable...generous in spirit and open-minded."

—Sara Maitland, *Commonweal*

THE WORD
ACCORDING
TO EVE

BOOKS BY CULLEN MURPHY

Rubbish! The Archaeology of Garbage
(with William L. Rathje)

Just Curious: Essays

The Word According to Eve:
Women and the Bible in Ancient Times and Our Own

THE WORD ACCORDING TO EVE

WOMEN AND THE BIBLE IN ANCIENT TIMES AND OUR OWN

Cullen Murphy

Foreword by Karen Armstrong

A PETER DAVISON BOOK

A Mariner Book

Houghton Mifflin Company

Boston   New York

First Mariner Books edition 1999
Foreword copyright © 1999 by Karen Armstrong
Copyright © 1998 by Cullen Murphy

For information about permission to reproduce selections from
this book, write to Permissions, Houghton Mifflin Company,
215 Park Avenue South, New York, New York 10003.

Library of Congress Cataloging-in-Publication Data

Murphy, Cullen.
The Word according to Eve : women and the Bible
in ancient times and our own / Cullen Murphy.
p.   cm.
"A Peter Davison book."
Includes bibliographical references and index.
ISBN 0-395-70113-9
ISBN 0-618-00192-1 (pbk)
1. Bible and feminism. I. Title.
BS680.W7M87   1998   220.8'3054—dc21
98-18015   CIP

Book design by Anne Chalmers
Typeface: Linotype-Hell Electra (W. A. Dwiggins)

Printed in the United States of America

QUM 10 9 8 7 6 5 4 3 2 1

FOR

Anna Jane Murphy

Anna Marie Murphy

Joan Byrne Murphy

Mary Bodnar Torres

"THESE ARE THE GENERATIONS..."
— *Genesis* 10:1

CONTENTS

Foreword

Karen Armstrong

THE SCORN DIRECTED AGAINST the practitioners of "political correctness" is understandable: at its worst and most unintelligent, political correctness undoubtedly breeds a self-righteousness that is unattractive and often ludicrous in its desire to avoid calling a spade a spade. But the caricaturing of political correctness also reflects a lost opportunity. The project as, perhaps, originally conceived could have been used creatively to make ourselves aware of ingrained prejudices and to revise the habits of the heart. One of the most crucial areas in which political correctness has in fact made a difference is the question of gender. Every time we find ourselves tempted to speak of "mankind," we realize how ubiquitous and inherent is our tendency to see the male of the species as normative. If the more inclusive substitutes, such as "humanity" or "persons," seem artificial and unnatural, we should use this unease to make ourselves acknowledge how deeply these sexist attitudes have penetrated the language and our modes of thought. The discipline of avoiding the old exclusive terminology and opting for the newer terms—however awkward —is a way of reeducating ourselves at a level that is deeper than the rational and the cerebral but which is the seat of these irrational and emotional prejudices. As a theologian, constantly required to speak about God, I still find myself after many years of effort wanting to call the deity "He," even though I know that this is theologically as well as politically incorrect. But I have also found that as I struggle to find an adequate substitute and fail (neither "She" nor "It" is truly satisfactory), I acquire in the process a fresh insight into the difficulty of speaking about the divine at all. Each time I encounter this problem, I find, therefore, that I have gained a new appreciation of the important truth that any discourse about the sacred stumbles under insuperable difficulties.

The feminist revolution has been one of the most significant developments of the late twentieth century. It has not only affected relationships between the sexes but has also influenced the social, political, and economic spheres at every level. It has also had an impact in theology. People have become aware of the sad fact that none of the major world faiths has been wholly good for women. Even though the founders of the religion may have had a positive message for women, men quickly hijacked the faith and made it endorse the old patriarchy. As a result, women have been marginalized religiously in a way that often runs counter to some of the deepest imperatives of a given tradition, by violating such principles as equality and compassion.

It is, perhaps, because men have sensed at some buried level that this oppression and denigration have been wrong and even sinful that this misogyny has been so virulent. The very violence of their chauvinism reflects a hidden worry about their behavior. In the Christian tradition, for example, women have not merely been regarded as inferior; they have been associated with evil. "Do you not know that you are each an Eve?" the third-century historian Tertullian demanded of the pious women in Carthage:

> You are the devil's gateway; you are the first unsealer of that forbidden tree; you are the first deserter of the divine law; . . . you destroyed so easily God's image, man. Because of you the Son of God had to die
>
> (*On Female Dress* I:1)

Saint Jerome (c. 342–420) told his disciples to have nothing to do with women; not only was marriage disgusting and sinful, but women should be relegated to a separate sphere. Priests should not minister to women, even if they were sick or in trouble. A woman's malign influence was too dangerous for most men to withstand. Saint Augustine of Hippo (354–430) had a very saintly mother and he was well aware that she had been largely responsible for his conversion to Christianity. Yet he did not feel it incongruous to write to one of his male friends: "What is the difference whether it is in a wife or a mother; it is still Eve the temptress that we must beware of in any woman" (Letter 243:10). Augustine can be called the founder of Western Christianity. When the Protestant reformers turned back to his teachings, they revived his misogyny along with his doctrine of grace. Thus it was Martin Luther (1483–1546) who coined the phrase that a woman's place was in the home. She was to be segregated from public life as a punishment for her inherent sinfulness:

> The rule remains with the husband, and the wife is compelled to obey him by God's command. He rules the home and the state, wages war, defends his possessions, tills the soil, builds, plants, etc. The woman, on the other hand, is like a nail driven into a wall. She sits at home . . . the wife should stay at home and look after the affairs of the household as one who has been deprived of the ability of administering those affairs that are outside and concern the state . . . In this way Eve is punished.
>
> (*Lectures on Genesis* 3:11)

From an early stage, therefore, Christian men were taught to project their own guilt and consciousness of sin on to woman, who, as "Eve," who was the first to succumb to Satan and eat the forbidden fruit, was to blame for the problem of evil. Even though Saint Paul, the earliest Christian writer, had declared in his manifesto that in Christ there was neither male nor female (Galatians 3:28), it did not take Christians long to lay aside this egalitarian vision. As a result, Christians have found it difficult to associate women with the sacred—an attitude that has persisted in our own time, as became evident during the acrimonious debates in the Church of England concerning the ordination of women to the priesthood.

Christians have not been alone in belittling and marginalizing women. Even though Jewish law protects the rights of women, some of the rabbis whose views are recorded in the Talmud spoke of the "second sex" with contempt and disdain: "A woman is a pitcher of filth, yet all run after her" (Shabbat 152a); "Women are greedy, eavesdroppers, lazy and envious" (Nedarim 31b). Women, we are told, were separated from men in the Jerusalem Temple because their presence could lead to an atmosphere of frivolity (Middot 2:5). Indeed, Jewish feminists argue that women are accorded the status of peripheral Jews in Jewish law, on a par with children and Canaanite slaves. Their Judaism is characterized by negation rather than by affirmation: they must not violate the Sabbath, eat nonkosher food, steal, murder, or commit adultery. But they are not obliged to perform the positive commandments, which bring the sacred into the life of a male Jew on a daily, hourly basis, such as studying Torah, praying the three daily services, or hearing the shofar on New Year's Day. Women's testimony is invalid in a Jewish court (Shavuoth 30a; Rosh Hashanah 22a), and they are excluded from the minyan, the quorum that is necessary for prayer and which is the basic unit of the Jewish community. The implication is that women are expendable, mere adjuncts of the community, their presence inessential for many of the core religious experiences of male Jews.

One of the reasons for this exclusion of women from the realm of the sacred is that the Judeo-Christian God has been conceived in such strongly masculine terms. The deity of the early books of the Hebrew Bible was irredeemably male: he was a god of war, connected with volcanic eruptions and violent acts. Only later, when the prophets of the eighth, seventh, and sixth centuries B.C.E. began to reform the ancient religion of Israel and create what would eventually be known as Judaism did this belligerent deity become a symbol of absolute transcendence, which went beyond all human categories, including that of gender. YHWH was sometimes given feminine traits, but even so, the predominantly masculine imagery persisted and most Jews, including Jesus, who referred to God as his Father, continued to assume that their God was a male person. Christians had an added problem, since their doctrine of incarnation taught that when God decided to take human flesh he chose a male body. This created special difficulties for the ordination of women. Since a priest is supposed to represent Christ to the people, it was argued that a woman could not adequately perform this function.

In fact, a priesthood that includes women is in this respect more theologically correct than an exclusively masculine one, since, according to one of the Creation accounts in the Bible, the sight of a man and a woman standing together at the altar will remind the faithful that both male and female human beings were created in God's image (Genesis 1:27). The slight frisson of shock or unfamiliarity that the spectacle of a woman priest often inspires should also be a salutary warning that all our notions of the divine must constantly be challenged and revised. No one human conception of God can ever be adequate. We need continuously to be reminded of this fact lest we bow down before an idol, created in our own image and likeness. The overtly male God of Judaism and Christianity is certainly no more than an idol if it inspires, as it has so frequently inspired, the exclusion of women from the most sacred offices, institutions, and practices of monotheistic religion.

Jews, Christians, and Muslims have long been conscious of this theological imbalance in favor of the masculine. Over the centuries, they have devised ways of correcting this. Thus Christians created the cult of the Virgin Mary, though, as we see in these pages, the image of the virgin mother has sometimes been problematic for women, who feel that it negates female sexuality. It is interesting that devotion to the Virgin Mary was initially developed in Europe during the twelfth century, when Christians were engaged in the Crusades: imagery of the macho God who demanded that the soldiers of Christ kill and maim the enemies of the faith was countered by the gentler image of Mary. "O clement, O loving, O sweet Virgin Mary" is the concluding line of the hymn "Salve Regina," which is traditionally ascribed to Adhémar, bishop of Le Puy, and Saint Bernard of Clairvaux, both of whom were deeply involved in the crusading enterprise. It is as though they deliberately invoked a divine tenderness that was so clearly missing from the terrifying God of the Crusaders. All over Western Europe, the great cathedrals, which were often dedicated to Mary, began to be built almost as a counter-Crusade. They demonstrated that it was possible to create holy places at home and that Jerusalem, which required the slaying of the infidel, was not the only sacred place in the Christian world.

Jews went even further than Christians by introducing a female element into God itself. In the Kabbalah, the Jewish mystical tradition, the Shekhinah (the divine presence on earth) is seen as feminine. In the sixteenth century, Kabbalists imagined the Shekhinah wandering in exile from the divine sphere, just as Jews lived in exile from their holy land in the Diaspora. They also imagined a future reunion of the Shekhinah with the Godhead as marking the apotheosis of history and an end to suffering and exile here below. Some Kabbalists in Jerusalem and Safed used to enact this mystical marriage of the Shekhinah on the Sabbath — going out into the fields to greet the divine bride, escorting her back to the city, and finally taking her into their own homes, where the dining room was decked with myrtle, like a wedding canopy. It was a ritual that induced hope by looking forward to the final Return of all things to the Source of being and one which powerfully reminded Jews that the divine could not be conceived in strictly masculine terms. Other Kabbalists reverently imagined other female aspects of the divine, which were employed in *ziwwug* (copulation) with their male counterparts. Again, this mating of the male and female elements within God symbolized a restoration of order. The Kabbalists constantly warned their disciples not to take all this literally. This was a fiction, designed to suggest a process of integration that could not be expressed in logical, rational terms and which also neutralized the overwhelmingly masculine imagery of the sacred.

The God of the Koran is envisaged in less personalized terms than the God of the Bible, so the question of theological gender is less pronounced. Indeed, some of the ninety-nine Divine Names attributed to God in the Koran have a distinctly female connotation. This is most strikingly evident in the *bismallah*, the invocation that precedes every recitation of the Koran: "In the name of God (*al-Lah*), the Compassionate (*al-Rahman*), the Merciful (*al-Rahim*)." In Arabic, *al-Lah* is grammatically masculine, but *al-Rahman* and *al-Rahim* are related etymologically to the word for "womb." Thus every time they hear their holy book read aloud or peruse it in private, Muslims are presented with a counterpoint, which juxtaposes the masculine and the feminine God.

Western people often assume that Islam is inherently misogynistic, but this is a misapprehension. The Prophet Muhammad was a man who loved and sought out the company of women; their emancipation was a project dear to his heart, and women were among the earliest converts to Islam. The Koran gives women rights of inheritance and divorce that their sisters in Christian Europe would not receive until the nineteenth century. There is nothing in the Koran to prescribe the veiling of all women or their seclusion in harems. These were practices that did not appear in the Islamic world until two or three generations after the Prophet, when Muslims copied the lifestyles of the Christians of Byzantium who had long veiled and secluded their women. Like the Christians, however, Muslims abandoned this early positive attitude and reverted to the old patriarchy. But even so, Islamic mystics and theologians sometimes imagined the divine feminine. In Shiite Islam, the figure of Fatima, the Prophet's daughter, attained cosmic status: she became the Muslim equivalent of Divine Wisdom, or Sophia. In the Sunni world, the highly influential twelfth-century philosopher Muid ad-Din Ibn al-Arabi saw the divine incarnated in a woman he saw during the *hajj* pilgrimage to Mecca; he wrote a series of impassioned poems to Nizam, the woman who had become a manifestation of God for him, in rather the same way as Beatrice Portinari would be for Dante. Ibn al-Arabi also taught that for men the female was a specially potent symbol of the divine, since it evoked in them a love that was ultimately directed to God, who was revealed in all creatures.

All this shows that religions change and develop over centuries. People feel free to innovate, to use their creative imaginations. Indeed, Ibn al-Arabi and other Muslim philosophers believed that the way to God led through the creative imagination. The great religions did not descend from heaven ready-made, nor were they cast in stone for all time. In each generation, people have to make an imaginative effort to make their tradition speak to their own unique circumstances. Today, however, many religious people find this idea disturbing. They often assume that men and women have always believed in and lived their faith in exactly the same way, and that there have been no further changes. Their duty is to go back to basics, remain true to what they perceive to be an unbroken tradition, and hold on to a timeless truth in spite of the blasphemous innovations that some of their coreligionists are introducing.

This present age is a time of particular religious transformation and ferment. We have seen incredible changes in the course of the twentieth century and now inhabit a world that would have been inconceivable to the men and women whose stories are recounted in the Bible. We can even see the earth from outer space—a symbol of an unprecedented change of perspective. Inevitably, this has meant a corresponding change in our religious ideas. Religion can be defined as the creative attempt to find ultimate meaning and value in the frequently tragic and seemingly senseless world in which we live. As our circumstances change, so too will the meaning we discover in our lives. For Jews and Christians, this will mean that they will read their Bible in a different way. They will find meanings there that no other generation has discovered. The miracle of a scripture is not that it was revealed by God at one moment of historical time—to Moses, to the prophets, to Paul or Muhammad. The miracle is rather that these ancient texts have for centuries been able to illuminate the lives of people living in conditions that the biblical writers themselves would never have been able to envisage. This requires inspiration on the part of the reader—not just on the part of the original authors.

The traditional ideas of God and religion have been challenged on several fronts during the late twentieth century. Science has made the literalistic reading of Genesis—itself a modern development—increasingly problematic. Cosmologists claim that there is no room for God in the universe they are discovering. The problem of evil has become especially acute: as we have witnessed suffering in Auschwitz, Bosnia, or Rwanda, it has become more and more difficult for many people to square this with the conventional ideas of providence and of a wholly benevolent, omnipotent God. New theologies are being devised to deal with these difficulties. A similar challenge has come from the feminist movement. Men and women have become sensitized in a new way to the exploitation, marginalization, and denigration of women in society. Women are beginning to enjoy a new equality, and this will drastically change both their view of the world and the world-view of men. This means that they cannot see the inequality and prejudice that has sometimes been sanctioned by religion in the same way as their grandparents did. Many realize that they will have to refashion a new religious identity, and to do that they will have to go back to the Bible.

Cullen Murphy has likened this feminist revolution in theology to the Reformation of the sixteenth century, another period of major change that made the old religious ideas of the Middle Ages seem inadequate and ineffectual to Protestants and Catholics alike. In order to be healthy, a new identity must be rooted in the old; there must be a life-giving continuity with the past rather than an ugly severance, and that is why the Protestant reformers went back to the Bible with such zeal. Even though they claimed to be rediscovering the faith of the Primitive Church, their reading of the Bible was essentially a sixteenth-century hermeneutic—it was steeped thoroughly and inevitably in the early modern ethos. That is why people found it so compelling.

The theologians and biblical scholars whom Murphy has sought out and interviewed are reading the Bible from the perspective of the late twentieth century and asking questions that other generations might not have asked. Is Eve really to blame for the fall of humanity? Is woman created from the rib of man (*'adham*) as an afterthought or as the culmination and perfection of the creative process? Were some of the books of the Bible actually written by women? Was Jesus a feminist? Were there women priests in the early church? They have come up with some surprising and challenging answers. Sometimes they disagree with one another, but that should cause no concern. These scholars are trying to reshape the religious world they have inherited and are confronting texts that for too long have been read from a chauvinist and even a misogynist perspective. True, the Bible does reflect a patriarchal world-view, but it is by no means as negative about women as such theologians as Tertullian or Augustine assumed. A great deal of this new hermeneutic does not filter down to the people in the pews; much of the work of these scholars is difficult and written for other scholars. Murphy has performed the valuable task of making some of their ideas accessible to the general reader.

In addition to recounting their ideas, Murphy has given us a biographical background, tracing the spiritual and intellectual paths that led each of these writers to their present vision of the Bible. The stories of the women scholars are strikingly similar: when they first became interested in biblical studies, there were virtually no women on the theology faculties and there was decidedly no interest in women's issues. Women such as Phyllis Trible or Elisabeth Schüssler Fiorenza were pioneers, venturing into new biblical and religious territory. Because of their work, there are an ever-increasing number of women in the field today, just as more women than ever before are preaching in synagogues and churches. For the first time in religious history, women are making their voices heard on a wide scale. This in itself will transform the religious vision of the next century.

Many believers—men and women—will disagree vehemently with these scholars' interpretations of scripture. They will cite the biblical texts Murphy lists on pages 14 and 15 that seem to give a divine seal of absolute approval to the subordination of women. But the Bible does not speak in one voice nor issue a single message. The work of the scholars discussed in these pages reveals the complexity of the biblical text, the layers of meaning and the ambiguities that have made it a source of inspiration and a bridge to the divine for so long. Had the Bible not had this flexibility and capacity for multiple interpretation, it would not have been able to speak to the condition of so many people in such varied circumstances over the centuries. But the religious problem of gender cannot be solved by citing this or that particular text. These issues evoke deep-seated anxieties, fears, and emotions that lie beyond the reach of rational discourse and argument. What is needed is to educate the heart, and, given the centuries of misogyny and prejudice, this will take a long time.

All the world religions agree that the one acid test of any theology, any spirituality, is that it leads the faithful to the practice of compassion and to the recognition of the sacred in others. A theology that has led to the denigration, exploitation, and oppression of half the human race for so long cannot pass this test. If the religions are truly to bring enlightenment to the whole of humanity, the problems arising from gender must be urgently addressed. That is why this is an important book.

THE WRITING
ON THE WALL

THE BIBLE IN MY HOME, our family Bible, was bought by my great-great-grandfather, Robert Murphy, nearly a hundred and fifty years ago. The first words written in it record his marriage, on June 9, 1852, to Ellen Costello, in Clifton, New York. The book is in remarkably fine condition, as only very old items can be, and the very dignity of its aging—the gentle foxing of the paper; the velvet dustiness of the leather; the mild pungency of the aroma, like that of sandalwood—lends to it an aura of timeless comfort.

This is the kind of Bible that comes to mind when we think of the words "the good book." It is the kind of Bible that we want for graveside obsequies and for swearings-in, the kind from which we expect to hear nondenominational intonations of "The Lord is my shepherd" and "Blessed are the pure in heart" and "Love thy neighbor as thyself," and whose prose may be savored for its expressive economy and its lapidary beauty. This family Bible is, as much as anything else, an artifact, a symbol of our civilization. As a physical object alone it can exert an emotional power quite distinct from what the words inside it may convey.

And then, of course, there are the words. It is a truism that those parts of the Bible which are most frequently encountered, and most readily apprehended, through the medium of Jewish or Christian religious rituals provide only a wan version of the Hebrew Bible and the New Testament as a whole, and only the dimmest sense of the Bible's volatility and intensity: the swiftness of its judgments, the peremptoriness of its anger, the cold purposefulness of its attention span, the impatience of its disdain for euphemism.[1] Although the Bible offers transcendent moments of prayer and parable, psalm and song, myth and revelation, it is also a document that cannot fail to register in the minds of modern readers as profoundly alien, the product of a world and of sensibilities that in many ways are manifestly not our own.

This is nowhere more the case than with regard to women.

The Bible is famous for being the world's most overstudied book— overstudied by male scholars and commentators, that is to say. It has not, however, been overstudied by women. Indeed, until recently, it was studied by female scholars hardly at all, let alone by female scholars who were interested specifically in what the Bible had to say *about* women. This has changed, to put it mildly, owing in large measure to the influx of women into fields of study from which they once were virtually absent and effectively barred. Today the Bible is being confronted not only by women who are theologians, who bring to the task an overtly religious perspective, but also, and more pertinently from the point of view of this book, by women who are biblical scholars, linguists, historians, archaeologists, and literary critics. The research of this latter group by now covers just about every conceivable aspect of the Hebrew Bible and the New Testament, from religious law and leadership to the economics of household life, from women exploited as servants and slaves to women exalted as prophets and queens, from the most brutal depictions of rape and murder to the most sublime seductions of romantic love.

These scholars are posing questions such as the following: In the inhospitable and tribalized world of early Israel, could women have been central and authoritative figures, despite the contrary picture usually painted by the Bible? Do certain passages in the Bible, together with the evidence of archaeology, preserve traces of what may have been a more egalitarian social regime than we might have imagined? Does the theology of the creation stories really mean that woman must be considered subordinate to man, as centuries of interpretation would have us believe? Might it even be incorrect to think of the first human being, Adam, as a male? How and where did women exercise the role of prophet, and what did exercising that role signify? In the New Testament, can the case be made that some of the female disciples of Jesus occupied a leadership status equal to that of the male disciples? If they did, how did their status come to be played down? Was feminine religious imagery more pervasive in early Christian times than we have tended to acknowledge? Can we ever know whether parts of the Hebrew Bible or New Testament were written by women?

I once asked David Tracy, the prominent Catholic theologian, what he thought would be the result of feminism's encounter with religion, and he said simply, "The next intellectual revolution."

In the course of its existence, which covers the larger part of three millennia, the Bible has been implicated in four intellectual revolutions of enduring and civilization-shaping consequence. The initial revolution is the one that gave impetus to the Bible in the first place, the formation of an intertwined people and book that set the Israelites apart from the rest of the ancient world in their conception of human character and destiny in the eyes of a unitary, indivisible God. The second revolution occurred within Jewish religion and produced what would come to be called Christianity, along with an additional set of texts, the New Testament, with its organic connections to the Hebrew Bible. The third revolution occurred within Christianity during the Reformation, and its manifold consequences included, for some believers, an exaltation of Scripture's authority and also broader access to the very words of Scripture, in the form of printed Bibles that the faithful could read in their own languages, fostering literacy throughout the Western world. The fourth revolution, under way since the Enlightenment, was instigated by advances in scientific discovery and historical investigation that offered Reason to counter the Bible's authority as an explanatory or descriptive text and therefore perhaps also its authority as a prescriptive one.

Is feminism truly the Bible's fifth intellectual revolution? That assessment may sound overblown, but in all likelihood it is not. Feminism's larger conversation with religion, brought about both by issues of faith and by issues that know no faith, touches every aspect of it, leaves no subject off the table. Feminism engages doctrine, liturgy, ministry, and leadership, and it engages them all at once.

There is obviously no single "canonical" version of feminism—the movement fractures and calves with an enthusiasm reminiscent of the left in the 1930s, and with the same sense of injury and righteousness and the same level of noise—and thus there is no single take on the Bible or any of its parts by scholars who look at biblical issues from a feminist perspective. Some are historians of a purely secular bent, who seem to care little for religion considered on its own terms but who are seized by the idea of women and religion as a historical reality and an intellectual problem. They want to understand how women in the Christian and Jewish traditions came to be consigned to an inferior status—one thinks of Thomas Aquinas's definition of woman as *mas occasionatus*, a "missed opportunity" for creating a male. (Or consider this entry from the edition of the *Encyclopedia Britannica* currently in print: "EVE: *see* Adam and Eve.") Some are theologians, or aspire to be theologians, whose religious impulses must be taken into account as an element of any inquiry. Some, surely, have other kinds of very personal issues at stake, such as the wish to carve out political and theological space for churchly advancement, say, or for the expression of sexual intimacy.

Phyllis Trible, one of the first biblical scholars whose work has been informed by feminism, uses an image from the Bible that would find emotional resonance among many and perhaps most scholars in this field, whatever their differences in method or outlook. Jacob, the son of Isaac and Rebekah and long an inhabitant of Mesopotamia, is described in the book of Genesis (32:22–32) as returning with his two wives and his eleven children to the land of his fathers. They have reached a ford at the River Jabbok, an eastern tributary of the Jordan, and Jacob sends everyone else across. That night, alone, he is accosted by a mysterious visitor—is it God?—with whom he wrestles until daybreak. Jacob's hip is put out of its joint, but he presses on. At last the night visitor asks Jacob to desist, and Jacob replies, "I will not let go unless you bless me." A few lines later the text reports: "And there he blessed him." With his bad leg, Jacob then continues on his journey.

The Bible too is an inscrutable and sometimes antagonistic visitor, Trible has said. Only wrestling with it offers hope of a blessing. And even then you may find yourself walking away with a limp.[2]

This book is not a work of theology. It is a work of reporting, about living people and the scholarship they do, the periods of history they encounter, the evidence they marshal, the insights they venture, and the distinctive, even peculiar academic culture they inhabit. There is no breast-beating in these pages, nor self-laceration, nor searches for the sacred feminine or the inner goddess, at least not on the part of the observer.

A word about that observer: I have written frequently about issues of religion in the pages of *The Atlantic Monthly*, drawn in part by religion's obvious significance as a cultural force but also by the large, ineffable questions at any religion's core, which perhaps at some level intrigue and haunt us all. I am male, Roman Catholic, married, and a parent, unembittered by the sting of personal grievance or the lash of impersonal oppression. I came to the subject of this book impelled by curiosity, not rage. But I frankly share the essential motivations of many of those whose work is discussed, and I share their perception of the Bible as a collection of historically conditioned books that are fully open to modern critical study. I do not claim to be a disinterested party.

A few years ago I wrote an essay in *The Atlantic* on the subject of women and the Bible, and it concluded as follows: "I write these last words on the day of my daughter's first communion in a denomination that still restricts the role of women, and I write them in the expectation that with regard to the position of women, matters will not remain—will simply not be able to remain—as in some places we see them now; in the expectation, to employ a biblical turn, that the present way's days are numbered."[3] The reference, of course, was to the story of the writing on the wall, in chapter five of the Book of Daniel—the writing, traced by a moving finger upon the plaster, that embodies a judgment and a sentence and foretells a course that is imminent and inevitable.

On a host of matters involving women and the Bible, the writing on the wall is there to be read. And more and more of it appears with every passing day.

THE WORD
ACCORDING
TO EVE

Chapter One

....

JOINING THE
PROCESSION

*Wherever the gospel is preached in the whole world,
what she has done will be told in memory of her.*
— Mark 14:9

*By God, if women had but written stories,
As have these clerks within their oratories . . .*
— *Chaucer, prologue, "The Wife of Bath's Tale"*

IF YOU HAPPEN to be an outsider looking in, you will have no difficulty finding occasions to feel like one at the annual joint meeting of the American Academy of Religion and the Society of Biblical Literature, which is the most important regular gathering of religion scholars and theologians in this country and probably in the world. I have attended this meeting for a number of years, and its rhythms and atmosphere are by now familiar. The season is always late autumn, the location always one of America's prime convention-center cities. The number of participants is always upwards of seven thousand, and with experience you can develop and indulge a taste for theodemographics — that is, for sight-sorting people into one of several archetypal categories. The categories are valid, even if your particular selection in any instance may not be: the bearded Ivy Leaguer with tenure; the nun in mufti; the Talmudic scholar; the evangelical publisher; the jobless supplicant; the thwarted but undaunted idealist; the seekers after validation for various lifestyles and orientations. A fat "program book" will have been provided in advance, its several hundred pages filled with a rich, conflicting schedule of papers to be presented, seminars to be convened, lectures to be delivered, caucuses to be endured — a dozen events an hour over a period of four days. Like a diner after a smorgasbord, you come away with sensations of both satiety and missed opportunity, and also, frankly, regret at some of the choices not forgone.

You also come away with a number of vivid impressions. The first has to do with what a vast enterprise the scholarly embrace of religion has come to be. A stroll through the exhibition hall takes you past the elaborate displays of hundreds of religious booksellers and software and database vendors. Some of the offerings are as strangely inviting as they are prohibitively inaccessible. A mail-order coupon from a Belgian publisher: "YES, I want to order the 3 volumes of *Novus Thesaurus Philologico-Criticus: sive lexicon in LXX et reliquos Interpretes Graecos ac Scriptores Apocryphos Veteris Testamenti.*" (Visa and MasterCard accepted.) At one booth I picked up a brochure from the publishers Chadwyck-Healey advertising the *Patrologia Latina Database on CD-ROM*, which can be obtained for $45,000. Evangelical publishing companies occupy a vast portion of the religious market, and when you have concluded your business at one of their booths, a representative will probably say, "It was good to visit with you" instead of "It was nice to meet you." Just about everything related to the Hebrew Bible, the New Testament, and other ancient materials is now available on electronic databases in whatever language and script you want. A salesperson may be talking about "hotspot links" and "zooming" and "search capabilities" when what you are looking at on the screen is a manuscript fragment from the famous cache found in 1947 at Qumran, on the Dead Sea. The experience gives the idea of "scrolling" a whole new dimension.

A second impression is that this gathering of scholars is a distinctive community, whatever may be the individual disparities in interests and outlook. That characteristic comes through most obviously in the way people communicate — in scriptural shorthand. Why make a wordy reference to "the story of Jesus and the Pharisees and the issue of sharing a meal with the tax collectors" when you can simply say "Matthew 9:10–13" and be confident that everyone will know what you mean? Why take up time relating the story of Adam and Eve and the serpent when "Genesis 3:1–7" will make the point? As a result, conversations can become dense, at times even mathematical. Much can be missed. I have been in conversations that remained essentially mystifying until sometime afterward, when I found a Bible and could rehydrate all the pellets of concentrate. Once, during the discussion of a paper titled "Gender and Power in the Gospel of Mark," which partly concerned the episode (Mark 5:25–34) in which Jesus heals a woman "who had had a flow of blood for twelve years," a responding scholar was saying something about there being a lack of any reference to male genitalia in the New Testament. Eager interruptants leaped to their feet, crying as one, "Galatians 5:12!" The room filled with laughter. Only after returning to my hotel room and consulting the Bible placed there by the Gideon Society did I discover that Galatians 5:12 is the passage in which Saint Paul, opposing circumcision for Gentile believers, expresses the wish that those who disagree with him "would castrate themselves."

The fact that a paper with the title "Gender and Power in the Gospel of Mark" was even given at a meeting of the Society of Biblical Literature brings up the third and indeed the overriding impression: the degree to which issues involving gender — specifically, issues involving women — have become a powerful seasoning, if not the dominant flavor, at the meeting of the American Academy of Religion and the Society of Biblical Literature. To be sure, as at any American academic conclave in the 1990s, a sense of open-mindedness is at once pervasive and implacable; every special interest has a working group, every opinion a champion who deserves at least a moment of respectful attention. (I wandered into one crowded meeting at a recent SBL convention at which a scholar was giving a spirited and contrarian defense of Judas Iscariot, and appeared to be holding his own.) But the engagement with women's issues stands out among every other discrete concern. "Feminist Interpretation and the Fourth Gospel"; "Women in Religious Offices in Western Asia Minor"; "Sexual Boundaries, Gender Trouble, and the Ruth-Naomi-Boaz Triangle"; "Prostitutes and Penitents in the Early Christian Church"; "The Personification of Cities as Women in the Hebrew Bible" — you cannot browse through the program book or stride through the corridors without becoming aware of the rapidly expanding influence of feminist scholars in the study of Jewish and Christian history, and of the reassessment of many issues that has ensued as a result, issues that speak not only to the role of women in history but also to the role of women in the modern world.

Biblical scholarship may remain a predominantly male endeavor —

feminist scholars refer to the "academic malestream" — but during the past three decades women have made substantial inroads. The female membership of the Society of Biblical Literature amounted to a mere 3 percent in 1970. It now exceeds 16 percent, still small but rising inexorably. The share of the society's student membership that is female — a harbinger, surely — is 30 percent. Until 1980, when it marked its centennial, the society had never held a panel discussion about any issues involving the Bible and women, and regardless of the subject matter, had never held a session in which a woman served as the moderator or chair.[1] By 1987, though, it was able to elect its first female president, Elisabeth Schüssler Fiorenza, who at the time was a professor at Episcopal Divinity School and who now teaches at the Harvard Divinity School. In 1993 the society installed its second female president, Phyllis Trible, of Union Theological Seminary, in New York City. Of the scores of women emerging annually with fresh doctorates in fields relating to the Hebrew Bible and the New Testament, almost all place issues of gender at the heart of their scholarly concerns.

The body of work that feminist biblical scholars have produced is by now substantial. Virtually all of it has been published within the past twenty-five years. Most has been published within the past ten or fifteen. The writing can at times be difficult; some scholars don methodology like chain mail. A certain amount of it also runs cold or hot with anger, or succumbs to the distracting indulgence of self-revelation, or goes off in directions ("*The Story of O* and Jeremian Pornography") that elicit delighted hand-wringing by unfriendly critics. But a strikingly large proportion of this work, whether in specialized journals or in books, has been written to be accessible to a broad range of readers outside academe.

The motivations, besides simple intellectual curiosity, that lie behind this work are not difficult to discern. There is the perception, hardly open to question, that the Hebrew Bible and the New Testament deal with women harshly, negatively, and unfairly in many spheres; the need to understand why they do; the conviction, among some women, that an alternative past awaits recovery. Among certain feminist scholars there is a belief, too, that recovering the past could help change the present —

for example, could help make the case for giving women access to positions in religious ministry from which they are now excluded. The work of feminist scholars, both individually and collectively, has been greeted in some quarters with impatience, irritation, dismissiveness, even contempt. But it has also established women's issues as a permanent focus of biblical studies. That it has done so is one important element of the broader engagement of feminism with every aspect of organized religion.

The women's movement has as yet had meager impact on a number of academic realms — can there be a feminist physics? a womanist mathematics? a gynocentric cosmology? — but the realm of religion has been profoundly affected. Some of the developments deriving from the convergence of feminism and religion might be regarded as occurring on the fringes of popular culture — for example, the proliferation of neo-pagan goddess movements. The new attention to the idea of goddesses has an academic dimension, although a controversial one, embodied most notably in the work of the late Marija Gimbutas, who was for many years a professor of European archaeology at the University of California at Los Angeles and the curator of Old World archaeology at UCLA's Cultural History Museum. Elements of Gimbutas's theorizing have obvious antecedents in the work of the nineteenth-century Swiss anthropologist J. J. Bachofen, whose 1861 treatise *Das Mutterrecht* represents the first modern investigation of women's rights and status in a broad array of prehistoric and ancient cultures. As set out in such books as *Goddesses and Gods of Old Europe* and *The Language of the Goddess*, Gimbutas postulates the existence of a goddess-oriented civilization in Neolithic Europe, between roughly 6500 and 3500 B.C., where people lived in peace and sexual harmony; it was destroyed at the peak of its florescence, she speculates, by a patriarchal culture ruled by weapon-wielding horsemen who swept out of the Volga basin. "We are still living under the sway of that aggressive male invasion," Gimbutas writes, "and only beginning to discover our long alienation from our authentic European Heritage."[2]

It is impossible to say how many people are caught up in the various New Age forms of feminist religion — not only goddess worship but also Wicca (witchcraft wielded with a benevolent, nature-oriented attitude) and the cult of Gaia (Mother Earth, our planet, conceived of as a living organism) — but popular books on these subjects by such writers as Clarissa Pinkola Estes, Lynn Andrews, and Barbara Walker sell by the hundreds of thousands. Sales of Estes's book *Women Who Run with the Wolves* have in fact exceeded the one million mark.[3] The women's spirituality movement, as it is sometimes called, finds expression in worship groups large and small. The Wicca entrepreneur who goes by the name Starhawk hosts gatherings that attract thousands of people. Some groups consist of a tiny band of like-minded acquaintances. The *Wall Street Journal*, whose theology sanctions the worship of something else entirely, reported on one such group:

> On a recent sun-splashed afternoon, Ms. Daufin, decked out in a grass skirt and bead necklace in the shape of fallopian tubes and ovaries, joins five others . . . for a fertility rite. They giggle as they plunge a 12-foot pole into a hole they have dug in "Mother Earth." Then Ms. Daufin, a journalism professor, dances with the other women around the Maypole. The worshippers include a graying ex-nun who calls herself Changing Woman. They purify themselves with burnt sage, sing in a circle, clutch their wombs, and beseech the Goddess to make their lives more fruitful. Their wails reach a feverish pitch and peak in a primal scream.[4]

It is hard to say whether this sort of thing has a future, although it is surfacing even in forums held under more or less orthodox auspices. A women's conference called "Re-Imagining" sponsored by the Methodist and Presbyterian churches in Minneapolis in 1993 came under attack from conservative elements in those denominations for its embrace of what some saw as neo-pagan ritual.[5] Pope John Paul II, apparently taking note of practices among some American Catholic feminists that draw on Native American traditions, has warned against "forms of nature worship."[6] But the truly significant consequences of the convergence of feminism and religion — those that have occurred closer to the mainstream of religious ministry and scholarship — are, I expect, irreversible. Two of them have received considerable attention, and although they are not my primary focus, they deserve some consideration.

The first is the influx of women into traditional divinity school programs and the ministry. Walk into the department of religion or the divinity school at any major university in America today and the bulletin board will paint the same picture: seminar after workshop after lecture after caucus on almost every conceivable matter involving women and religion. At present women are forbidden to enter the ministry in about eighty Christian denominations (including Roman Catholicism, the Greek and Russian Orthodox churches, and the Seventh-Day Adventists) and are prohibited from the rabbinate in Orthodox Judaism, but they are admitted to the ministry in more than eighty other Christian denominations (including the American Baptist, Episcopal, Presbyterian, Evangelical Lutheran, and United Methodist churches) and to the rabbinate in Conservative, Reform, and Reconstructionist Judaism.[7] The number of women in seminaries preparing for the master of divinity degree, which typically leads to ordination, grew from less than 2,700 in 1976 to more than 7,300 in 1995. Women today account for more than a third of all students in seminary programs nationwide, and at some of the most prestigious divinity schools, such as the University of Chicago Divinity School, Union Theological Seminary, the Pacific School of Religion (in Berkeley), and the Divinity School at Vanderbilt University (in Nashville), they constitute an absolute majority and are decisive in establishing an institutional tone. Here is another way of looking at recent trends: between 1992 and 1996, the number of women enrolled in master of divinity programs grew by 15 percent, whereas the number of men enrolled in such programs actually declined. The aggressive feminization of divinity school presages a feminization of the pulpit. Although exact numbers are impossible to nail down, it has been estimated that at least 35,000 and as many as 45,000 women are serving as ministers and rabbis in America. Already women constitute upwards of 10 percent of the clergy in Protestant denominations, a proportion that will inexorably expand.[8]

The second much-publicized consequence of the convergence of feminism and religion, which is organically bound up with the first, has been the demand for translations of the Bible (an overwhelmingly androcentric text in its worldview and expression) that employ "inclusive" language — that is, translations that do their utmost to avoid terminology that might seem, and is certainly seen by some, to be sexist.

Such issues of language have for decades aroused exasperation in all parties. One text that should be better known is a lecture given by Nelle Morton at Harvard Divinity School in 1973. Morton sought to turn the tables, proposing a thought experiment. She asked the members of the audience to imagine themselves as a lone male divinity school student coming to terms with an institution whose language and outlook happen to be feminine:

> What is evoked in you as you gradually become aware that the language in such an institution has a distinctly feminine character . . . that feminine words function for both masculine and feminine . . . that every time a professor says *womankind* she means, of course, "all humanity"? When one enrolls in a seminar on "The Doctrine of Woman" the professor intends at least to deal with men also. When one sings of the Motherhood of God and the Sisterhood of Woman, one breathes a prayer that all men as well as women will come to experience true sisterhood.[9]

A common concern about the language specifically of the Bible has roots that actually go deep; for instance, the founder of the Quaker movement, George Fox, introduced inclusive language into scriptural texts as one element of that tradition's egalitarian impetus.[10] Purists and strict constructionists might argue that no warrant exists for altering the original biblical language in order to satisfy the desires of later communities, but accepted precedent exists, others say, for doing just that — to the extent of replacing, as the Jews began to do twenty-five centuries ago, one form of the name of God (*Yahweh*, expressed in the tetragrammaton YHWH) with another (*Adonai*, meaning "Lord") in spoken language, to avoid the risk of profanation.[11] At the same time, of course, some tendencies toward linguistic accommodation of the zeitgeist have verged on self-parody.

The history of Bible translation is long and intricate, and as with attempts to reconstruct the evolutionary genealogy of any species, that history involves many distinct phyla; some 250 new translations of the New Testament into English alone have been published during the past four centuries.[12] (At this writing, projects are under way worldwide to translate the Bible into some 1,200 languages that do not yet possess a vernacular version.)[13] The most important phylum in English is the one that runs from William Tyndale's sixteenth-century translation of the New Testament and the first five books of the Hebrew Bible, done directly from the former's original Greek and the latter's original Hebrew rather than, as previously, from the intermediary Latin version of both known as the Vulgate, through the King James Bible (completed in 1611), and then on to the English Revised Version (the first translation to reflect the fruits of modern biblical scholarship, resulting in some 30,000 emendations of the King James Bible in the New Testament alone; it was completed in 1885), the American Standard Version (1901), the Revised Standard Version (completed in 1952), and the New Revised Standard Version (completed in 1990). Every new translation has had its critics, often for theological reasons, picky and profound, but also because existing versions tend to become over time something like a comfortable sweater that occupants dread to replace.[14]

The Revised Standard Version (RSV), for instance, is acknowledged by most authorities to be a triumphant work of scholarship, and it is probably the most popular translation in the English-speaking world, but it was wryly and memorably taken to task in the 1950s by a Baptist missionary and translator, William C. Taylor, for its dogged pursuit of gentility and for what today would be called its political correctness. As Taylor noted, the RSV eschewed such familiar biblical words as "flesh," "carnal," "fornication," "seed," "only begotten," "virgin," "confess," and "remission."[15] The RSV can also be, for all its philological accomplishments, a little hard on the ear. It reads very much like the hybrid of linguistic modernity and linguistic familiarity that it is. Its language does not reproduce, even in the palest mimicry, the cadences and textures of the Bible as originally composed (as the recent translation by Everett Fox, *The Five Books of Moses*, ambitiously does).

The feminist movement was essentially dormant when work on the RSV was proceeding. The term "sexist," whose natal citation in the Oxford English Dictionary is given as 1965, was decades away from coinage. The *New* Revised Standard Version, in contrast, was conceived at a time of feminist ferment. When the NRSV appeared, it immediately made headlines for its adoption of inclusive, gender-neutral language in all instances save when the text is referring to God. Thus, for instance, where the RSV uses the words "I will make you fishers of men" (Matthew 4:19), the NRSV instead uses the words "I will make you fish for people." Where the RSV uses the words "There is no other name under heaven given among men by which we must be saved" (Acts 4:12), the NRSV uses the words "given among mortals." Where the RSV uses the word "brethren," the NRSV uses the expression "brothers and sisters."

As we might imagine and could safely have predicted, this approach elicited derision, scorn, and impatience in many quarters. "There can be *no question*," wrote Roland H. Worth, a minister and historian, in an analysis of the NRSV in 1990, "that the New RSV has a *multitude* of odd sounding phrases due to its effort to appease the extreme militants. Some feminists insist that 'we' (i.e., people at large) will get used to it — and perhaps so. However, *mutilating* the text is something no faithful Christian should *ever* get used to, even when it's in the interest of what he himself believes."[16] Phyllis Schlafly, who in the 1970s and 1980s waged a much publicized and ultimately successful fight against the Equal Rights Amendment and who remains a conservative activist on a variety of social issues, undoubtedly speaks for many when she observes: "'We don't want to have to pray to 'Our Parents which art in heaven.'"[17] The NRSV has been explicitly shunned by the Vatican as a text for use by Catholics.

The NRSV has not, however, gone as far as some other versions of the Bible. Perhaps the most radical document in this regard, one that breaks through the line that divides "translation" from "improvisation," is *An Inclusive Language Lectionary*, sponsored by the National Council of Churches. A lectionary is a collection of readings designed for use in liturgy; as of 1995, some 95 percent of the New Testament and 60 percent of the Hebrew Bible had been released by the National Council of Churches in lectionary form. The several volumes of *An Inclusive*

Language Lectionary are insistently devoid of male-oriented language no matter what the original biblical context, and they do not exempt God from revision. The words "God the Father" become "God the [Mother and] Father." The denotation of Jesus as "Son of God" is changed to "Child of God." The sentence "For God so loved the world that he gave his only Son" (John 3:16) becomes "For God so loved the world that God gave God's only Child." The *Inclusive Language Lectionary* is sensitive to issues other than sexism. What was formerly a reference in the Bible to a "cripple" becomes "a person with a disabling condition." The many references to "darkness" are also paraphrased, darkness being considered to have possible racial overtones.

From a feminist point of view, as we shall see, there are many issues pertinent to translation other than inclusive language. It is also true that there is no monolithic feminist view on inclusive language to begin with. Even as many object to language that serves to exclude women from the Bible unnecessarily, so do others object to allowing the Bible to masquerade as a document that seems less androcentric and friendlier to women than in fact it is. As the biblical scholar Elizabeth Castelli, of Barnard College, has noted, the translation project is therefore "nuanced and delicate, striving not to obscure the nature of the text while at the same time trying not to construct and reify further sexist expectations and assumptions through the use of language that erases, marginalizes, or trivializes women's lives, agency, and contributions."[18] Phyllis A. Bird, a biblical scholar who teaches at the Garrett Evangelical Seminary in Illinois, has made the same point: "Attempting to solve the problem of the Bible's sexist language through translation alone may only serve to mask the deeper problem and prevent critical engagement with the underlying issues."[19]

Women in the pulpit and new translations of the Bible and of other religious texts are the kinds of developments that reliably make news. But the work being done by women in biblical scholarship and related fields — work that requires immense erudition — remains far less well known.

In her book-length essay *Three Guineas* (1938), Virginia Woolf ponders a solicitation from a private girls' school for money and from there takes up the issue of three causes to which she might donate the sum of one guinea each, which leads in turn to a broader consideration of opportunities for women and what might be done with those opportunities. She conjures an image of the long, eons-old, endlessly regenerating procession of men into the professions — "There they go, our brothers who have been educated at public schools and universities, mounting those steps, passing in and out of those doors, ascending those pulpits, preaching, teaching, administering justice, practising medicine, transacting business, making money" — and observes of modern women, now taking up many of those same pursuits, that "there, traipsing along at the tail end of the procession, we go ourselves." Woolf allows herself to savor this prospect for a few sentences, but then resumes in a more judicious mood: "The questions that we have to ask and to answer about that procession during this moment of transition are so important that they may well change the lives of all men and women for ever. For we have to ask ourselves, here and now, do we wish to join that procession, or don't we? On what terms shall we join that procession? Above all, where is it leading us, the procession of educated men?"[20]

These are questions that in fact might be asked by women and men alike, and that some feminists have never been shy about raising. They are especially pertinent when it comes to the study of the Bible.

The Bible has always been a compelling object of contemplation, both because questions of religious faith are involved and because it is a window onto much of human history, albeit one whose refractions may distort and occlude. With respect to issues of gender, the Bible is also, of course, highly "problematic," to use a word that no feminist scholar I've spoken with can help uttering in a tone of ironic politeness, and one that gets employed quite a lot. (If this word alone were subtracted from the proceedings, the annual SBL meeting would end an hour or two sooner.) It is a central tenet of contemporary feminism that a patriarchal template — a worldview shaped consciously or unconsciously by males and reflecting male interests and reinforcing male power — governs the way people have come to think as individuals and as societies. The Bible is no stranger to patriarchy; indeed, it is the text that gave us the men known as the patriarchs — Abraham, Isaac, Jacob. It is an androcentric document in the extreme. It was written mostly, if not entirely, by men. It was edited by men. It presents God in most instances, though with some remarkable if often unheralded exceptions, as male. It describes a succession of societies over a period of roughly 1,200 years in which public life was dominated by men. And because the Bible's focus is largely on public rather than private life — a trait it shares with most historical works published up until the mid-twentieth century, when a focus on "social history" gradually began displacing the Great Man approach — it talks predominantly about men. In the Hebrew Bible, only 151 of the roughly 1,400 people who are given names are women. The number of named women in the New Testament (48) is, proportionately, about twice as great, which still leaves them a small minority of the named figures. Hundreds of other women (564 in all) are mentioned in the Bible as a whole, but the text does not provide a name, a comparatively infrequent occurrence for men.[21] The biblical books Esther and the Song of Songs are famous for containing no reference to God; the books of Obadiah, Jonah, Habakkuk, Zephaniah, and Haggai in the Hebrew Bible deserve mention for a parallel but largely overlooked achievement, which is to avoid making any reference to women.

As a prescriptive text, moreover, the Bible has been interpreted as justifying the subordination of women to men. It has been interpreted as explaining the creation of woman as an afterthought, an act of secondary importance, with woman's very substance being subsidiary to that of man; as defining the purpose of woman to be the servant of man; as laying the blame for the human fall from grace in the Garden of Eden on the woman, Eve, who is portrayed as having first succumbed to the temptations of the serpent. It has been interpreted over the centuries as forbidding a role for women in preaching and ministry. The word "interpreted" may put too benign a gloss on passages that are in many cases fully capable of speaking for themselves, and hardly bashful about doing so.

The practice of summoning a biblical passage to nail down an argument is known as "prooftexting"; the text, as it were, serves as the proof of the rightness of one's position. Defenders of the sanctity of the Sabbath may invoke, say, Exodus 23:12, in which God says to the Israelite people, "Six days you shall do your work, but on the seventh day you shall rest." Those taking a dim view of homosexuality may invoke, say, Leviticus 20:13, in which it is stated, "If a man lies with a male as with a woman, both of them have committed an abomination." Prooftexting is hardly the overt and accepted staple of public discourse that it was in American life a century ago (when it would have seemed as natural to participants in some aboriginal version of the *Jim Lehrer NewsHour* as the use of polling data and social scientific theorizing does now), but no matter: it remains a legacy even where it is not an overt presence. Were someone to undertake the compilation of something along the lines of a Ten Most Wanted list of biblical citations antithetical to women — Ten *Least* Wanted may be more to the point — the attempt would prompt a rolling of the eyes for its inadequacy in many circles. Yet there is a reason that certain citations come up time and again.

* "Then the Lord God said, 'It is not good that the man should be alone; I will make him a helper fit for him'" (Genesis 2:18).
* "So the Lord God caused a deep sleep to fall upon the man, and while he slept took one of his ribs and closed up its place with flesh; and the rib which the Lord God had taken from the man he made into a woman and brought her to the man" (Genesis 2:21–22).
* "The man said, 'The woman whom thou gavest to be with me, she gave me fruit of the tree, and I ate.' Then the Lord God said to the woman, 'What is this that you have done?'" (Genesis 3:12–13).
* "I will greatly multiply your pain in childbearing; in pain you shall bring forth children, yet your desire shall be for your husband, and he shall rule over you" (Genesis 3:16).
* "If a woman conceives, and bears a male child, then she shall be unclean seven days . . . But if she bears a female child, then she shall be unclean two weeks" (Leviticus 12:2–5).
* "But I want you to understand that the head of every man is Christ, the head of a woman is her husband" (1 Corinthians 11:3).
* "For man was not made from woman, but woman from man. Neither was man created for woman, but woman for man" (1 Corinthians 11:8–9).

* "The women should keep silence in the churches. For they are not permitted to speak, but should be subordinate, as even the law says" (1 Corinthians 14:34).
* "I permit no woman to teach or to have authority over men; she is to keep silent" (1 Timothy 2:12).
* "Wives, be subject to your husbands as to the Lord. . . . As the church is subject to Christ, so let wives also be subject in everything to their husbands" (Ephesians 5:22–24).

The general assumption of what many would describe as women's subsidiary ontological status has biblical manifestations that emerge in countless specific laws, in countless sayings and proverbs, and in passing remarks uttered by biblical figures. Consider those "begats" ("And unto Enoch was born Irad; and Irad begat Mahujael; and Mahujael begat Mathushael; and Mathushael begat Lamech . . ."), in which procreation is depicted as an accomplishment for which men deserve all the credit. In the New Testament, the duties and the proper place of women are delineated by what are known as household codes, rules governing private behavior in and outside the home. In the Hebrew Bible, the book of Leviticus by its nature is concerned with rules — it is, in essence, a book of instructions and laws, for the use of priests — and among its many strictures are those governing personal behavior as it relates to cultic purity and impurity and hence governing menstruation, sexual relations, and childbearing. Women, in the view of these codes, represent a very real threat to purity. A palpable sense of threat ("Give not your strength to women") emerges too even from the accessible poetry of Proverbs, a more congenial and kindred book than Leviticus to a modern reader. The famous "woman of worth" passage at the very end of the book (Proverbs 31:10–31), which defines the qualities of an ideal wife, is noteworthy for expressing this ideal exclusively from the point of view of the husband and the household:

> *The heart of her husband trusts in her,*
> *and he will have no lack of gain.*
> *She does him good, and not harm,*
> *all the days of her life.*

She seeks wool and flax,
and works with willing hands.
She is like the ships of the merchant,
she brings her food from afar.

The Bible is the best-selling book in the world. It has been and still is presumed by hundreds of millions of people to speak with authority, both explicitly through precept and implicitly through what it holds up by way of example. That authority, though it falls along a broad spectrum of fastidiousness, has helped to enforce what it prescribes. There is no getting around the disturbing character for women of much of the Bible, short of an interpretive reading (a "hermeneutic," to use the term of art) that may represent something of a stretch — what one biblical scholar has called an act of "hermeneutical ventriloquism."[22] Feminist scholars who persist in attempting to engage the Bible do so with a "hermeneutic of suspicion," to use Elisabeth Schüssler Fiorenza's frequently invoked term.

For many people in the modern world, as Ralph Waldo Emerson observed more than a century ago, the Bible "comes with a certain official claim against which the mind revolts." But the Bible is, of course, also something else, quite apart from any religious authority that has been vested in it. It would obviously be of immense historical, social, and linguistic interest even if it had emerged from the sands, hitherto unknown, a mere fifty or hundred years ago, or yesterday, and even if it pertained to peoples with whom our own society felt no sense of shared identity or destiny. It is, after all, a document produced by a succession of related and important ancient cultures, and it casts light on those cultures, though not in the straightforward way (or the apparently straightforward way) that modern documentary records cast light on developments in modern times. Those ancient cultures created many of the mental and social structures that have shaped the world in which we live. As a focus of historical or anthropological inquiry, then, the Bible helps to prompt certain questions and offers a venue and a resource for seeking certain answers.

A lot of those questions involve women, now that some scholars have decided that such questions are worth asking. What evidence does the Bible yield about the reality of daily life for women, beginning in that penumbral time before writing came to the Israelites, its oral culture preserved nonetheless in bits and pieces? Did women exercise more power than we might imagine, or than the Bible tends to acknowledge? What tasks were women responsible for, and what role did those tasks play in the advance of society? How did Israelite women and men conceive in gender terms of this anomalous deity of theirs — a singular God who somehow held out against the polytheistic legions of powerful neighbors? As codified, why did the laws of household and cult take the forms they did? Are there hints in the Bible of stories and traditions about women and their roles that have for some reason been lost to us? Are there times when we hear, directly and unmediated, a female voice speaking across the ages? What social factors drew some Jewish women to the movement that grew up around Jesus of Nazareth, and did any of those factors derive from the status of women *as* women in ancient Palestine? What opportunities, if any, did Jewish and Christian women have to exercise leadership in religious circles?

The subjection of the Bible to historical and critical scrutiny, a revolution that began during the nineteenth century, was until recently undertaken almost entirely by men. It did not occur to these men that the way the Bible treats women or depicts women — or, just as important, the way it *fails* to treat or depict women — might be a matter for study. Indeed, it did not occur to them that how the Bible deals with women was in any way untoward, just as it might not have occurred to them that how they themselves dealt with women might be in any way untoward.

In the preface to his book *Ancient Christian Gospels* (1990), the New Testament scholar Helmut Koester offers an anecdote that inadvertently captures some of the spirit of this disregard. The anecdote refers to members of an academic movement that developed in Germany earlier in this century and that encompassed many biblical scholars: "When I visited the University of Göttingen recently, Professor Gerd Luedemann showed me some of the original photographs of the scholars of the *'Religions-geschichtliche Schule,'* of whom published pictures are well known. In several instances the originals pictured these scholars together with their wives — but their spouses had been cut out of the published photographs."[23]

It is perhaps unfair to read too much into those doctored photographs. Appropriate symbolism, though, is frequently unfair. As it happens, a number of remarkable nineteenth-century women, none of them biblical scholars by training, showed interest in biblical questions about which men showed little interest at all, and their work provides a starting point for the investigations being done in our own time. We might think of them as being the first to notice those cut-out images all over the floor.

Chapter Two

....

THE SORCERER'S
APPRENTICE

We have made a fetish of the Bible long enough.
— Elizabeth Cady Stanton

*Time and trouble will tame an advanced
young woman, but an advanced old woman
is uncontrollable by any earthly force.*
— Dorothy L. Sayers

EIGHTY YEARS OLD and bedridden, her legs no longer capable of supporting the 240-pound bulk of her body, Elizabeth Cady Stanton was scarcely disposed to attend the annual convention of the National American Woman Suffrage Association being held in Washington, D.C., in January of 1896. It was perhaps just as well. Even if she had shown up on her own two feet, the likelihood was that they would be knocked out from under her. Stanton, together with her longtime friend and collaborator, Susan B. Anthony, had founded the Woman Suffrage Association a quarter of a century earlier, and Stanton was now its president. But she knew that many of the delegates to the Washington meeting were in no mood to be bound by feelings of historical obligation.

The association was gathered at the Church of Our Father, a Universalist meeting house at 13th and L Streets, N.W., and the meeting was the largest that the organization had ever held. One delegate had traveled all the way from Alaska. Another had come from Bermuda, a British colony that had just given women the right to vote in island elections. Reports about the convention were sent by telegraph to big-city newspapers throughout the country. (Susan B. Anthony pasted clippings of many of them into a folio-size scrapbook, which is preserved at the Library of Congress.) And one of the choicest pieces of news was that a resolution designed as a direct rebuke of Elizabeth Cady Stanton had come before the assembly.[1]

Anthony argued eloquently against it. "I shall be pained beyond expression if the delegates are so narrow as to adopt this resolution," she said. "You had better not begin resolving against individual action, or you will find no limit. This year it is Mrs. Stanton; next year it may be I or one of yourselves who may be the victim." But her words were to no avail. The resolution was passed by a vote of fifty-three to forty-one. Here is what it said: "This association is non-sectarian, being composed of persons of all shades of religious opinions, and has no official connection with the so-called *Woman's Bible*, or any theological publication."[2]

What was this *Woman's Bible*, and why had it caused such a fuss?

Stanton had for years been interested in the role played by religion, and by institutionalized Christianity in particular, in the subordination of women in virtually all spheres of endeavor in the larger society. As she wrote in the introduction to the first of the *Woman's Bible*'s two volumes, published in 1895,

> The Bible teaches that woman brought sin and death into the world, that she precipitated the fall of the race, that she was arraigned before the judgment seat of Heaven, tried, condemned and sentenced. Marriage for her was to be a condition of bondage, maternity a period of suffering and anguish, and in silence and subjection, she was to play the role of a dependent on man's bounty for all her material wants, and for all the information she might desire on the vital questions of the hour, she was commanded to ask her husband at home. Here is the Bible position of woman briefly summed up.[3]

The methodology employed by Stanton and her collaborators was to comb through the Hebrew Bible and the New Testament for passages in which women or women's issues figure and then to subject those passages to commentary and analysis. Does a certain passage — for instance, the disobedience of Eve in Genesis 3 — really mean what it has been said to mean by centuries of male interpreters? Is it possible to see such passages in another light? Which stories and episodes might best be regarded, from a woman's point of view, as simply unacceptable and therefore be jettisoned from the canon — jettisoned, that is to say, from the body of text that should be regarded as authoritative?

The Woman's Bible is a remarkable document for a number of reasons, not the least of which is its broad range of tone, which can move from the sensibly revelatory to the magisterially sarcastic in a matter of sentences. Stanton was not a wit as that word is today understood, but she could express herself with bite. She was also adept at wielding the prized attributes of feminine domesticity as a cudgel against the men she read about in the Bible and against the Bible's male writers and interpreters.

Of the construction of Noah's Ark (Genesis 6:14–16), she observed, "The paucity of light and air in this ancient vessel shows that woman had no part in its architecture, or a series of port-holes would have been deemed indispensable."[4] Her scorn for hypocrisy ranged freely across historical boundaries. Of the episode (Exodus 32) in which the men of Israel melt down the women's jewelry to create the idolatrous golden bull, she wrote, "It was just so in the American Revolution, in 1776, the first delicacy the men threw overboard in Boston harbor was the tea, women's favorite beverage. The tobacco and whiskey, though heavily taxed, they clung to with the tenacity of the devil-fish."[5] Even God did not quite measure up. Stanton once refused to attend a suffrage meeting at which the opening hymn was to be "Guide Us, O Thou Great Jehovah," observing that Jehovah had "never taken any active part in the suffrage movement."[6]

In the eyes of the National American Woman Suffrage Association, Stanton's caustic commentary, which won for her work attentive scrutiny and commercial success, was proving to be a source of considerable embarrassment. The first volume of *The Woman's Bible*, covering the Pentateuch, had immediately become a bestseller and had gone through seven printings in six months. Not surprisingly, it was denounced by religious leaders across the country — this at a time when traditional religion was experiencing something of a revival in America and the ranks of the suffrage movement were showing signs of growing evangelical Christian influence. *The Woman's Bible* was a cause of scandal, and Elizabeth Cady Stanton was vilified on editorial pages and from pulpits around the country. "The clergy denounced it as the work of *Satan*,"

Stanton recalled in her memoirs, "though it really was the work of Ellen Batelle Dietrick, Lillie Devereux Blake, Rev. Phebe A. Hanaford, Clara Bewick Colby, Ursula N. Gestefeld, Louisa Southworth, Frances Ellen Burr, and myself."[7]

Was it possible that the damage to Stanton's reputation would undermine the cause of women's suffrage, with which she had been so deeply identified? "As an organization," said Rachel Foster Avery, a delegate to the Washington meeting, "we have been held responsible for the action of an individual (an action which many of our members, far from sympathizing with, feel to be unwise) in issuing a volume with a pretentious title, covering a jumble of comment . . . without either scholarship or literary value, set forth in a spirit which is neither reverent nor inquiring."[8] That was the issue that preoccupied the delegates in Washington in January of 1896. In the end, as noted, fifty-three delegates had no doubt but that, yes, *The Woman's Bible* would indeed damage the cause of women's suffrage. The vote by the suffragists to distance themselves from Stanton — in effect, to censure her — was never repealed.

Stanton, indignant, pressed on, actually seeming to relish the stir she was creating. Among the cache of her letters preserved at Radcliffe College is one written in April 1896 to the women's rights activist Antoinette Brown Blackwell, a longtime friend of Stanton's. "I am in the midst of divers controversies," the letter begins, in the large, sprawling, powerful hand of a woman in her fourth decade, not her ninth, "with Bishops and Priests who combat my oft repeated assertion that 'no form of religion as yet has taught the equality of women.'" And she went on, "Our politicians are calm and complacent under our fire but the clergy jump round the moment you aim a pop gun at them 'like parched peas on a hot skillet.'"[9]

A second volume of *The Woman's Bible* appeared in 1898, covering the books from Joshua in the Hebrew Bible to Revelation at the end of the New Testament. "All through the centuries," Stanton wrote in the introduction, "scholars and scientists have been imprisoned, tortured, and burned alive for some discovery which seemed to conflict with a petty text of Scripture."[10] Stanton's fate was more prosaic: she was marginalized from the suffrage movement ever after, and Susan B. Anthony took her place in the public esteem of activists. It is not going too far to say (as some have suggested) that *The Woman's Bible* is the reason that an image of Susan B. Anthony and not Elizabeth Cady Stanton graces the one-dollar coin that was first minted in 1978. Perhaps it is just as well. Stanton might have been uncomfortable peering out from the coin over the words "In God We Trust."

Directly or indirectly, and sometimes in complicated ways, the Bible has been bound up with the larger movement for women's rights from the very beginning. The English mystic Julian of Norwich (b. 1342), whose *Revelations of Divine Love*, with their unusual meditations on the "motherhood" of Jesus, is regarded as the first literary work in English indisputably to have been written by a woman, acknowledged the obvious impediment to her efforts posed by the harsh dictum of Paul in the epistle to Timothy: "I permit no woman to teach, or to have authority over men; she is to keep silent. For Adam was formed first, then Eve." Julian, though, went on to ignore this stricture, asking, "Because I am a woman should I therefore believe that I ought not to tell you about the goodness of God?"[11]

A century and a half later, a troublesome and somewhat idiosyncratic German physician and lawyer named Henricius Cornelius Agrippa von Nettesheim published his treatise *The Glory of Women*, which among other things sought to undermine the use of Scripture as a basis for male privilege (without undermining the authority of Scripture itself). Von Nettesheim observed that because the trajectory of creation in the Bible moves from the inferior to the superior, the creation of Eve *after* Adam demonstrates woman's higher status. He also noted that the man, Adam, was inherently flawed: he was, after all, missing a rib.[12]

In the seventeenth century, the English founders of the egalitarian Quaker movement confronted passages in the Bible that had long justified social relations between the sexes of less than complete equality, whether in the home or in the realm of religion. They reinterpreted or dispensed with the most egregious passages, and they employed what today would be called inclusive language in Scripture readings.[13]

The same issues involving women, supported by the same woven net of scriptural texts, have come up repeatedly over the centuries. When Judith Sargent Murray tried to make a case for the more widespread education of women in her essay "On the Equality of the Sexes," in 1790, she ran into opposition premised on biblical passages that were interpreted as establishing and justifying the subordination of women to men — notably the story of Eve's disobedience in the Garden of Eden, which was held to have led to Adam's disobedience. This act was accounted an aboriginal sign of female weakness. Murray, a spirited native of Gloucester, Massachusetts, who had learned to read and write only because her father had hired a tutor for her brother so the boy could prepare for Harvard, attempted to vitiate Eve's culpability with a counterreading of the same passage, noting that Eve's behavior was motivated by a quest for understanding ("It doth not appear that she was governed by any one sensual appetite; but merely a desire of adorning her mind; a laudable ambition fired her soul, and a thirst for knowledge impelled the predilection so fatal in its consequences"), whereas Adam, who ate the forbidden fruit that Eve offered to him, acted out of "bare pusillanimous attachment to a woman!"[14] It is hard for any reader not to be struck by Adam's ignobility in general — his abject cowering and impulsive finger-pointing. Murray did not win her argument in the public arena, and widespread education of women did not begin to occur for another half-century, but her use of an alternative reading pioneered a strategy that some nineteenth-century women would adopt and that is employed by a number of feminist biblical scholars today.

To use the word "feminist" in an eighteenth- or nineteenth-century context is obviously anachronistic; for all we know, it is even becoming anachronistic in a late-twentieth-century context, given the often angry differences of opinion that now exist within something that once styled itself a "movement." In retrospect, we can say this: the first stage in what today we would regard as a feminist approach to the Bible was to view the problems the Bible posed for women not so much as inherent in the text as inherent in the way the text had been interpreted and wielded by men. The issue was joined again, almost inadvertently, beginning in the 1830s, when a number of prominent women sought public roles in the campaign for the abolition of slavery. And it came up in yet another context, beginning in the 1850s, when prominent women assumed public roles in the campaign in favor of temperance. These women ran up against a problem with respect to the Bible that had less to do with either abolition or temperance than with their taking a stand, as women, on something — *anything* — in public in the first place.

Wasn't a woman's proper place inside the home? This was the question that reform-minded, activist women ran into time and again as they sought a platform for their views — a pulpit in a church, a dais in a meeting hall, a bandstand on the town common. The case of the Grimké sisters, Sarah and Angelina, is instructive. Natives of Charleston, South Carolina, and members of a distinguished slaveholding family, the Grimkés eventually moved to Philadelphia, became Quakers, and in 1837 embarked on a tour of several northern states to speak out against slavery, sometimes scandalously addressing a "mixed" audience of men and women.[15]

In Massachusetts, one of the most firmly abolitionist states, the Grimkés were slammed by a broadside in the form of a pastoral letter from the leadership of the Congregational Church. It cited Paul's injunction against women's preaching in 1 Corinthians 14:34: "Women should keep silence in the churches. For they are not permitted to speak, but should be subordinate, as even the law says." It cited Paul's encapsulation of the wifely role as defined in 1 Peter 3:1–6: "Wives, be submissive to your husbands . . . Sarah obeyed Abraham, calling him lord." It cited the naturally fallen state of women in general, as evidenced by the examples of Eve and Jezebel (the brazen wife of King Ahab and the instigator of an Israelite lapse into idolatry). "We can not, therefore, but regret," the pastoral letter declared, "the mistaken conduct of those who encourage females to bear an obtrusive and ostentatious part in measures of reform, and countenance any of that sex who so far forget themselves as to itinerate in the character of public lecturers and teachers."[16] The poet and abolitionist John Greenleaf Whittier — Bard of Freedom, as he would be remembered — wondered how the Grimké sisters could forget "the great and dreadful wrongs of the slave in a selfish crusade against some paltry grievance . . . some trifling oppression, political or social, of their own."[17]

These were not isolated sensibilities. In 1840, three years after the

Congregationalist condemnation, the American female delegates to the World Anti-Slavery Convention, held at Freemasons' Hall in London, were actually refused permission to sit with the rest of their delegation, on the grounds that it would be "promiscuous" and would mischievously pluck women from the safe confinement of "woman's sphere." Abolitionists also feared that any association of the abolitionist cause with radical ideas about the proper place of women would detract from the main effort — a harbinger of the problem that suffragists faced when confronted by *The Woman's Bible*. (The abolitionist leader William Lloyd Garrison would have no part in women's exclusion from the Anti-Slavery Convention; he pointedly took his seat in the ladies' gallery.)[18]

The refusal to seat women at the World Anti-Slavery Convention sharply turned the attention of one person in attendance, Elizabeth Cady Stanton, then on her honeymoon, toward the issue of women's rights and the role of religion in subverting them. As she later recalled, "The clerical portion of the convention was most violent in its opposition. The clergymen seemed to have God and his angels especially in their care and keeping, and were in agony lest the women should do or say something to shock the heavenly hosts."[19] It was at this anti-slavery meeting that Stanton was introduced to the Quaker activist Lucretia Mott, who would be her partner in the first women's rights convention, held at Seneca Falls, New York, in 1848. This convention, whose substance elicited public commentary in tones ranging from censure to ridicule, inaugurated the modern women's movement in America.

The Grimkés and other activist women responded to critics with biblical passages of their own. For every 1 Corinthians 11:3 ("The head of every man is Christ, the head of a woman is her husband") they lobbed back a Galatians 3:28 ("There is neither Jew nor Greek, there is neither slave nor free, there is neither male nor female; for you are all one in Christ Jesus") or a Joel 2:28 ("I will pour out my spirit on all flesh; your sons and your daughters shall prophesy"). They held up the example of women in the Bible who occupied prominent, indeed, decisive public roles — women like Miriam, the sister of Moses, who is called a prophet (Exodus 15:20) and helps lead the Israelites out of the land of Egypt, and Jael, the wife of Heber the Kenite, who brings the Canaanite general

Sisera to a violent and ignominious end (Judges 4:21); women like the prophet Huldah, the wife of Shallum, "keeper of the wardrobe," who delivers herself of an urgent oracle for King Josiah (2 Kings 22:14–20), and Esther, serendipitously the wife of the king of Persia, who saves the captive Israelites from slaughter at the hands of Haman the Agagite (Esther 8).

Activist women also raised the larger theological question of what the Bible is "about": is it fundamentally a text that is *about* the oppression and subordination of one sex by another, or is it a text whose driving theme is one of liberation and emancipation? The issue, in other words, was one of what today would be called biblical theology — that is, a theology focused less on issues of doctrinal or prescriptive punctilio than on the larger message of the Bible considered as an act of unfolding revelation.

These ideas are spelled out in Sarah Grimké's reply to the pastoral letter of the Congregationalist ministers, which was published in 1837 under the title *Letters on the Equality of the Sexes and the Condition of Women*. Grimké reiterated the point that the chief problem with the Bible for women was not, in her view, the document itself (which she, like most people of the time, held to be the inspired word of God) but the fact that the Bible had been held as a male monopoly. Men had done all the translating, and who knows what errors might have resulted, whether by accident or by design, or simply because of an unselfconscious mindset conditioned by the cultures in which the men had lived. And, of course, from the period of the Talmud and the church fathers on forward, men had done virtually all of the interpretation of the Bible. This conception of the nature of the Bible's challenge — that the problem was not the document itself but errors in the reading and application of it — was in fact explicitly endorsed at the Seneca Falls Convention in these words: "*Resolved*, That woman has too long rested satisfied in the circumscribed limits which corrupt customs and a perverted application of the Scriptures have marked out for her . . ."[20]

How could the challenge of this "perverted application" be met? Only by women's taking on the task of biblical study and interpretation themselves. In order to do so, of course, they would need the proper tools, meaning at the very least a knowledge of Hebrew and Greek, the original languages of the Hebrew Bible and New Testament, respectively. These tools were not going to be easy to obtain.

One who did obtain them but in the end put them to little direct use was the remarkable Antoinette Brown, the woman to whom Stanton wrote her "peas on a hot skillet" letter. Raised in rural New York among a family greatly influenced by the revivalism of Charles Grandison Finney, Brown was encouraged to seek an advanced education and eventually enrolled at Oberlin College, in Ohio, where Finney taught theology and where Lucy Stone, a future suffragist leader, was a classmate. (Stone would, among other things, become an advocate for women's retention of their maiden names; she kept the name Stone after her marriage but preceded it with "Mrs.") Oberlin in the 1840s was perhaps the most egalitarian and avant-garde institution of higher learning in America, a magnet for those who believed in the essential interlocking unity of the various reform efforts that seemed to enjoy an efflorescence all at once: abolition, temperance, women's suffrage, birth control, physical culture, vegetarianism, colonic irrigation. "No period has existed since the creation of the world when it was so easy to do good," the *Panoplist and Missionary Magazine* had announced in 1814, a sentiment that for many embodied a lifetime's worth of moral tone.[21]

Antoinette Brown, who (like Lucy Stone) would later marry into the polymorphously self-improving Blackwell family, which provided leadership for many of the reform movements, embarked at Oberlin upon a career in the ministry, mastering the requisite languages and writing her senior essay on the troubling "women should be silent" passage in 1 Corinthians. She argued in this essay that the kinds of speech Paul sought to quell could only have been "excesses, irregularities, and unwarrantable liberties," since the right of women to prophesy and preach was clearly sanctioned elsewhere in Scripture. Brown's view of a woman's permissible public role in religion won few endorsements. "Associated as I have been this winter frequently with ministers," she wrote to Lucy Stone, "I have not found one who has been both ready and willing to talk over the matter candidly." Brown completed the theology program at Oberlin in 1850 but was not awarded a degree; Oberlin awarded degrees to women only in classical studies. (The theology degree was belatedly conferred on Brown in 1908.) In 1853 Brown became the first woman to be ordained a minister in the United States and assumed parish duties at a small Congregational church in South Butler, New York. But she seems to have experienced almost at once a crisis of the spirit and soon resigned her position, never to venture in this direction again.[22]

Still, women like Brown and the Grimkés were emblematic of a force that had been set in motion. In her book *The Feminization of American Culture*, the cultural historian Ann Douglas, of Columbia University, describes a thickening nineteenth-century alliance between educated women and liberal clergymen: "She could become aggressive, even angry, in the name of various holy causes; he could become gentle, even nurturing, for the sake of moral overseeing."[23] As the historian Dorothy C. Bass, who teaches at Valparaiso University, has pointed out, the reformist zeal of revivalist Protestantism had come to rely heavily on the activism and organizational skills of large numbers of women on behalf of various causes, and these women and their daughters and grand-daughters were eager to accomplish more. The abolitionist Lydia Maria Child likened the process to the story of the sorcerer's apprentice, in which the apprentice, having seen the sorcerer transform a broom into a servant able to bring him water, successfully performs the transformation himself, but is soon dealing with a flood because he can't turn the servant back into a broom. "Thus it is," Child wrote, "with those who urged women to become missionaries, and form tract societies. They have changed the household utensil to a living, energetic being; and they have no spell to turn it into a broom again."[24]

The first stage of feminist thinking about the Bible, as noted, is encapsu-lated in the view that the Bible has been damaging to women because it has been mistranslated and otherwise misused. The second stage, not long in coming, can be stated as the view that the Bible is damaging to women by its very nature. This belief was nurtured in part by the broader intellectual climate surrounding the study of the Bible by modern, often secular scholars.

After the Reformation, as Bible study by nonclerics became acceptable and widespread, at least among Protestants, and as religious doctrine became less resistant to scrutiny (again among Protestants), the Scriptures began to attract scholarly attention of a recognizably contemporary kind. The initial stages of this contest between reason and revelation were complex, and the motivations of those involved on the side of reason ran the whole range from faith through skepticism to unbelief.

Ultimately, the authority of the Bible — its claim to be the literal word of God and to present an account that was to be regarded as objectively true — was undermined in two ways. First came the scientific study of the natural world (for example, the discovery of the motion of the planets), which threw doubt on the Bible's literal truth. Then came historical and textual study of the Bible itself, as if it were any other ancient document — a document in this case consisting of many different parts composed at different times by different people who, whether inspired by God or not, could hardly help but be influenced by the norms and biases and worldviews of the societies in which they lived. The undermining of the Bible's literal authority and the legitimation of (indeed, the insistence on, in some quarters) a skeptical cast of mind with regard to biblical tradition constitute an intellectual revolution that has not yet fully played itself out.

The scholars who began this revolution did not give the least thought to what their work might mean for women. They were interested in differentiating the authorship of various parts of the Bible and in trying to determine when the various parts had been written. They were concerned, for instance, with untangling what appeared to be the several braided sources that composed the first five books of the Hebrew Bible, the so-called five books of Moses, which Moses manifestly could not have composed himself. They also wished to work out the relationship of the three Synoptic Gospels — Matthew, Mark, and Luke — to one another, theorizing that Mark was the earliest and that the other two had drawn on Mark and also on a collection of Jesus' sayings, now lost, to which they gave the name Q (from the German word *Quelle*, meaning "source"). They were interested too in bringing the new insights of Middle Eastern archaeology and comparative linguistics to bear on the biblical text itself, to produce new and more accurate translations.

The particularities of such endeavors aside, biblical criticism's very conception of the Bible as in some measure (perhaps entirely) a *human* construct had obvious ramifications for those in the women's movement who perceived attitudes based on biblical authority — on the Bible as representing God's literal word — to be the single biggest obstacle to changing the status of women in modern society. Elizabeth Cady Stanton was, of course, one of these people. The child of a strict Presbyterian lawyer and judge who eventually disinherited her for her various efforts at social reform, Stanton became mindful at an early age of the disadvantages accruing to her sex and situation. She was independent-minded on the subject of women's rights (deleting the word "obey" from the ceremony at her marriage to Henry Brewster Stanton) even before her thinking became embodied in anything like a women's movement. Her interests were diverse — birth control, childrearing, psychology, temperance. "All reforms," she once observed, "are interdependent."[25] She never lost the doughty, naive, maddening optimism so characteristic of nineteenth-century reformers, and doubtless so essential to their successes.

Stanton was aware of the new biblical criticism and had read widely in the field, though by no means could she be considered (nor did she consider herself) a biblical scholar. She displayed a certain sympathy with but was not overpowered by the ideas of Matilda Joslyn Gage, who in her book *Woman, Church, and State* (1893) evoked a supposedly blessed epoch, now lost: "A form of society existed at an early age known as the Matriarchate or Mother-rule. Under the Matriarchate, except as son and inferior, man was not recognized in either of these great institutions, family, state or church. . . . Woman was ruler in each."[26] (Gage, by turns confident and censorious, earnest and sardonic, and suffused with an implacably blithe spirituality, seems to have missed her time by about a century.) Stanton could read Latin and Greek, though not Hebrew or German, the latter being the language in which so much biblical criticism, then as now, was written. As if they represented little more than common sense, Stanton intuitively shared biblical criticism's basic assumptions about how the Bible had come to be written and its all-too-human character.

At the same time, being an immensely practical woman, she recognized the enduring power of the Bible among people who would find such assumptions repugnant. "So long as tens of thousands of Bibles are printed every year," she wrote, "and circulated over the whole habitable globe, and the masses in all English-speaking nations revere it as the word of God, it is vain to belittle its influence."[27] Long after the Bible had ceased to mean anything to her as a spiritual resource, she still shuddered with horror when she saw one being placed on a chair to elevate a child.[28]

Many people tried to dissuade Stanton from undertaking *The Woman's Bible*, and many of those whom she asked for assistance turned her down. With the help of a handful of women, none of them true biblical scholars, she pushed ahead. "Accordingly," she wrote, "I began to read the commentators on the Bible and was surprised to see how little they had to say about the greatest factor in civilization, the mother of the race, and that by no means complimentary."[29] She worked in her room in her son's apartment at the southwest corner of Broadway and Ninety-fourth Street in New York, a building with an elevator that she marveled at and that was absolutely essential for a woman of her age and condition — heavy, lame, and afflicted with heart disease. On Stanton's desk was a plaster cast of her hand grasped in friendship with the hand of Susan B. Anthony, a cast that is on display today at the original Stanton homestead, in Seneca Falls, an exceedingly modest preserve of the National Park Service.

Stanton and her team devoted volume one of *The Woman's Bible* to the first five books of the Bible: Genesis, Exodus, Leviticus, Numbers, and Deuteronomy. Each entry began with a biblical passage pertaining to women quoted in full, coming in most cases from the new English Revised Version of the Bible, which was the first English translation to reflect the new biblical scholarship. In some instances the translation used was the homespun product of a somewhat eccentric Connecticut activist named Julia Evelina Smith, whose achievement, published in 1876, has otherwise gone largely unacknowledged by biblical professionals (and as a work of translation represents an evolutionary dead end).[30] Following the quotation came a commentary, frequently the product of Stanton's pen.

Of the story of Isaac meeting Rebekah at the well (Genesis 24:42–49), where Rebekah draws water for him, Stanton notes that the image has formed the basis for many charming paintings. She writes of Rebekah: "It was certainly a good test of her patience and humility to draw water for an hour, with a dozen men looking on at their ease, and none offering help." And she goes on: "Women as milk-maids and drawers of water, with pails and pitchers on their heads, are always artistic, and far more attractive to men than those with votes in their hands at the polling booths."[31]

Genesis 36:18 reveals that the wife of Esau was named Aholibamah and goes on to list the names of her sons. Stanton writes: "The name Aholibamah has a suggestion of high descent, but the historian tells us nothing of her virtues or idiosyncrasies of character, but simply that she was the daughter of Anah, and the wife of Esau, and that she was blessed with children, all interesting facts, which might have been intensified with a knowledge of some of her characteristics, what she thought, said, and did, her theories of life in general. One longs all through Genesis to know what the women thought of a strictly masculine dynasty."[32]

In Leviticus 24:11 the mother of a man brought before Moses for blasphemy is identified, by way of afterthought, as Shelomith, the daughter of Dibri, of the tribe of Dan. Stanton writes: "The interesting fact here is that a woman is dignified by a name, the only one so mentioned in the book of Leviticus. This is probably due to the fact that the son's character was so disreputable that he would reflect no lustre on his father's family. . . . If there had been anything good to tell of him, reference would no doubt have been made to his male progenitors."[33]

Judges 4 relates the story of the Israelite leader Barak, who was reluctant to lead his forces against the Canaanites until the prophet Deborah bolstered his courage by joining him in battle. Stanton writes of this episode: "We never hear sermons pointing women to the heroic virtues of Deborah as worthy of imitation. Nothing is said in the pulpit to rouse them from the apathy of ages, to inspire them to do and dare great things, to intellectual and spiritual achievements, in real communion with the Great Spirit of the Universe. Oh, no!"[34]

Judges 13 speaks of a woman at the center of a significant story, in which an angel of the Lord promises to bring an end to the woman's barrenness and to give her a child, who is to be known as Samson. The woman is known to us only as the wife of Manoah and the mother of Samson. Stanton writes: "I suppose it is from these Biblical examples that the wives of this Republic are known as Mrs. John Doe or Mrs. Richard Roe, to whatever Roe or Doe she may belong. If she chance to marry two or three times, the woman's identity is wholly lost."[35]

1 Kings 10:2 describes the visit of the queen of Sheba to the court of Solomon, where "she told him all that was on her mind." Stanton notes: "This is the first account which we have in the Bible of a prolonged rational conversation with a woman on questions of public policy."[36]

Stanton's search for women whom the Bible portrayed in an estimable manner is sometimes conducted with a playful twist. In Numbers 22 we find the story of the seer Balaam and his far more prescient ass, in which the ass's refusal to continue down a path despite Balaam's repeated beatings "to turn her into the way" saves Balaam from death at the hands of an angel of the Lord. "The chief point of interest in this parable of Balaam and his ass," Stanton writes, "is that the latter belonged to the female sex. This animal has been one of the most remarkable characters in literature. Her virtues have been quoted in the stately cathedral, in the courts of justice, in the editorial sanctum, in both tragedy and comedy on the stage, to point a moral and adorn a tale."[37]

Stanton's commentaries throughout *The Woman's Bible* are tart and acerbic. We need to spend only a little time with her published and unpublished writings to see her also as, for the most part, one of the more casually indomitable reformers of her time. And she was the mother of seven children, a fact that keeps peeking through. In 1 Samuel 2:19, a passage in the story of Hannah and her son begins, "His mother used to make for him a little robe, and take it to him each year." Stanton writes, "The historians and commentators dwell on the fact that Hannah made her son 'a little coat' and brought one annually. It is more probable that she brought him a complete suit of clothes once in three months, especially trousers, if those destined to service in the temple were allowed to play sports."[38]

At the same time, Stanton and her collaborators — upper-middle-class white Protestant women, invariably endowed with three names —

were very much products of their race and class and confined by familiar social prejudices, including those against non-Protestant Christians and against Jews and the Jewish tradition. "The only value of these records," Stanton observes of certain passages in the biblical accounts of Israelite history, "is to show the character of the Jewish nation, and make it easy for us to reject their ideas as to the true status of woman, and their pretension of being guided by the hand of God, in all their devious wanderings."[39] Earlier, the abolitionist Stanton had found herself inadvertently allied with white supremacists in opposing the Fourteenth and Fifteenth Amendments: why support extending the franchise to black males if it was not extended to all women at the same time? The women's rights movement was deeply split on this issue, and Stanton's rhetoric was ugly and racist.[40] Plainly, Stanton could be as blind to the disturbing character of some aspects of her social environment, and her own outlook, as she could be perceptive about others.

As noted, no one involved in *The Woman's Bible* had any formal training in biblical studies. Indeed, throughout the nineteenth century and well into the twentieth, those who raised the issue of the Bible and its role in female subordination were nonscholars, almost to a woman. Real biblical scholars, even the handful of women among them, showed no interest. A figure like Antoinette Brown Blackwell represents a glaring exception (and she, of course, left the field of biblical studies and seems to have left religion behind as well). Frances Willard, the leader of the Women's Christian Temperance Union, in 1889 urged young women "to make a specialty of Hebrew and New Testament Greek in the interest of their sex," and some young women in fact did make a specialty of Hebrew and New Testament Greek.[41] Applying those skills "in the interest of their sex" was another story. The established female scholars approached by Stanton to help with *The Woman's Bible* turned her down — "afraid," Stanton wrote, "that their high reputation and scholarly attainments might be compromised by taking part in an enterprise that for a time may prove very unpopular."[42]

The ranks of female biblical scholars were in any event not large, to say the least. The Society of Biblical Literature and Exegesis, the fore-runner of the present SBL, was founded in 1880 and did not induct a female member, Anna Ely Rhoads, until 1894. The number of women grew only slowly. Perhaps not surprisingly, most of the women in the field were employed at women's colleges. Wellesley College in particular had a strong and accomplished Department of Biblical History, Literature, and Exegesis, established by the redoubtable Mary Emma Wooley in 1895.[43] Many of the female biblical scholars were active in various reform movements; some had what might be called an incipient feminist consciousness. But those who have combed through the journals have found no record of interest among women in a feminist interpretation of Scripture. In the *Journal of Biblical Literature* you find early articles by women on such subjects as "The Messianic Ideal of Isaiah" (1917) and "Origin of the Name Pharisee" (1920) but nothing like the articles so common in our own time, nothing like "The 'Weaker Sex' in the *Testament of Job*" (1993) or "Judah as Wife and Husband: Deconstructing Gender in *Malachi*" (1996).

Why should this have been the case? The explanation involves a combination of oxygen depletion and firebreak. The animating spirit embodied in Stanton's person is hard to overestimate; Stanton died in 1902. Meanwhile, university life remained inimicable to all but the hardiest women in all but a few exceptional niches. And the demeanor of traditional religion in the broader American culture was at the turn of the century becoming more, not less, imposing. At the same time, the campaign for women's suffrage was about to bring an illusory sense of culmination to the women's movement as a whole. It had once seemed the most improbable of causes: "Why, Lizzie, thee will make us ridiculous," Lucretia Mott had complained when Stanton insisted on adding a resolution calling for women's suffrage in the original Seneca Falls declaration.[44] But within two decades of Stanton's death, women's suffrage was a reality. Antoinette Brown Blackwell lived long enough to cast a ballot (for Warren G. Harding) in the presidential election of 1920.

Whatever the reason, for roughly a century feminist criticism of the Bible, on the one hand, and biblical scholarship by women, on the other, constituted two widely separated worlds, worlds that would not begin to converge until the 1960s. When they did converge, some of the attention focused on Stanton and her work on Scripture was not wholly to her advantage — for instance, the attention paid to Stanton's prejudicial opinions. And when they did converge, the atmosphere was not always marked by the sense, inescapable in Stanton's prose, that the momentum of history gives cause for optimism. "Everything points," Stanton wrote a few months before her death, as she began to conceive plans for an expurgated Bible, devoid of pejorative references to women, "to a purer and more rational religion in the future, in which woman, as mother of the race, will be recognized as an equal in both Church and State."[45]

Chapter Three

....

BY THE HAND
OF A WOMAN

From a woman sin had its beginning,
and because of her we all die.
— *Ecclesiasticus 25:24*

Has the Lord indeed spoken only through Moses?
— *Numbers 12:2*

UNION THEOLOGICAL SEMINARY, in New York City, lies between Broadway and Claremont Avenue above 120th Street, in a neighborhood that might be thought of as upper Manhattan's religion district. It occupies two square blocks. The Jewish Theological Seminary of America stands across the street to the northeast, taking up much of a third block. Across the street to the southwest, taking up a fourth block, stands the Interchurch Center, which in recent years has housed scores of religious organizations, including groups devoted to social work, to missionary work, and to publishing and broadcasting. (The undistinguished, clunky, nineteen-story-tall structure is sometimes called "the God box"; its occupants, when you see them emerging at lunchtime or at work's end in the late afternoon, seem multicultural, well-meaning, and pallid.) Across the street directly to the west, occupying a fifth block, is Riverside Church, long a bulwark of social activism with a mildly hallowed cast. The Sunday sermons preached at Riverside Church have often been appropriate for quotation in the *New York Times*. Riverside's senior minister in the 1970s and 1980s, William Sloane Coffin, was an early and outspoken opponent of the Vietnam War.

Union is perhaps the archetype of the liberal, nondenominational theological seminary in America. Once under the wing of the Presbyterian Church, it emerged into independence amid the contentious late-nineteenth-century debates over the application of modern scholarship to the Bible, which at one point centered on Union's influential and modernist biblical scholar and librarian Charles Augustus Briggs (who was tried for and acquitted of heresy by the Presbyterian Synod).[1] Among Union's archetypal characteristics at present is the fact that its student body in recent years has become increasingly female: almost 55 percent of the more than four hundred students are women.[2] Institutionally, it embodies the mixture of comfort and conflict characteristic of its sister seminaries. The architecture is monastic, preserving outwardly in cool stone a way of life that no longer prevails inside. I can never visit the place without thinking of any number of passages from John Updike's novel *Roger's Version*, about a divinity-school professor. Among them is this:

> He reaches the broad stairs of carved oak, turns on the landing underneath the tall arched window, almost a slit, of bevelled granite and gray lozenge glass, and walks, in his rustling camouflage jacket, along the main hall downstairs. From behind the classroom doors arises, in binary fashion, laughter or silence. The walls are dotted with the tacky residue of old posters, with bits of Scotch tape and tinted Xeroxed paper. New, competing posters overflow the appointed display boards, advertising rallies to protest pollution in Maine and interference in Central America, and discussion groups concerning "hunger awareness" and "goddess thealogy."[3]

In the Union library's reading room, whose shelves hold the leather-bound classics required for exegetic work and where the marble pates of learned men gleam around the perimeter, it is perhaps possible to believe that this is still the seminary of Paul Tillich and Reinhold Niebuhr, a seminary for white men pursuing traditional careers in the ministry and theology. But even the statuary shows evidence of newer and broader concerns. There are now busts of the anti-slavery crusaders Sojourner Truth and Harriet Tubman, neither of whom was a reverend divine or even a significant donor to the seminary. In the hallways of the living quarters, tricycles and plastic toys betray a radically changed demography; Fischer-Price is not a reference to some venerable exegete.

The omnipresent flyers announcing meetings also tell a newer story: "Hunger Strike Demanding Action for Peace and Reunification in Korea"; "Union Condemns Police Brutality"; "Feminists for Animal Rights"; "Lesbian and Gay Caucus Sez Howdy"; "Wanted: Experienced teacher of Classical Greek to tutor a serious grad student." On one visit I saw pinned to a wall a critique of the current New York governor in the form of a parody of the Twenty-third Psalm:

> *George Pataki is my shepherd, I shall not want.*
> *He leadeth me beside still factories.*
> *He restoreth my doubt in New York politics.*
> *He guideth me to the path of unemployment.*
> *He surroundeth my wage with freeze.*

The people at Union, you sense, are busy, committed, occasionally even funny. They do not lack up-to-date agendas.

Phyllis Trible is the Baldwin Professor of Sacred Literature at Union. Her office is tucked high in a corner of the Union complex; you have to switch elevators and take a narrow-gauge spur line in order to reach it. On a wall of her office hangs a photograph of a kindly white-haired man in a dark suit and tie: James Muilenburg, who was a professor at Union when Trible was a student here, in the late 1950s and early 1960s, and who taught the first class she attended at the seminary. "I'll never forget that class," Trible recalled during one of several visits. She speaks with clarity and precision in an accent shaped by her native Virginia, a provenance of which she is proud in the special way that Virginians have. (Listening to Trible talk the first time I met her prompted me to ask, in some deluded imitation of Henry Higgins, if she was from North Carolina. She straightened in her chair in a gesture of wounded pride, and one eye took on a wide and chilly cast.) "He walked in with a stack of syllabi under his arm and he put them down on the table and started quoting Hebrew poetry, the 'Sword of Lamech' passage in Genesis."

> *I have slain a man for wounding me,*
> *a young man for striking me.*

If Cain is avenged sevenfold,
truly Lamech seventy-sevenfold.
— Genesis 4:23–24

"And he dramatized the whole thing — took the sword and plunged it in. He asked us where that sword reappeared, and jumped to Peter in the New Testament. I was utterly captivated and have never gotten over it to this day." Trible is only one of many female biblical scholars I've met who, whatever problems being a woman may have caused them in academe (and it has caused some of them considerable trouble), warmly acknowledge a close intellectual relationship with a male mentor.

Trible is the author of two books that would appear in anyone's canon of feminist biblical studies: *God and the Rhetoric of Sexuality* (1978), which is an attempt to recover feminist perspectives from a number of biblical stories, and *Texts of Terror: Literary-Feminist Readings of Biblical Narratives* (1984), which is an attempt to grapple with stories of a more disturbing kind. Even colleagues who have no affinity with her work, who differ radically in outlook, may acknowledge a debt, as evidenced by Trible's election in 1993 to the presidency of the Society of Biblical Literature. Ask graduate students in their twenties or established scholars in their thirties or forties how they came by their interest in women's issues and biblical studies, and the answer will often turn out to involve an article or a book by Trible. That her work is so widely read owes not only to the subject matter, although that of course is paramount, but also to her confidence of expression. Trible was among the group of scholars and writers whose lively, outspoken discussions at Rabbi Burton Visotzky's monthly seminars in New York evolved into the *Genesis* series created by Bill Moyers and broadcast on PBS. Not for her the dense gray scrivenings of academe. She writes with brightness and clarity and a dash of color.

It is important to recognize where Trible stands in a spectrum that ranges, as she explained to me, "from some fundamentalists who claim that they are feminists but say that they have no problem with the Bible to those at the other extreme who are unwilling to concede the Bible any authority at all." Trible is in the middle, perhaps the most uncomfortable place of all. She knows that for a woman many portions of the Bible are profoundly disturbing, and there is no way around them. How can you put an inspirational gloss on the story of Tamar, the princess who is raped by her brother Amnon and left desolate (2 Samuel 13:1–22), or the story of Hagar, the Egyptian slave who bears Abraham the son named Ishmael but who is later cast out of the household when Sarah, Abraham's wife, proves to be fertile after all (Genesis 16:1–16; 21:9–21)?

At the same time, Trible is hardly a member of the rejectionist camp. She believes that the Bible can be "reclaimed" as a repository of spiritual sustenance for women. She makes the points, too, that some of the Bible's problems are not of its own making and that some of its resources for and references to women are hidden. She pulled down a copy of the Revised Standard Version during one conversation and opened it to Deuteronomy 32:18, a passage in the long recitation known as the Song of Moses, which the prophet utters just before his death, and read aloud the following: "You were unmindful of the Rock that begot you, and you forgot the God who gave you birth." She said, "Those words 'gave you birth' are from a Hebrew term for 'writhing in labor,' so the translation, though accurate, is tame. But here is how the Jerusalem Bible translates it" — and she pulled down another book — "'The God who *fathered* you.'"

Since the early 1960s two generations of women have fully entered the field of biblical studies; a third is beginning to make its presence felt. Phyllis Trible is part of the first generation, and she was present at the very start of it. She was born and raised in Richmond, Virginia, in a family whose religious tradition was Southern Baptist, but Southern Baptist of a theologically moderate sort. She remembers an incident from her childhood that would one day, in a sense, reappear in her work. Every summer Trible was sent to a coeducational camp in the Blue Ridge Mountains that was run by several Southern Baptist churches. The boys at the camp were called RAs, which stood for Royal Ambassadors. The girls were called GAs, which stood for Girls' Auxiliary. "All the little boys," Trible recalls, "would hear the great ministers of the church, who would come to preach to them or teach them, and the little girls would just be put aside with somebody to take care of them — a retired missionary who told us stories. And one day the missionary said, 'Little girls, everything God made during the Creation got better and better, from the monsters of the sea to the wild animals of the earth. Now what was the last thing God created?' And we all chirped up and said 'Man.' And she said, 'No — woman!'" Across four centuries, the arguments of Heuricius Cornelius Agrippa von Nettesheim echoed in the Blue Ridge.

Trible attended Richmond public schools, where Latin was taught beginning in the seventh grade, and after high school she went on to Meredith College, a Baptist school for women in Raleigh, North Carolina, that her minister's wife had attended. Choosing Meredith turned out to be a wise and momentous decision. Women's colleges throughout America had for decades been employment havens for the many women with doctorates who found themselves effectively shut out of much of the rest of academe. Meredith's faculty, filled with women who had earned advanced degrees from Yale and Cornell and Duke and Pennsylvania and who would today be teaching at such institutions, was of a considerably higher quality than that of many male or coeducational schools of similar size, which had access to a supply of men from which the best had already been skimmed.

As it happened, though, Trible's great mentor at Meredith was not a woman but a professor in the department of religion named Ralph McLain, who was in touch with the best in theological education in the country and who encouraged a number of his students, Trible among them, to think seriously about going on to a seminary. Specifically, he urged Trible to attend not a Southern Baptist seminary, which at the time would not have offered solid academic programs for women, but the more liberal Union Theological Seminary. Trible embraced the idea. She entered a master's degree program at Union in the fall of 1954, one of only a half-dozen women in a class of a hundred. She would ultimately be the only one of these women to pursue a full-fledged academic career. She did not spend much time, she recalls, in the contemplation of her anomalous situation but was sustained by the work itself and by some of those who taught her. "Later — a generation later —

women began to talk about how hard it was, being a woman, but there were more women by then to have that conversation. It was a conversation I couldn't have. And to have dwelled on it would have been paralyzing, would have ended the whole thing."

During her student years at Union, Trible did take one class from Reinhold Niebuhr and did attend lectures by Paul Tillich, but the greatest influence from the outset was James Muilenburg, the Davenport Professor of Hebrew and Cognate Languages. It was Muilenburg who eventually helped persuade Trible to enlarge her horizons and expand her ambitions. When she arrived at Union, her conception of what the future held for her, to the extent that she had formed such a conception at all, was teaching Bible and religion at a good prep school. Under Muilenburg's guidance she fell in love with the course of study in the Hebrew Bible. She began asking herself, Why not think about doctoral work?

The study of the Hebrew Bible and the New Testament is an extraordinarily difficult undertaking, and there are no acceptable shortcuts. At a minimum you need to know Hebrew, Aramaic, and Greek, the languages in which the various books were first written. Almost all scholars of the Hebrew Bible have more ancient languages than just these — Akkadian, say, or Ugaritic or Assyrian or Hittite, languages whose structure and vocabulary and cultural underpinnings can offer insight into the world and the words of the Bible. New Testament scholars also have Latin and perhaps Coptic, a form of Egyptian written with the Greek alphabet and a few other letters. And, of course, knowing German and French is standard, because so much biblical scholarship down through the years has been written in those languages. The "Languages" line on a biblical scholar's curriculum vitae can be imposing, and even modesty may glow beneath a nimbus of accomplishment (as, for example, when Trible mentioned offhandedly that she had needed "a touch of Syriac" for her dissertation).

The ancient languages are by no means always straightforward affairs. Ugaritic, one of the languages Trible pursued, was unknown until 1929, when a ploughman accidentally opened up some ancient tombs at a place called Ras Shamra, in northern Syria, which led to the excavation of the cosmopolitan city of Ugarit and the discovery of a royal archive containing thousands of clay tablets. The Ugaritic tablets, which date back to about the fourteenth century B.C., before written Hebrew, provide a great deal of religious and literary material about the world of ancient Canaan that is important for understanding the Bible's prose and, even more, its poetry. This material is also important for understanding some of the Bible's theology, because the religion of the Israelites was in many ways both a reflection of and a reaction against that of the Canaanites (Baal, one of the false gods that the Israelites were reliably prone to worship, was a Canaanite deity) and employed a great deal of Ugaritic language and imagery. Psalm 29 — "The Lord sits enthroned over the flood; the Lord sits enthroned as king for ever" — was in all likelihood originally a Ugaritic hymn, and King David's famous curse after the death of Saul — "Ye mountains of Gilboa,/Let there be no dew or rain upon you" — draws on a prior curse uttered in a Ugaritic epic.[4]

Ugaritic is written in cuneiform — wedge-shaped marks pressed into clay — but not all cuneiform writing is alike, scholars quickly discovered. Most of it is syllabic or ideographic in nature and requires hundreds of distinct symbols. Ugaritic happens to be an alphabetic script and requires only about thirty symbols. Once this unprecedented characteristic of a cuneiform script was recognized, it took the German linguist (and former military cryptanalyst) Hans Bauer less than a week to crack the code.[5]

Establishing the alphabet only takes you so far, however. Written Ugaritic, like ancient written Hebrew, is "unpointed," that is, it is a consonantal language, without vowels. To make sense of the text, the reader has to do the pointing, has to figure out what the vowels are. To give an example in English, the reader has to decide whether "CP" is the word for "cup" or "cape" or "cope" or "cap." You can run into further trouble because sometimes there aren't space breaks between words. (By way of analogy, consider the English letters GDSNWHR; do they stand for "God is now here" or "God is nowhere"?) Sometimes you find consonantal parallels with words in cognate languages, and these may help show the way; indeed, knowledge of Ugaritic and other languages has permitted scholars to translate some words in the Hebrew Bible that had eluded precise translation since antiquity. (For instance, the resolution of a puzzle in Ugaritic recently helped to resolve one in the Song of Songs. For years, translators could only guess at the meaning of a Hebrew verb that appears only once in the Bible, in Songs 4:1: "Your hair is like a flock of goats, which _____ from Mount Gilead." The discovery of several examples of a probable cognate verb in Ugaritic, whose precise meaning is also unknown but has something to do with the sea, allowed scholars to work out a translation in both languages. The passage should read, "which *flow in waves* from Mount Gilead.")[6] Sometimes, of course, you are on your own. The task of mastering ancient languages can be grueling. It takes years of study, and persistence, and patience.

There is more. To subject the Bible to the historical-critical method — that is, to treat it objectively, not theologically, as if it were any other ancient text — requires familiarity with a number of well-defined (and still developing) techniques. The first of these is textual criticism, which in essence means establishing an accurate text, as close to the presumed original as possible. This is not easy. Between the original text of the various books of the Bible and the earliest extant manuscripts lie centuries of copying and recopying. Scribes make errors that might seem improbable or peculiar if all of us had not made similar errors ourselves in the mundane documents of school and daily life. A seeming mistake that is not really a mistake gets "corrected." The eye fleetingly wanders, then takes up where it thought it was but wasn't. The jargon of textual criticism is laced with an abundance of chewy denotational necessities, such as the terms "haplography" and "dittography" (haplography, in the words of one standard survey, is "a mistake in writing, when a copyist wrote once what should have been written twice; the opposite of dittography"), or the terms "homoeoarchton" and "homoeoteleuton" ("an accidental omission by a copyist caused, respectively, by similar beginnings or similar endings on words; the copyist's eye skipped from the first to the second, leaving out the intervening material").[7] Whether deliberately or by accident, documents acquire an element of corruption. There has long been disagreement about where the Gospel of Mark and the Epistle to the Romans were initially supposed to stop.

One way or another, textual criticism of the Bible has been occurring from the very outset; the task, if not the term, was very much on the minds of those responsible for the transmission of the various biblical texts from age to age and language to language. Another analytical technique, known as form criticism, is more recent. It grew largely out of the work of the German biblical scholar Hermann Gunkel (1862–1932), who took an interest in certain work being done by scholars in Germany on the oral transmission of folktales. Form criticism looks at the various typologies of what scholars presume were originally oral materials — for instance, parables, hymns, acclamations, healing stories, legal sayings, prophetic sayings, legends — that are incorporated into a given text. It attempts to relate these materials to the setting in life, or *Sitz im Leben*, that each type of material is thought to have occupied, such as preaching, instruction, and worship, and it also looks at parallels with extrabiblical materials.

A related methodology is source criticism, which focuses on the disparate strands of biblical material as they may have looked when they first achieved written existence. As with form criticism, you work presumptively backward, by deduction. You ask of the text such questions as Who wrote it? In what place? At what time? Under the influence of what literary models? Clearly the book of Genesis differs from that of Job, as Job differs from Psalms and Psalms from Samuel. Even within books the hand of more than one person can be seen at work. It was through the use of source criticism that scholars came to the conclusion that the first five books of the Bible drew upon the work of essentially four different authors.

A further technique, tradition criticism (also known as redaction criticism, when the subject is the New Testament), builds on the others, looking at a biblical text with respect to the editorial process, or redaction, that produced it from the available compositional elements. The assumption on which redaction criticism rests is that the editors were intent on producing works of particular and coherent theological substance and point of view, and that this point of view can be apprehended through an understanding of "the collection, arrangement, editing, and modification of traditional material."[8] Of course, apprehension works the other way as well: a prior grasp of the theology may inform a scholar's reconstruction of the editing. The Gospel of Mark seems to have been written with an audience of Gentile readers in mind, possibly in Rome; it tends to be critical not only of Palestinian Jews in general but also of the apostles, whose inadequate behavior it mentions repeatedly. Matthew, in contrast, is exceedingly Jewish in tone, is didactic, and is concerned with presenting a glorified Jesus.

By 1960 Trible had completed her course requirements and had undertaken a doctoral dissertation — on the Book of Jonah, as it happens, in part because so very little had been written about it. "I would go to the library," she remembers, "and look up Jonah, and often there were no books at all, which delighted me no end." Also, Jonah is short (it consists of only four chapters), so Trible was able to apply all the various methodologies of biblical criticism and also a method known as rhetorical criticism, an approach pioneered by Muilenburg that grows organically out of form criticism but concentrates less on a text's parts in isolation and more on how a text functions as a literary whole.[9] Whereas much of historical-critical scholarship has understandably been concerned with identifying ingredients, using reverse evolution and retroactive surmise — has been concerned, in other words, with "unscrambling the omelette," as the anthropologist Sir Edmund Leach once put it — rhetorical criticism has sought to pay new attention to the omelette itself.[10]

While writing her dissertation, Trible was teaching at a girls' prep school, the Masters School, in Dobbs Ferry, New York. When she completed her doctorate, she took up a position at Wake Forest University, a coeducational liberal arts institution in Winston-Salem, North Carolina. Wake Forest was then a Baptist school (it now has no denominational ties), and it possessed substantial resources, owing to large amounts of tobacco money endowed by the Reynolds family. The religion department was big enough and strong enough that individual faculty members could concentrate on their specialties rather than dilute their teaching by offering a wide range of courses — say, ethics *and* theology *and* world religions *and* New Testament *and* Hebrew Bible. In 1971, when Andover Newton Theological Seminary, a Baptist and Congregational institution near Boston, had an opening for a professor of Old Testament, the seminary selected Trible, and it was at Andover Newton that she first blossomed into a scholar known for her distinctively feminist approach to the Bible.

Here we need to back up for a moment. There is nothing in Trible's doctoral dissertation that gives any clue to the later direction of her work, save that in technique it is an exercise in rhetorical criticism.[11] The dissertation was completed in 1963, the same year in which Betty Friedan published *The Feminine Mystique,* which in many ways helped to reignite a feminist movement that had faltered badly since its high point in the period immediately after World War I, when the constitutional amendment granting women's suffrage was at last ratified in the United States.

If the women's movement as a whole had faltered, biblical studies with any sort of feminist motivation scarcely survived at all. A handful of women toiled in the field, and they trained other women, but their professional concerns did not involve thinking about women. The one figure who sought to carry on, in her own idiosyncratic way, the work of Elizabeth Cady Stanton as embodied in *The Woman's Bible* was the missionary physician and social reformer Katharine C. Bushnell, whose book *God's Word to Women: One Hundred Bible Studies on Woman's Place in the Divine Economy* (1916) went through several printings and enjoyed a limited vogue. Bushnell, a descendant of the submarine designer David Bushnell, was an evangelical Christian and a onetime student of the redoubtable Frances Willard. She had first been made aware of male bias on the part of Bible translators during a long period in China, in the course of checking a Chinese version of the Bible against the Greek one. She turned next to English translations, and then, when she realized that translation flaws could not account for all the problems of biblical meaning she encountered, to broader issues. "Why," she asked, "should fossilized theologians be allowed to drag their antiquated notions across the pages of every biblical commentary which is published for the use of Christians?" At the time of her death in 1946, at the age of ninety, Bushnell was still active but largely forgotten. Her last pastor, K. Fillmore Gray, offered a grimly frank assessment of her legacy: "Her work was like a rock dropped to the bottom of the ocean. Kerplunk, it was gone, the end of it."[12]

Betty Friedan's *The Feminine Mystique* contained little that was explicitly about women and Scripture, beyond noting that "women of orthodox Catholic or Jewish origin do not easily break through the housewife image; it is enshrined in the canons of their religion," but as the historian Carolyn De Swarte Gifford has pointed out, the implication of the biblical narrative in male domination went back to Stanton and earlier.[13] In 1964, Gifford notes, a biblical scholar at Smith College, Margaret Brackenbury Crook, proposed what she called a "reconnaissance" of the position of women in Judaism and Christianity, making full use of a broad array of modern scholarship. In her book *Women and Religion*, Crook wrote: "A masculine monopoly in religion begins when Miriam raises her indignant question: 'Does the Lord speak only through Moses?' Since then, in all three of the great religious groups stemming from the land and books of Israel — Judaism, Christianity, and Islam — men have formulated doctrine and established systems of worship offering only meager opportunity for the expression of the religious genius of womankind."[14]

Crook, a native of England and the first woman to undertake the full training for the Unitarian ministry, was seventy-eight years old when *Women and Religion* was published. She had done her university work at Oxford but was given a degree from the University of London, because Oxford at the time did not give degrees to women. Crook did not consider herself a feminist.

Mary Daly, an American studying for doctorates in philosophy and theology at the University of Fribourg in Switzerland, most certainly did consider herself a feminist. In the mid-1960s, Daly began publishing outspoken feminist commentaries on the role of religion, especially Catholicism, in the oppression of women. The publication of her first book, *The Church and the Second Sex*, caused something of a sensation, in no small part because Daly was by then a professor of theology at Boston College, a Jesuit school. About the Bible she had to say what others had said before: "The authors of both the Old and the New

Testaments were men of their times, and it would be naive to think that they were free of the prejudices of their epochs." She made reference to "the mounting suspicion in the minds of many that Christianity — particularly as it is embodied in the Catholic Church — is the inevitable enemy of human progress."[15]

Publication of *The Church and the Second Sex* resulted in Daly's being fired from her job at Boston College, which caused widespread demonstrations and what Daly described in a preface to a later edition of the book as "an archetypal battle between principalities and powers," with herself happily cast in the role of "witch and madwoman."[16] The case, she recalled in an article for a special women's issue of *The New Yorker* in 1996, "received national/international/supernatural publicity."[17] Whether despite or because of the demonstrations and the publicity, Daly was soon rehired, with reluctance (and with tenure).

For a number of years Daly was a popular lecturer in certain church circles. She has continued to write books and to maintain a following, although now primarily outside of those circles. Her position as a reformer within Christianity has given way to advocacy of a post-Christian perspective and to espousal of "Gyn/Ecology" and "the Witch within ourSelves, who spins and weaves the tapestries of Elemental creation."[18] Her presence today in the theology department at Boston College is an uneasy one. My impression is that if there are some at Boston College who might pause at a hypothetical offer by the devil to arrange for Mary Daly's disappearance in return for the loss of their immortal souls, it is only because they are wondering, What's the catch?

Phyllis Trible went to Andover Newton at a time when her own thinking as an incipient feminist was beginning to mature and when Mary Daly was at the height of her influence and a significant presence in Boston theological discussions. From this conjunction came Trible's first real foray into feminist biblical studies. "When I went to Andover Newton," she recalls,

it was required of new faculty people that they deliver a scholarly paper. Now, one of the reasons I made the decision to come to Boston was my interest in feminism. A lively conversation was going on there.

Mary Daly, who at the time defined "feminist," was speaking everywhere. But the debate, the discussion, was mostly going on in theological, not in biblical, studies. The assumption was that the Bible was kind of hopeless in this discussion.

So when I was invited to give that paper, several things came together. One was hearing many speeches by Mary Daly in which the Bible was tossed off as the beginnings of patriarchy, and hence *only* patriarchal and worthy of dismissal or denunciation. I asked myself, If that is so, how come I love the Bible? Because two things are beyond question for me: I *am* a feminist, and I *love* the Bible. And they were saying, "Well, these things are incompatible." Or "You can love the Bible as a scholar, but you can't love it existentially." And I knew that I did. So then the challenge for me was to try to articulate that. There must be something more that can be said. I had some clues from the text that started surfacing in my mind. I was looking at Genesis 2–3 to see if I could articulate an interpretation of that story that was not patriarchal, because at some level I sensed it within myself. If that story is, as people have told us and continue to tell us, so patriarchal, how come I like it?

Trible's first public consideration of the Creation stories in Genesis 2–3 came in a lecture titled "Depatriarchalizing in Biblical Interpretation." Trible has spoken of how the Bible might be reclaimed as a spiritual resource for women, and this lecture, later published in the *Journal of the American Academy of Religion*, was an attempt at doing so.

Since early Christian times the accounts in Genesis of the creation of human beings and of their expulsion from the Garden of Eden have been used to explain and justify the subordination of woman to man and to fix responsibility for humanity's fallen state firmly on the shoulders of woman. Eve came to be seen as responsible for what Christian theology deems original sin, the transgression that would stain all future generations. In her "Depatriarchalizing" lecture, Trible argued, however, that properly understood, the two very different Creation stories in Genesis do not actually say what centuries of interpretation have made them say.

In the first of these stories, man and woman are created at the same time ("male and female he created them"), but in the second story, the man, to be called Adam, seems to have been created first, from clay, and the woman, who is later given the name Eve, seems to be an afterthought, created from the man's rib. Is woman to be considered subordinate to man simply because in one of the two stories she was created after he was? This was certainly the point of view of Augustine, and even the feminist Simone de Beauvoir accepted this interpretation at face value: "Eve was not fashioned at the same time as the man; she was not fabricated from a different substance, nor of the same clay as was used to mold Adam: she was taken from the flank of the first male. Not even her birth was independent."[19] But if mere subsequence implies inferiority, Trible argued, then why are human beings not regarded as subordinate to animals, since Genesis 1:24–27 plainly declares that human beings were created after the animals were? This member of the Girls' Auxiliary had not forgotten that retired missionary's early lesson.

Of course, the issue of precedence in the order of creation and whether it matters is almost beside the point, because it is a mistake, Trible wrote, to think of the first human being, Adam, as male. She points out that the Hebrew word *'adham*, from which "Adam" derives, is a generic term for humankind, denoting a being created from the earth, and is used at the beginning of Genesis 2 to describe a creature of undifferentiated sex. Only when the Lord takes a rib from *'adham* to make a companion are the sexes differentiated, and the change is signaled by the terminology. The creature from whom the rib was taken is now referred to not as *'adham* but as *'ish* ("man"), and the creature fashioned from the rib is called *'ishshah* ("woman"). "Making her entrance in the last episode of scene one," Trible wrote, "she is the culmination of the entire movement, in no way an afterthought." And Trible went on: "Unlike all the rest of creation, she does not come from the earth; rather Yahweh God *builds* the rib into woman. The Hebrew verb *build (bnh)* indicates considerable labor to produce solid results. Hence woman is no weak, dainty, ephemeral creature. No opposite sex, no second sex, no derived sex — in short, no Adam's 'rib.' Instead, woman is the culmination of creation, fulfilling humanity in sexuality."[20] In this reading, then, the sexes begin in equality.

Be that as it may, there comes almost at once the moment of temptation, when the serpent entices the woman with the allurements of the forbidden fruit, promising that it will "make one wise"; and the woman eats, and gives fruit to her husband, who also eats. "The serpent beguiled me, and I ate," the woman tells an angry God, who in retribution orders the expulsion of the man and woman from Eden, amid memorably wroth divine poetry that spells out some of the harsh future consequences of the fall from grace for ordinary men and women.

For these consequences the woman was eventually saddled with blame. "Indeed," wrote the fourth-century bishop Ambrose, one of the fathers of the church, "after the woman was made, she was the first to violate the divine commandment. She even dragged her husband along with her into sin, and showed herself to be an incentive to him."[21] Recall the words of 1 Timothy 2:12–14: "I permit no woman to teach or to have authority over men; she is to keep silent. For Adam was formed first, then Eve; and Adam was not deceived, but the woman was deceived and became a transgressor." The early Christian writer Tertullian addressed women in a fiery, uncompromising vein: "You are the devil's gateway; you are the unsealer of that forbidden tree; you are the first deserter of the divine law; you are she who persuaded him whom the devil was not valiant enough to attack: you destroyed so easily God's image, man. On account of your desert — that is, death, even the Son of Man had to die."[22] "O Eve," says Adam in Milton's *Paradise Lost*, fixing the blame, "in evil hour thou didst give ear to that false worm." And he goes on, extending the taint to all of her sex: "Thus it shall befall/Him who to worth in women overtrusting/Lets her will rule."[23]

With regard to the Genesis story, Trible was determined to accept every challenge, to fight every battle. Yes, it is the woman who first succumbs to temptation, but notice the qualities that the text reveals in her. She is "intelligent, informed, perceptive." She plays the role of "theologian, ethicist, hermeneut, rabbi." The man, in contrast, is silent, weak, evasive. After the act of disobedience, God delivers his judgment: death enters life, the earth is cursed, and the relationship of woman and man deteriorates. It is only at this point, with the departure of 'ish and 'ishshah from their initial and intended condition, that the sexes fall out of equality. It is only then, in this disobedient state, that the man establishes his dominance. Oppression of women by men is not what was meant for humanity, even if it is what we have come to. "Rather than legitimating the patriarchal culture from which it comes," Trible concludes, "the myth places that culture under judgment."

≈∞

Trible's specialty, as noted, is rhetorical criticism, which pays particular attention to a document's literary architecture. During one conversation Trible walked me through some passages that together may offer an instance of a biblical woman's falling victim to editorial manhandling. The passages tell the story of Miriam, the sister of Moses and Aaron, a woman who was perhaps considered by the Israelites to have been the equal of her brothers but of whom few traces survive in the Bible as it has come down to us.

We meet Miriam in the Book of Exodus. It is she who persuades Pharaoh's daughter to raise the infant Moses, left in a basket among the rushes on the banks of the Nile, as her own, and to bring along Moses' mother as a nurse: "Then his sister said to Pharaoh's daughter, 'Shall I go and call you a nurse from the Hebrew women to nurse the child for you?'" Miriam is not at this point given a name; the woman who saves the infant's life is identified only as his sister. And as the story of Moses proceeds, Miriam disappears — until the crossing of the Red Sea. Then, when the Israelites reach the far shore, Pharaoh's armies having been destroyed, there is a song of rejoicing, the poetic Song at the Sea (Exodus 15), sung by Moses and the people of Israel. It begins, "I will sing to the Lord, for he has triumphed gloriously;/the horse and his rider he has thrown into the sea." No sooner has Moses finished than we encounter a small fragment of text that appears to be out of place. The fate of Pharaoh's armies is for some reason quickly retold, and then, with the Israelites once again safely on shore, "Miriam the prophetess, the sister of Aaron," begins to sing the very same Song at the Sea. She sings the first two lines. The text then moves on to other business.

There are several interesting things here, Trible told me. One is that we learn for the first time that the sister of Aaron, who must also be the sister of Moses, has a name, and it is Miriam. (In the rhetoric of the

Bible, the act of giving a name to a person can be of great significance, and the significance is heightened in this instance by the fact that so many biblical women function as nameless character actors.) We also see that she is called a prophet and that this occurs well before Moses himself is first called a prophet, even if the precise meaning of "prophet" in the context of Exodus remains unclear. This piece of text about Miriam represents, Trible said, the dogged survival of an earlier version of the Exodus story. Indeed, scholars have argued that in the most ancient Israelite traditions, the singing of the Song at the Sea was probably ascribed not to Moses but to Miriam. (As an aside, Trible observed that the first work on the attribution of the Song at the Sea to Miriam dates back to the mid-1950s and was done by men. She added pointedly, "I'm not one to say you can't use the previous generation of scholarship — not at all.") Whether through insight or serendipity, Miriam's prominent function was acknowledged by George Frideric Handel in his oratorio *Israel in Egypt*, which, as the historian of religion Jaroslav Pelikan has noted, makes her the *choregos*, "like the leader of the chorus in Aeschylus or Sophocles."[24]

A hint of an alternative version of the Exodus story has recently come to light in one of the Dead Sea Scrolls, among the fragments that make up the manuscript known as 4Q365. These fragments, when arrayed alongside the established text, give evidence of a longer song of Miriam at the place where the two-line refrain is found now. Although it strongly echoes portions of the Song at the Sea, its surviving handful of truncated lines also signals other themes, including, in the phrase "and he exalted her to their heights," an indication that God acted to save his people in part through a woman, Miriam. This "by the hand of a woman" theme is a trope that turns up in other examples of the genre known as victory song, and its point, as one scholar, George J. Brooke, of the University of Manchester, has noted, is twofold: "Not only does it show that God protects the weak, but that he protects the weak through the weak." The reversal here, in other words, involves not only the Israelites and their enemies but also the status quo within Israelite society.[25]

In any event, as Trible pointed out, Miriam soon moves with the people of Israel into the desert, whereupon she disappears from the

Book of Exodus. But she reappears later in the Bible, in connection with what seems to be a severe clash within the leadership, from which she emerges the loser — which accounts, perhaps, for her diminished prominence. The reappearance occurs amid the jumble of the Book of Numbers, wherein Miriam and Aaron are heard to question the authority of their brother, asking the question that Trible and others ask more broadly: "Has the Lord spoken only through Moses?" The Lord does not punish Aaron, but Miriam is struck down with a skin affliction, possibly leprosy, for her rebelliousness, and later dies in the wilderness of Zin.

Yet there are signs that the memory of Miriam in the Israelite consciousness remains an active and uplifting one. Miriam has always been associated with water, Trible noted — remember the basket among the rushes? remember the Song at the Sea? — and the text immediately following the notice of Miriam's death again brings up the subject of water. It reads, "Now there was no water for the congregation." In standard editions that sentence starts a new paragraph, as if the subject is suddenly being changed. "Written Hebrew doesn't have such breaks," Trible said. "The paragraph marking after the end of the Miriam story is artificial. It makes you miss the idea that what is happening is connected to Miriam's death. Nature is mourning the loss of Miriam."

Thereafter in the Bible, Miriam appears only in hints and fragments, most significantly in Micah 6:4, where God puts her on a par with Moses and Aaron as leaders in early Israel: "I brought you up from Egypt, I set you free from the land of slavery, I sent Moses, Aaron, and Miriam to lead you." Miriam also survives in ordinary life, in the obvious but easy-to-overlook form of the continuing popularity of her name and its variants. The New Testament, compiled more than a millennium after Miriam's death, is populated with a multitude of women named Mary — the Hellenized version of the Hebrew Miriam. "It is probably safe to estimate," Pelikan has written, "that for two thousand years 'Mary' has been the name most frequently given to girls at baptism, and, through the exclamation 'Jesus, Mary, Joseph' . . . and above all through the *Ave Maria*, which has been repeated literally millions of times every day, the female name that has been pronounced most often in the Western world."[26]

It is no coincidence, Trible has argued, that the Magnificat, the great canticle of Mary the mother of Jesus, whose similarities with the Song of Hannah (1 Samuel 2:1–10) have long been noted, also borrows imagery directly from the Song at the Sea. From the Song at the Sea: "Thy right hand, O Lord, glorious in power,/thy right hand, O Lord, shatters the enemy." From the Magnificat: "He has shown strength with his arm,/he has scattered the proud in the imagination of their hearts."

Miriam, Trible said, is only one of a number of powerful women in the Bible who are alluded to almost in passing, the modesty of the references at odds with the importance of the roles these women seem to have played. The references hint at the existence of a class of women in Israel whose history has in essence been lost, or can today be recovered only by means of the most delicate salvage, even then yielding mere wisps of insight. That the references survive at all — that the editors believed that some mention of these women *had* to be made — is itself suggestive. "It shows," Trible said, "that the stories just couldn't be completely squelched."

Much as we hear the polite word "problematic" applied to material in the Bible that some feminist scholars deem to be negative, so we hear the polite word "optimistic" applied to interpretations that some scholars deem to be too positive. "In Trible's hands the Bible almost turns into a feminist manifesto," writes Ilana Pardes, of Jerusalem's Hebrew University, in the course of an otherwise not unsympathetic treatment of Trible in her book *Countertraditions in the Bible*.[27] Trible is not unfamiliar with this assessment, or with the broader charge that she falls on the wrong side of the divide between exegesis, which involves establishing the intended meaning of a text, and eisegesis, which involves reading a desired meaning into a text. Her views about the Creation stories have an articulate camp of supporters, including, up to a point, such prominent literary critics as Mieke Bal, but they face a considerable camp of critics.

Some of the arguments take place amid thickets of linguistic arcana and have to do with such things as the definition and manner of usage of words like *'adham,* or with how the Hebrew term that has been translated as "fit helpmate" should really be understood as it applies to Eve. Other arguments address the internal logic of some of Trible's contentions, pointing out that she seems willing to infer some messages but not other, equally suggestive ones from the literary construction of the text. The literary critic Susan Lanser agrees with Trible that, strictly speaking, by eating of the forbidden fruit Adam and Eve commit exactly the same sin and bear exactly the same measure of personal responsibility. But why then should the punishment be so disproportionate, with man condemned, if that is an apt word, to dominance over woman and woman condemned to submission?[28] The Hebrew Bible scholar David Jobling, of St. Andrew's College in Saskatchewan, working from the same textual platform, acknowledges the presumed parity of the sinful act per se but cannot accept that moral equality is the only or even the main point the passage is intended to convey: "This, of course, is true in itself, but it takes no account of the asymmetry of the offences. The woman sinned first, and was implicated in the man's sin; the man did not sin first, nor was he implicated in the woman's sin. Why should the text be saying nothing significant through this clear asymmetry when — especially for a skilled rhetorical critic like Trible — much smaller details have large significance?" Jobling goes on to ask Trible this question: "Who, in a patriarchal culture, composed the feminist story which she takes the text to be; and how was it received, by a patriarchal culture, as its basic myth of origins?"[29]

Pamela J. Milne, a professor of Hebrew Bible at the University of Windsor in Ontario, has expressed doubts about how widely comprehensible Trible's subtleties might be even now. "When Phyllis was talking about teasing elements out of the text, these bits about Miriam," Milne commented during a 1994 symposium sponsored by the Smithsonian Institution, "I thought to myself, if we took this book out into the streets of this city and asked people to read this or that text, what are the chances they would see these things on their own? It takes great literary insight to find these kinds of things in the text." Trible replied, "So-called people on the street, or laypeople, come up with all sorts of surprising readings of the text. They play hunches that scholars may never have dreamt of. The scholar may think that she has teased something out, but later she learns that a particular Bible study group in a particular church always thought that was the case anyway."[30]

In a sense, one of Trible's responses to the charge of incautious optimism is her second book, *Texts of Terror*, a feminist reading of the stories of tragic women in the Bible — stories that have no happy endings and whose lessons are far from redemptive. In recounting such episodes, Trible intends "to recover a neglected history, to remember a past that the present embodies."[31]

One story is that of Hagar, the Egyptian slave by whom the patriarch Abraham fathers a child, Ishmael, believing his wife, Sarah, to be barren (Genesis 16:1–16; 21:9–21). Sarah eventually conceives, and at her instigation Hagar and Ishmael are cast out into the wilderness, where only the Lord's intervention saves them from death. Trible notes that Hagar is the first woman in Scripture to receive an annunciation and the first "historical" woman after the Creation allegory to bear a child. "Yet she experiences exodus without liberation, revelation without salvation, wilderness without covenant, wanderings without land, promise without fulfillment, and unmerited exile without return."[32]

Another story is that of Tamar, a daughter of King David, whose brother, Amnon, conceives an angry passion for her (2 Samuel 13:1–22). He contrives to get her alone, and his intentions become plain. "No, my brother, do not force me," Tamar pleads, "for such a thing is not done in Israel; do not do this wanton folly." But Amnon pays no heed. He rapes her and then in effect discards her. David, upon learning what has happened, becomes angry but does nothing.

A third story is that of an unnamed concubine (Judges 19:1–30) in Bethlehem who is raped, murdered, and dismembered. This act leads to war among the Israelites, and to more rape and more slaughter. "Of all the characters in Scripture," Trible writes of the unnamed woman, "she is the least. Appearing at the beginning and close of a story that rapes her, she is alone in a world of men. Neither the other characters nor the narrator recognizes her humanity. She is property, object, tool, and literary device."[33]

And then there is the story of the daughter of Jephthah (Judges 11:

29–40), who is given no name yet must pay the ultimate price. Jephthah, an Israelite general, has vowed to the Lord that in gratitude for a victory over the Ammonites he will make a sacrifice, "a burnt offering" of whoever first comes to greet him when he returns home. That person turns out to be his daughter, who "came out to meet him with timbrels and with dances." Although the Lord stayed the hand of Abraham before he could offer his son in sacrifice, no intervention saves Jephthah's daughter from her father, "who did with her according to his vow which he had made." In later commentaries, in both the Hebrew Bible and the New Testament, Trible notes, Jephthah is praised for his faith, for not turning away from the Lord, and his daughter is forgotten.

Is there any more point in holding up biblical stories for contemporary censure than there is in mining them for overlooked gems that, if given just the right polish, can be made to shine in a certain contemporary light? With Phyllis Trible's work expressly in view, the biblical scholar Phyllis A. Bird has ventured a word of caution: "The contemporary theologian-exegete is reminded that the Bible is often quite uninterested in, or unable to comprehend, the questions pressed upon the text from modern perspectives and experiences."[34] Trible's response might be that such a reminder is absurdly confining and makes sense only if we assume that the relationship people have with the Bible, or should be encouraged to have with the Bible, is a relationship with something dormant and musty. Trible thinks of the Bible in vastly different terms — as if it were a pilgrim forging new relationships over time. There are ways, she believes, of articulating a conversation between feminism and the Bible in which each critiques the other.

It is, of course, not hard to see how feminism might critique the Bible. When I asked Trible once what critique the Bible could possibly offer of feminism, she replied that people sometimes have a tendency to make too much of feminism, to put it up on a pedestal. The Bible calls attention to that propensity. "It warns," she said, "against idolatry."

Chapter Four

....

THE MOTHERS
OF ISRAEL

I would lead you and bring you into the house
of my mother, and into the chamber
of her that conceived me.
— Song of Songs 8:2

The observer must distinguish between
what people actually do and what
people say that they do.
— Sir Edmund Leach

I HAD KNOWN in an abstract sort of way that the events associated with any square mile of soil in Israel were sufficient to provide an ample history for a medium-size planet, but the reality was brought home during a drive through Israel's Jezreel Valley on my way to Nazareth and, a few miles beyond, to the hilltop ruin of ancient Sepphoris. It was in the Jezreel Valley, beneath Mount Gilboa, that King Saul fell upon his sword rather than risk capture by the Philistines. A few miles from Mount Gilboa is the Spring of Harod, where, at the Lord's insistence, the judge Gideon winnowed his army from 32,000 to 300 men before successfully attacking the Midianites. To the west, where a strategic pass opens onto the Jezreel Valley, lies what is left of the ancient city of Megiddo, the earliest of whose twenty-five layers of occupation dates back to the Bronze Age. The final battle between the forces of good and evil "on the great day of God the Almighty" is supposed to take place in the shadow of the Hill of Megiddo — *Har Megiddo*, that is to say, or Armageddon: "And they assembled them at the place which is called in Hebrew Armageddon" (Revelation 16:16). The most recent battle in the area was of less apocalyptic consequence. It occurred toward the end of

World War I, in September 1918, when Field Marshal Edmund Henry Hynman Allenby surprised and routed a Turkish army at Megiddo Pass. Elevated to the peerage, Allenby was thereafter known as First Viscount Allenby of Megiddo and Felixstowe.

The Jezreel Valley also happens to be a place where women figure prominently in the Bible. Visible to the north of the Spring of Harod is Mount Tabor, below which the judge and prophet Deborah, with her reluctant general Barak, led the Israelites to victory over the Canaanite army commanded by Sisera — an event (Judges 4–5) culminating in Sisera's death at the hand of another woman, Jael, who drove a tent peg into his head "till it went down into the ground, as he was lying fast asleep from weariness." Forty years of peace ensued.

> *The peasantry ceased in Israel,*
> *they ceased*
> *until you arose, Deborah,*
> *arose as a mother in Israel.*

The long poem spoken after the battle, a victory song, derives from an oral tradition that is among the oldest in the Bible, dating, scholars believe, from the twelfth century B.C., roughly contemporaneous with the events the words recount.

Not far from Mount Tabor is the village of Ein Dor, where the Bible describes a woman performing a quasi-religious role. Before his final battle, King Saul (1 Samuel 28) consulted a witch or medium — to his deep regret, because she summoned the judge Samuel, who foretold Saul's horrific fate and that of his sons and his army at the hands of the Philistines. "Then Saul fell at once full length upon the ground, filled with fear." Beyond Ein Dor, just off Route 71, the main road that runs through the Jezreel Valley between Beit She'an (on whose walls Saul's body was hung) and Afula, is the mound, or tel, that harbors the remains of Jezreel, the winter capital of King Ahab and his wife. This was Jezebel, a woman whose name today is commonly associated with wanton wiles and idolatry, although her true offense seems to have been a ruthless exercise of power together with loyalty to the gods of her ancestors (she was not an Israelite but a Phoenician).

Within a few miles of Jezreel is the village of Nain, where, according to the Gospels (Luke 7:11–17), Jesus brought back to life a widow's only son. This is merely one among many stories in the Hebrew Bible and New Testament that draw attention to the unusual and often precarious status of widows in ancient Israel: on the one hand, they could be freer from male authority than some other women and were capable of operating independently in the public sphere, but on the other hand, they were profoundly susceptible to poverty and exploitation. The very first words of the Book of Lamentations, which describe Jerusalem after it has fallen to the Babylonians and its people have been carried off to captivity, speak metaphorically to the condition of widowhood: "How lonely sits the city that was full of people!/How like a widow has she become,/she that was great among the nations!"

Nazareth, where Jesus grew up, lies on the Jezreel Valley's northern edge. It is a city divided among Jews, Christians, and Muslims, with a complex but functional local politics, and during the past few years it has been palpably bustling (dust, jackhammers, cranes) in preparation for the official "Nazareth 2000" celebrations, which will mark the second millennium, according to the calendar if not the historians, since the birth of Jesus. A league to the northwest of Nazareth is Zippori, where Carol Meyers, a professor of biblical studies and archaeology at Duke University, has gone to conduct archaeological excavations every summer for more than a decade. In Greco-Roman times, Zippori went by the name Sepphoris, and in later antiquity by the name Diocaesarea. Today a citadel of Byzantine vintage crowns the hilltop and affords an extraordinary view of Galilee in all directions; you can even see, far to the northeast, the summit of Mount Hermon, where the Israeli-occupied portion of the Golan Heights meets Syria.[1] On close inspection you realize that some of the citadel's building stones are in fact not building stones at all but oblongs of carved marble — empty Roman sarcophagi. The past doesn't go unused for long in this part of the world, which is both its fascination and its dilemma.

Sepphoris was an important city in historical times — it was the capital of Galilee — and it survived the Great Revolt of A.D. 66–70, which led to the destruction of the Temple in Jerusalem, by siding with the

Romans and surrendering to imperial forces, whereupon it was renamed once again, this time becoming Irenopolis, the city of peace. Carol and her husband, Eric Meyers, who is also an archaeologist, have discovered at Sepphoris some of the finest mosaic floors from the Roman era known to exist in the Middle East. They have also excavated sites nearby — specifically, at Tel Ein Zippori — that go back to the Middle Bronze Age, when the Israelites were emerging as a people and when what are thought to be the earliest passages of the Bible became a part of popular consciousness and of an oral tradition.

This is the period that first drew Carol Meyers's interest to the subject of the role and status of women in Israelite society, and to the question of how that role and status are reflected in the Hebrew Bible — an interest that finds expression in her book *Discovering Eve: Ancient Israelite Women in Context* (1988), which interweaves textual analysis, archaeology, and cultural anthropology into the kind of multidisciplinary study that today characterizes some of the most striking work in social history. In more recent research, employing the same integrated perspectives, Meyers has moved beyond the formative period of Israelite society, in roughly the years 1250–1000 B.C., in order to focus on the position of women during the evolution into monarchy.

What most catches your attention about Meyers's work is the way it liberates your view of women in Israelite society from a template imposed by our own time. It allows us to see women in the context of another age, another cultural frame of mind.

To conduct an archaeological dig is to be something of a general, albeit at times a frustrated one: there are plenty of young and healthy troops, in the form of graduate students, undergraduates, and volunteers, at your command, but to retrieve knowledge effectively, they must work at a plodding and painstaking pace. There are details in that dirt, and to make sense of the details you need to deploy maps and grids and screens and recording charts. During the six-week duration of the annual excavation at Sepphoris, the digging day starts at 5 A.M. and runs until 1, when the sun and the heat simply become too much to endure. Carol Meyers toils alongside the dozens of assistants, everyone taking turns wielding picks and shovels, cameras and computers, and, as much as anything else, the preeminent symbol of the archaeologist's craft, a triangular trowel from the Marshalltown Trowel Company, of Marshalltown, Iowa. Meyers seems naturally suited for this sort of work. Her build is lithe and athletic, her temperament patient and equable. Her children are now grown, and she has the look of someone who will negotiate middle age with productive serenity for another seventy or eighty years.

Archaeological work can be intense, she explained one day, yet for the most part it is also strangely aimless, without a fixed short-term goal. At times the task at hand looms plainly — let's finish uncovering that marvelous mosaic floor we discovered last year; let's finish digging out that amphitheater — but more often what lies ahead is unknown, and unknowable in advance, and the quest for information is completely openended. The forms that the evidence comes in, such as a broken piece of pottery or a patch of discolored dirt, seem frequently unremarkable, at least on their face. "People come up to me and say, 'What are you looking for?'" Meyers says, "And I say, 'I'm looking for whatever's there.'"

Every archaeologist, of course, gets a thrill when coming across something beautiful or spectacular, and Carol and Eric Meyers have perhaps come across more than their share of such things. In the ruins of an ancient synagogue in upper Galilee in 1981, for instance, they discovered the 1,200-pound pediment of an ark made of carved stone, used to house Torah scrolls, which dates back to the third century A.D. This discovery happened to coincide with the release of the movie *Raiders of the Lost Ark*, with predictable results, including a feature story about Carol and Eric in *People* magazine. ("They scoff at the *Raiders* image of archaeologists as scientific buccaneers on the prowl," the magazine reported, but the photographer posed Eric wearing Indy-style garb, with a coiled whip hanging off his shoulder and his arm around Carol, who was dressed in the role of the long-skirted, barefooted sidekick, Marion.)[2] Still, it is usually not the Torah scroll arks but all the other material, the detritus of the everyday lives of ordinary people, that does the most important work in helping to reconstruct the past.

I first met Carol Meyers a few months before she began digging the

Bronze Age site at Sepphoris. We were in her Gothic office at Duke University, where she is a professor in the religion department and the associate director of women's studies; the window of her office overlooks the quad, with its oversized tiers of painted benches that each fraternity maintains for its members. (What would archaeologists ever make of *them?*) The office is small — Meyers once compared it to the size of a typical room in an Iron Age cluster dwelling in Palestine — and the crowded shelves around us held books like *L'architecture domestique du Levant* and *Catalogue of Ancient Near-Eastern Seals in the Ashmolean Museum* — the sort of books that have always evoked for me an image of baked earth and native porters.

At that first meeting, Meyers described the conditions under which she and her colleagues labored. When you step off the plane onto the tarmac in Israel, she said, it is always a visual and epidermal shock. Even with the achievements of modern irrigation, and even in the rainy season, much of the landscape is forbidding: barren, rocky, thorny. In the summer it is *hot.* And in the winter, as people abroad often do not realize, it is *cold.* There is wind and hail and sleet. When Herod the Great captured Sepphoris from a rival, Mattathias Antigonus, in 37 B.C., the decisive battle was fought during a snowstorm.

Conditions are at their most extreme in the hill country of Judea and Samaria, where the Israelites first emerged, inhabiting the unforgiving uplands because the Canaanite city-states controlled the fertile bottom-lands. Precisely who the Israelites originally were and where they came from have been matters of intense debate for decades, and the debate in recent years has become more heated.[3] The biblical story of the children of Israel capturing the Promised Land in a decisive military campaign under the leadership of Joshua at some point during the thirteenth century B.C. — an account once taken for granted — was overtaken first by a widely accepted counterpostulate of a gradual and mostly peaceful influx of Israelite pastoralists into the Canaanite highlands and then by the more radical idea that the Israelites were themselves Canaanites who rose in revolt during what was essentially a class war.

It is not hard to imagine the modern political sensitivities that can be touched or inflamed by theorizing about Israelite origins and ethnic identity — and about who was where, in what order, and at what time. What can be said, however, is that the Israelites, whoever they were, appeared in the land of Canaan as a distinct people by around 1200 B.C. Until the advent of the monarchy a quarter of a millennium later, the demands of social organization fell almost entirely upon the family — or, more precisely, upon clusters of related families. There was no central government, no structured politics, little sense of a public domain. In this marginal ecological niche, with scarce water and thin soils, the proto-Israelites clung to a tenuous subsistence. They terraced the hills to make fields. They built cisterns lined with slaked lime plaster to hold water.

In this inhospitable world, Meyers believes, many men and women functioned in social parity within family households. The books of the Bible that describe this period of Israel's history — Judges and Joshua, primarily — do not, of course, necessarily show this to be the case. Having achieved final form centuries later, they depict a society in which most of the visible roles were played by men. But as Meyers explained during our first conversation, there is frequently a significant disjunction between a society's public stance and the everyday social reality, and everyday social reality in ancient Israel has only recently become a subject of scrutiny. In biblical studies as in many other kinds of scholarship, social history has been a latecomer, and it is in social rather than political history that women tend at last to emerge from the background. The prominent historian of family life Carl Degler has observed that social history and women's history are inextricably entwined, and are together changing the very definition of history.[4]

The economic functions of men and women before the dawn of the monarchy and complex political institutions would have been separate and distinct, Meyers argues in Discovering Eve, with the men disproportionately responsible for tasks involving brute strength and the women disproportionately oriented toward tasks involving technology, specialized skills, or social sophistication: experimenting with plants and seeds; shearing wool and weaving cloth; processing and preserving food. Women would have taken responsibility for managing a complex household whose membership, as excavated floor plans suggest, usually went beyond the nuclear family.[5]

The Book of Leviticus, the ancient manual for Israelite priests, provides some unexpected insight into the relative valuation of women and men. Leviticus is a formidable work, with its long enumerations of arcane rituals and behavioral codes. Its concern for the maintenance of cultic purity involves a detailed consideration of many aspects of human sexuality and whether or when they have ramifications for purity and impurity. As the biblical scholar Judith Romney Wegner, the author of *Chattel or Person?: Women in the Mishnah*, has observed, Leviticus treats "the entire class of women" as a subgroup subject to certain forms of regulation.[6] For reasons that remain mystifying, my old family Bible falls open naturally to a page in Leviticus where the following passage (12:1–5) has been marked: "The Lord said to Moses, 'Say to the people of Israel, If a woman conceives, and bears a male child, then she shall be unclean seven days. . . . But if she bears a female child, then she shall be unclean two weeks.'"

Leviticus 27, though, partakes of a somewhat unusual character: it is an appendix, probably older than other parts of Leviticus, that calculates the value in shekels, for purposes of contributions to the religious establishment, of the labor provided by women and by men, which it puts at 40 percent and 60 percent, respectively. Leviticus 27 has typically been seen, Meyers writes, as suggesting flatly that men are more valuable than women. But in truth, she goes on, such a perception ignores the time and energy "bound up in reproductive contributions." Drawing on ethnographic studies of agrarian communities, Meyers argues that "this kind of economic gender parity, with females contributing about 40 percent of productive labor, marks societies with the highest status for women."[7]

Women would also have shared with men the responsibility for teaching children the formal and informal information of early life, as reflected in the Bible: "My son, keep your father's commandment, and forsake not your mother's teaching" (Proverbs 6:20). Would women's teaching have involved the tools of basic literacy? The question is unanswerable in these terms, though the Bible holds some modest hints of a degree of literacy among at least some of the ordinary populace in very early times. Hebrew, with its twenty-two-letter alphabet, was easier to write than the contemporaneous nonalphabetic languages. It is certainly not far-fetched to wonder whether the Israelite mother's teaching role is associated at all with the biblical conceptualization of wisdom itself as a woman (and Wisdom, in turn, is bound up intimately with God). In sum, in premonarchic Israel, as in village societies today where the household represents the basic political and economic unit, women would have claimed central and authoritative roles.[8]

Meyers observes further that the God of Israel, in sharp contrast to the gods of all other contemporaneous religions, was ultimately perceived as asexual. Moreover, when God had to be described metaphorically, both male and female imagery was used. The prominence of God as father is a very late development in Israelite religion, she argues, and the concept makes only rare appearances in the Hebrew Bible, where the term "father" is used in association with God less than a dozen times.

When Meyers makes these and related points, in her writing and in conversation, you can see indications of a fault line — or at least a zone of major sensitivity — produced by feminism's encounter with religion. The sensitivity has to do with the "origin of patriarchy" issue. Where did the long history of female inequality and the long history of the oppression of women by men originate? Some of those inspired by visions of defunct utopian cultures in which worship of goddesses is said to have prevailed give one crude answer. In their view, the triumphant monotheism of the Israelites, centered on a wrathful Father God who drove the goddesses away, ushered in the present patriarchal age. Some Christian feminists, in considering the emergence of the Jesus movement and the values it may have espoused, also use the religion of the Israelites as a foil, often unwittingly and sometimes even despite protestations to the contrary. The result, as Judith Plaskow pointed out in a frequently cited broadside in Lilith in 1980, has sometimes been to make feminism "another weapon in the Christian anti-Judaic arsenal."[9]

Meyers, who does not find patriarchy to be a particularly useful analytical construct to begin with, notes that the editors of the Bible have preserved traces of what she believes was a relatively egalitarian family structure. The Book of Judges, which reached its final form around the time of the Babylonian exile (586–538 B.C.), purports to depict life in Israel half a millennium earlier and in fact contains material that is very old. It brings attention to an unusually large number of prominent and powerful women. As we have seen, one of these, Deborah, was referred to as both a prophet and a judge. The judges in these earliest times were not magistrates but rather those few individuals whose authority extended beyond household and tribe and might be thought of as somehow "national." A number of scholars have even speculated that one portion of Judges, the Song of Deborah, was composed by a woman. Resolving such matters of authorship is at this point impossible.

To Israelite women's economic productivity we must add the essential element of reproduction. Meyers reads the Bible mindful of the precarious demographic circumstances confronting the early Israelites. "It's wrong," she says, "to impose our idea of the individual on a society in which that may not have been a driving force in human development. The 'me-ness' or the 'I-ness' of our contemporary life cannot be superimposed on another era. The demands of community survival meant cooperation and a sense that what people were doing was in order for the group to survive. I get annoyed at some feminist critics who don't consider the whole social-history perspective. They see things like 'Be fruitful and multiply, and fill the earth' as meaning that the sole purpose of a woman is to conceive children. And all her interactions with God or with her husband seem to be to bring that fact about. They say, 'Well, a woman is just giving up her body for her husband.' I would counter by saying that in an agrarian society large families are essential, and that the Israelites were settling into marginal lands that had never been developed before. Whether they would make it or not depended on a certain population base. So the injunctions for fertility — and remember, they are addressed to both men and women — can be seen as a way of encouraging something that was beneficial, if not essential, for community survival."

Meyers has argued that the oft-cited "pain in childbearing" passage in Genesis 3:16, which reads

> *To the woman he said,*
> *"I will greatly multiply your pain in childbearing;*
> *in pain you shall bring forth children,"*

has long been mistranslated and has been "typically read through the interpretive lenses of Augustine and Milton and other postbiblical commentators" — men who saw God's words as a special curse because of woman's role in the expulsion from the Garden of Eden (which was theologized among Christians in the idea of the Fall). She notes that the Hebrew word translated as "pain" is translated as "toil" in the next verse, when God is talking not to the woman but to the man and is referring to the labor required for daily life. She also notes that the Hebrew word translated as "childbearing" refers not to the process of childbirth but to the fact of pregnancy. Her alternative translation would run as follows: "I will greatly increase your toil and pregnancies; along with travail shall you beget children."[10] Her point is not that the lot of women encapsulated here was a happy one, but that the passage, when properly expressed, "describes and prescribes the realities of highland farming." The realities were hard. Infant mortality approached 50 percent. Excavations of burials show that female life expectancy, owing in part to the risks involved in repeated pregnancies, was perhaps thirty years, ten years less than the life expectancy for men.[11]

Meyers told me that whenever she is on an archaeological dig in the Middle East, she inevitably begins to imagine herself as one of those women of ancient Israel, at least in terms of short-term physical stress. During an excavation she is working the same remorseless terrain as the Israelites did three thousand years ago, the two sexes side by side. The toil is unremitting and tedious, the environment dry and dusty. The days when scores of local laborers were supervised by aristocrats in pith helmets are long gone. Archaeology is a complex enterprise, group-oriented in the extreme. Being a mother, Meyers for years had other responsibilities as well: young children for whom she had to care on the site, sometimes hanging on her hip, sometimes having to be nursed, even as excavations proceeded. She experienced, in other words, the ancient but also the very modern female reality of having to cope with an armful of often competing tasks.

People on a dig depend on one another physically, for their very safety, in ways that most people usually don't. The abiding fact of interdependence offered a lesson that one of Meyers's daughters, Dina, has written about. In 1985, when Dina was thirteen, the Sepphoris team uncovered the mouth of an ancient underground cistern, one of several that have since come to light. Cisterns are always an important find, because while they are in use things fall into them — pots, coins, household objects, small carvings — and drop softly through the water to settle unbroken on the silted bottom. (I once dimly glimpsed a visitor's plastic sunglasses on the bottom of a water-filled Roman cistern underneath Jerusalem, and I remember fancifully imagining the day in the future when exhilarated excavators would coax them into their possession.) Frequently the cisterns discovered in the Middle East have been unused for two or three thousand years. At Sepphoris, the archaeologists were eager to get inside and look around. The entrance was small, but someone pointed out that Dina was very slim — maybe she could be lowered into the cistern to have a look around. And so she was. What she remembers is not only the excitement of being about to see things that had not been seen for millennia but also the stark apprehension, and the need to have implicit trust in the people who tied the knots and played out the rope — the people who had to be able to hoist her back up through the tiny shaft.

Carol Meyers's children have been on archaeological excavations since they were babies, so the life and the work became second nature to them. Meyers herself did not participate in an excavation until 1962, just after her sophomore year at Wellesley. She was then Carol Lyons and had lived most of her life in Kingston, Pennsylvania (population 15,700), where her father was a dentist. She signed up essentially as a lark, as part of an expedition sponsored by Harvard University's Peabody Museum. The dig took place at a site called Hell Gap, in Wyoming, where the remnants of human habitation went back nine thousand years. The site was so old that it had been abandoned long before the advent of pottery; the only artifacts that anyone could expect to find were chips of flint tools and stone circles that had once been hearths. Excavating a site like this doesn't involve moving mountains of dirt to expose baths and brothels and frescoed atria; it involves kneeling or lying on the ground with a paintbrush or a toothbrush, brushing dirt away, hour after hour, until tiny slivers of flint-knapping debris, or maybe just a few delicate circles of discolored ground, are fully exposed.

Meyers realized that for all its drudgery and unavoidable tedium, she loved archaeology. The following two summers she participated in excavations in Israel: at Tel Beit Yerah, an early Bronze Age site on the Sea of Galilee; at Ashdod, which is an ancient Philistine city on the Mediterranean coast that is frequently mentioned in the Bible (for instance, in 1 Samuel: "When the Philistines captured the ark of God, they carried it from Ebenezer to Ashdod"); and at Tel Arad, a fortified city of comparable age in the Beersheba Valley, where scores of shards with Hebrew writing from the preexilic period, a rare trove, have been found. Meyers knew by then that she wanted to become an archaeologist.

An important additional point: the dawn of Meyers's interest in archaeology coincided with the emergent significance of what would become known as the New Archaeology, which focused more on understanding cultural processes and systems than on establishing cultural chronology, more on social and domestic issues than on issues of politics and diplomacy, and more on understanding how aggregations of small sites once functioned as living societies than on discovering spectacular treasures at big sites. The very term "New Archaeology" elicited disdain from some of the old guard ("that precious and prissy phrase," to use the words of the Cambridge University archaeologist Glyn Daniel), but the principles behind the term have been broadly absorbed by younger generations of scholars.[12] This approach shaped Meyers's outlook from the beginning, though it was years before it began to redirect Palestinian archaeology as a whole.

The first major work of social history devoted to the Israelites was not published until 1979. This was Norman K. Gottwald's *The Tribes of Yahweh*, a fat, sprawling, ambitious book with a tone that is authoritative, confident, and more than a little combative. It is not hard to see how this book blew biblical social history onto the scene. Gottwald's index entry under "Women, in Israel" constitutes almost a road map, by categorical destination, to future feminist historical studies of the Bible:

societal roles of
  charismatics/prophetesses
  childbearers
  converts to Israel
  dancers
  dividers of spoil
  eponymous ancestors
  harlots
  inheritors/holders of property
  initiators of kin protection
  members of extended families
  military commanders/fighters
  mourners
  pious believers
  singers of songs of triumph
  widows
  wives

Wellesley College also had a profound effect on Meyers, for reasons she couldn't have predicted. Although students at most campuses today would drop their jaws at the thought, during the 1960s, when Meyers was a student, all undergraduates at Wellesley were required to take a certain number of common courses in order to graduate. By the time Meyers got there, these courses had been winnowed down to four: English composition, a physical education course called "Fundamentals of Movement," and, somewhat improbably from our current perspective, two Bible courses, "Introduction to the New Testament" and "Introduction to the Old Testament." The durability of these last two was a legacy of the wishes of Henry and Pauline Durant, who in establishing Wellesley College in 1875 sought above all to educate women "for the glory of God and the service of Jesus Christ." On the foundation stone of Wellesley's original structure are carved the words "This building is humbly dedicated to our Heavenly Father, with the hope and prayer that He may always be first in everything in this institution." Article one of the bylaws of the college states that there shall be "study of the Sacred Scriptures by every undergraduate."[13] This directive survived for nearly a century, even as a genteel tutorial regime dominated at first by people invariably referred to in Wellesley's histories as "Miss" gave way to a robust faculty of accomplished academics more interested in professionalism than in piety. The first woman to present a paper at a meeting of the Society of Biblical Literature (1913) was a Wellesley professor, as was the first woman to publish a paper in the society's *Journal of Biblical Literature* (1917). Brochures from the late 1940s and early 1950s show young undergraduates dressed and coifed like June Allyson, in suits with padded shoulders, poring avidly over the college's copy of the sixteenth-century Melanchthon Bible. By the time compulsory Bible study was ended, in 1967, it was the last compulsory course left in the Wellesley curriculum.[14]

Anachronistic though the Bible courses may have been in the eyes of some, they opened a new world for Meyers — not a spiritual experience but a profoundly intellectual one. Her education in religious matters had consisted of little more than weekly classes at the Conservative synagogue in Wilkes-Barre, Pennsylvania, to which her family belonged, which she was not much interested in and which she eventually rebelled against. She became determined to unify her two passions, archaeology and biblical studies, a decision that mystified her parents, who wondered what she could ever do with such training.

Upon graduating from Wellesley in 1964, Carol married Eric Meyers, a Dartmouth graduate who was studying for an M.A. at Brandeis and whom she had met just a few months earlier — he had been pressed into service as a cantor at an event at Wellesley, and Carol had overheard him singing. He shared many of her academic interests; on their first date they attended a lecture at Harvard on Hebrew seal inscriptions. Carol Meyers began work on an advanced degree in biblical studies and archaeology at Hebrew University in Jerusalem and then continued at Brandeis, picking up more of the academic tools she would need and adding Syriac and Aramaic to the Hebrew and Akkadian she already had. She was usually the only woman in her class — a particular jolt for a Wellesley graduate, accustomed to classes consisting *only* of women. She had no female professors.

Meyers became accustomed to such singularity in her chosen academic environment. At various senior professional and editorial board meetings, she may still on occasion be the only woman. Although many women now hold assistant professor and associate professor status in Meyers's field, there are not many who are full professors, as she is. Looking back on her career, she can point to few acts of outright discrimination because of her gender. "I've known of women with horror stories," she says, "but I personally did not experience them." She did recount in one conversation how she and her husband, before they met, had independently applied to a summer program in Jerusalem and had both been accepted. By the time the program started, they had married. The director, on learning what had happened, told Carol bluntly, "If I had known you were going to get married, I would never have given you a scholarship. I would only have given it to your husband." The assumption was that a woman was unlikely to make use of formal training over the long term, and that a married woman in particular was a hopeless investment.

(I have heard similar stories from many others. The case almost everyone cites is that of Elaine Pagels, whose book *The Gnostic Gospels*, published in 1979, is perhaps the work touching on issues of women and biblical religion that has thus far received the widest audience. Pagels earned a doctorate in religion from Harvard in 1970 but was allowed into the religion program only with a great reluctance, which had nothing to do with her qualifications. The dean who eventually accepted her as a doctoral student actually turned her down the first time she applied. In this field, he explained in a letter, women didn't last. Pagels went ahead and reapplied a year later. Needless to say, in the late 1960s, when she started work on her doctorate, there were no women on the faculty of Harvard's program in religion.)

Meyers participated in fieldwork whenever she had the chance — at Tel Arad again; at Tel Gezer, an ancient crossroads city (its king was killed by Joshua, according to Joshua 10:33) whose excavation was for years largely in American hands and served as a training ground for hundreds of students; and for many summers at Meiron, which was a Hellenistic and Roman settlement in the upper Galilee. The first winter

Carol and Eric were married, they worked together as part of the crew assembled by Yigael Yadin to excavate Masada, the mesa-top fortress overlooking the Dead Sea that Jewish rebels held against a Roman siege for three years, from A.D. 70 to 73. Yadin himself behaved like a military commander, marching his crews 1,300 feet up the mountain on the steep earthen ramp the Roman engineers had built, in the freezing temperatures before dawn. He worked everyone relentlessly in the gathering heat and sometimes in a pummeling rain, the kind that turns dusty wadis into momentary torrents, which the occupiers of Masada diverted into the fortress's vast cisterns.

It was only when Meyers began teaching at Duke University in 1976 that she became aware of the need and the potential for women's studies with respect to the Bible. The initial impetus in this direction was not really even hers. As she recalls, "When I joined the faculty here, my colleagues said, 'Listen, you have to put a couple of courses in our curriculum that are of your own design, so why don't you think about' — remember, I was the only woman in the department, and this was the mid-1970s now — 'why don't you think about doing some course on women, like "Women and the Bible" or something like that?'" Meyers was a junior faculty member; following advice along these lines seemed the prudent thing to do. When she started trying to put such a course together, however, she found almost no material to work with. Very little research had been done on women and the Bible, no doubt in some measure owing to the belief that there was little to do, or that it was not very important. It is a rare and exhilarating sensation when a scholar realizes that a new field beckons and that the footsteps upon it have been few. Meyers decided to step onto the field herself.

The matter of gender in archaeology has been particularly elusive, for several reasons. As was the case with other disciplines, until the past few years the people who defined the field of archaeology tended to be male. Some female archaeologists, such as Katherine Kenyon, the excavator of Jericho, became important and influential figures, to be sure, but there were not large numbers of them, and issues of gender were not the focus of their work. Gender was ignored for so long that unstated but implicit assumptions became part of a standardized background tableau. As the anthropologists Janet V. Romanowicz and Rita P. Wright have observed, "Archaeologists have tended to project twentieth-century Euroamerican gender structures onto the past, thus making gender roles unchanging, uninteresting, and irrelevant to a study of cultural dynamics."[15] That comment points to a problem of real substance. "Women's" activities such as weaving and making pots have been so familiar for so long — so domestic, so unexceptional — that we understandably no longer see them as the revolutionary breakthroughs they were, changing the way whole societies behaved. In her recent book *Women's Work: The First 20,000 Years*, the archaeologist and linguist Elizabeth Wayland Barber pursues redress by going a considerable way toward restoring the loom, a technology whose development has been in women's hands, literally, from the outset, to its deserved position of cultural and economic prominence. The anthropologist Miriam B. Peskowitz, in her book *Spinning Fantasies: Rabbis, Gender, and History*, has also delved into loom archaeology, for new perspectives on women's lives and status in Roman-period Judaism.

Another obstacle to an appreciation of gender in archaeology is that artifacts, especially primitive ones, are often not "gender-noisy." If you pick up an implement employed for some process of daily life — a spindle whorl, a grinding stone, an axe — you don't necessarily know whether it was being used in the specific context of its discovery by a man or a woman, by a child or an adult, by a stranger or a local inhabitant, by all of the above, by two or three of the above, by none of the above. This is a problem. Therefore, archaeology in and of itself has limits in terms of women's social history. For the biblical periods, of course, archaeologists can use the biblical text as a supplementary source, to try to figure out whether the archaeological reality can be identified somehow in terms of an object's maker and user. Often, suggestive parallels can be made with observations drawn from comparative ethnology — that is, from the study of living traditional cultures, whether settled or nomadic, pastoral or agricultural, which archaeologists presume to resemble certain aspects of ancient ones. For some things, it is safe to make assumptions. "When we find a spearhead," Meyers says, "we're likely to be able to say with some confidence that a man was using it. But there are problems even with that. It could be that a woman was polishing it when it came to be left where it was."

Meyers gave me an example of the intricacies of ambiguity: "Think of something as basic as pottery. These pottery containers are what make people able to store things from season to season, to serve things, to eat things, to cook things. Without pottery, civilization would not have developed as it did. So who made the pots? Ethnographers tell us that in more than 90 percent of all traditional societies studied, women are the village potters. Yet biblical texts would lead us to an opposite conclusion." Jeremiah, a book probably composed before and during the exilic period, in the late seventh and early sixth century B.C., contains texts that talk about potters, and the potters are clearly men: "I went down to the potter's house, and there he was, working at his wheel" (18:3). Some include metaphors for God as potter — "Behold, like the clay in the potter's hand, so are you in my hand, O house of Israel" (18:6) — and since God normally has male attributes, we assume that if God is being compared to a potter, then potters must also be male. "But those kinds of texts, to my way of looking at them," says Meyers, "might reflect only the urban environment from which they arise. Jeremiah is a Jerusalem-based prophet. I have no doubt that once you have professionalization and specialization in pottery-making, it does then get controlled by men, and that men had guilds and so on. But in a nonurban environment, in a small village environment, I would still make the case for the fact that pottery would have been a female enterprise, despite the implications of the sorts of biblical texts found in Jeremiah. I take seriously the anthropological evidence — that is, what anthropologists have done in describing life and gender roles in settings seen as similar to those one sees in ancient Israel — as a critical way to bridge the gap and fill in the gap between artifact and text."

Carol Meyers's research interests have lately moved beyond the formative centuries to the era of the Israelite monarchy, which was instituted around 1020 B.C. According to the Bible, Israel was governed by a unified monarchy first under Saul, then David, and then Solomon; after the death of Solomon, around 920 B.C., the land was partitioned into northern and southern kingdoms. The northern kingdom, called Israel, fell to the Assyrians in 722 B.C., whereas the southern kingdom, Judah, lasted until its defeat at the hands of the Babylonians, in 587 B.C., after which much of the Israelite population endured exile in Babylon. This period, covering four and a half centuries, is the one described in the two books of Samuel and the two books of Kings. Together with the books of Deuteronomy, Joshua, and Judges, these books make up what is known as the Deuteronomistic history. The presumption, on stylistic and other evidence, is that the author or compiler of Deuteronomy also wrote or compiled these other books from the perspective of exile, with a view to explaining the Israelite people's fate as a consequence of the rupture of their covenant with God.

Like the period of Israelite emergence, much of the monarchic period has become a subject of controversy, with the spectrum of opinion ranging from those who accept (with whatever cautionary footnotes and qualifications) the Bible's account of the emergence of the Davidic monarchy as somehow reflecting historical events to the much smaller group of so-called minimalists, who dismiss the entire account as basically ahistorical myth. What allows this controversy to persist is the fact that for the period prior to about 925 B.C., almost no universally accepted independent evidence — evidence, for example, in the form of inscriptions from ancient Egypt or Babylon — attests to any of the political history recounted in the Bible. Two ninth-century inscriptions, one of them discovered just a few years ago at Tel Dan, in northern Israel, do seem to refer to a House of David. For various reasons this evidence is regarded as tentative by the most ardent among the minimalist camp.[16]

Still, the Israelite polity indisputably became a monarchy, and under its kings, political structures became increasingly centralized and urban centers increasingly important. A market economy grew up alongside the subsistence one. The Bible explains the development of a monarchy as a response to a growing threat from hostile neighbors and to the need for a more efficiently organized society. God says of Saul, "He shall save my people from the hand of the Philistines; for I have seen the affliction of my people, because their cry has come to me" (1 Samuel 9:16). But as Meyers traces the story, the process could well have been more organic. "In those days there was no king in Israel; every man did what was right in his own eyes": these lines (Judges 21:25) laconically summarize a situation that the advent of increased social complexity would necessarily doom. Archaeological surveys of the Judean hill country east of Jerusalem, conducted after Israel wrested control of this territory during the Six Day War in 1967, have shown that the number of settlements in this region nearly doubled from the early Iron Age to the later Iron Age, and that the new settlements were on far less desirable sites than the older settlements. Population expanded, a fact indicated also by the spreading use of terraced fields for crops and an increasing number of cisterns. As the population grew and technology advanced, not every settlement could remain self-sufficient, prompting specialization, local and international trade, and new needs for adjudication and government.[17]

Consider, as Meyers urges, the cascade of consequences from something as basic as the need for better plows, which itself develops because of the need to exploit greater amounts of marginal land. Better plows meant a higher demand for iron, which in turn meant international trade, because iron-ore deposits in Palestine are scarce. "Throughout the tribal lands," Meyers has written, "there arose a need for adaptive mechanisms that would transcend the activities of local, related kinship groups" — a need, to put this into blunter language, for rulers.[18]

During this period too, at least in urban settings, the relative positions of women and men became more unequal, coming more to resemble the kind of society we see in many biblical texts. This was a society in which women achieved status mainly through marriage and childbirth and were subject to considerable legal disadvantages with regard to property ownership and the disposition of their own persons. It is hard, though, to know how closely the situation in, say, Jerusalem, reflected life in other places. Jerusalem, Meyers explained to me in one of our conversations, was an anomaly. After the Assyrians overran the Northern Kingdom, in 722 B.C., the population of Jerusalem, the capital of the Southern Kingdom, was swollen with refugees. The city grew to be ten times as large as the next largest city in Judah. Its inhabitants no longer had close ties to the land, and women no longer retained a central role in economic life. Jerusalem knew chaos and extreme poverty and great social stratification. The city sheltered large numbers of resident foreigners. There was something called public life, and it was in the hands of men. This is the time and place in which scribes fashioned much of the Hebrew Bible. No wonder, Meyers argues, that the picture it conveys is androcentric.

Even so, she points out, as many as 90 percent of the people of Israel continued to live in agricultural villages in the countryside. She is cautious about applying the label "patriarchal" either too broadly or too loosely. Often the social patterns in the city were quite different from those that survived in the country. The term "patriarchal" may be legitimate in some places and times and not in others. Who knows what this nineteenth-century construct means when applied to a premodern society? Moreover, a focus on patriarchy, whatever the term connotes, serves to "mask other kinds of power differentials among family members," hiding relationships that may prove revelatory when they are explored. What about divisions of wealth and class, divisions by age and generation, divisions among those who stood to inherit a bigger portion and those who stood to inherit a smaller? A relentless invocation of patriarchy, Meyers says, "does a disservice to a complex piece of literature, the Bible, and to a society that existed for a thousand years and changed and grew."

Our gaze is also deflected by the Bible's focus on public life, which is the aspect of biblical life that commentators for centuries were primarily interested in. But private life can be found if you set out expressly to track it down, reading the Bible in search of passages that bear on it and then concentrating on them intently. I have often found myself thinking of such subject matter as residing in "information tels." The landscape of the Middle East, as noted, is dotted with thousands of mounds, or tels, harboring the remains of ancient towns and cities that may have been occupied for thousands of years before they succumbed at last to pestilence or military defeat or economic collapse. These tels, no matter how small and insignificant, would yield up a story if only they were probed fastidiously and ingeniously by a knowledgeable excavator. Many of them, of course, never will be probed with any persistence, for they simply are too numerous.

Yet if someone were to look? In the course of her career, Carol Meyers has contributed long analytical essays to a number of the standard reference volumes in the biblical field, and she is the general editor of an important new reference work, A *Dictionary of Women in Scripture*. But in some ways the contributions that most quickly fill the Bible with ordinary life — make it come alive with sounds and smells and images — are the short entries she has written for the *Anchor Bible Dictionary* on small objects mentioned in a cultic context, which on occasion afford a brief glimpse of the mundane and, more specifically, of women. Here is a case where someone has dug an exploratory trench not through the Meggido of information tels but through the most insignificant of grassed-over mounds. Thus, Meyers has written the entry on anklets in the Bible. And on aprons in the Bible. On bells in the Bible. And on canopies. On censers. Checker work. Fillets. Firepans. Grating. Hooks. Jambs. Lavers. Loops. Moldings. Rings. Screens. Shovels. Snuffers. Trays. Twined linen.

Let's look at anklets, a piece of women's jewelry that adorns the ankle, as a bracelet adorns the wrist. The subject is at first glance an unpromising one, because the Hebrew word for anklets, *'ekes*, occurs only once in the entire Bible, in Isaiah 3:18: "In that day, the Lord will take away the finery of the anklets, the headbands, and the crescents; the pendants, the bracelets, and the scarfs." (A word used only once in a text is known by the Greek term *hapax legomenon*, meaning "word that appears in a single place"; about a quarter of the roughly 5,800 distinct, non-proper-name words used in the Bible are used only once.)[19] To this single reference Meyers is able to bring the findings of archaeology and other disciplines. You learn about aspects of metallurgy and craftsmanship. You learn about the discovery of figurines of female Canaanite gods who are wearing anklets. If you wished, you could move on to the much larger subject of metal and terra-cotta renderings of female musicians from ancient Palestine, about which Meyers has written elsewhere. As for anklets, the ones seen on Canaanite figurines are worn in sets of three or more, and this leads back to another biblical passage — and explains, no doubt, what the writer has in mind when describing the daughters of Zion "tinkling with their feet."[20]

When the Bible does afford an expansive glimpse of private life — which is, admittedly, only a modest amount of the time — a patriarchal society is not necessarily what we always see. The poetry of the Song of

Songs offers such a glimpse, which is one reason that the study of this untypical book of the Bible has become a small growth industry among scholars interested in issues of gender. The Song of Songs contains a great deal of very old material, passed along in the form of certain archaisms, which poetry tends to preserve more reliably over long periods of time than does prose, which is relatively malleable. It is especially noteworthy for the amount of text (about two thirds of its 117 verses) written in a woman's voice, and in the first person. The Song of Songs is the only book of the Bible in which a female voice appears to speak directly, without interpretive or narrative assistance. The poetry has such a feminine interiority that it is hard to imagine the words flowing from the hand of a male singer or poet or composer. Some of the terminology is suggestively feminine and even hints at female authority. For example, whereas in most of the Bible the standard term for household is *bet'ab*, or "father's house," the term used in the Song of Songs is *bet'em*, or "mother's house."[21] The poet writes (3:4):

> *Scarcely had I passed them,*
> *   when I found him whom my soul loves.*
> *I held him, and would not let him go*
> *   until I had brought him into my mother's house,*
> *   and into the chamber of her that conceived me.*

Indeed, there has been speculation that the Song of Songs was written by a woman (although many associate the book with Solomon).

Regardless of the author's gender, the love poetry in the Song of Songs expresses an emotional bond not between a master and a subordinate but between equals (2:16–17):

> *My beloved is mine and I am his,*
> *   he pastures his flock among the lilies.*
> *Until the day breathes*
> *   and the shadows flee,*
> *turn, my beloved, be like a gazelle,*
> *   or a young stag upon rugged mountains.*

Chapter Five

....

WORDS OF
WISDOM

Does not wisdom call,
does not understanding raise her voice?
— *Proverbs* 8:1

A woman's writing is always feminine; it cannot help being feminine;
at its best it is most feminine; the only difficulty lies
in defining what we mean by feminine.
— *Virginia Woolf*

THE RUINS of ancient Nineveh, the capital of the Assyrian empire, lie across the Tigris River from what is today the Iraqi city of Mosul. When the Assyrian empire was brought down in the seventh century B.C. by invading Babylonians, Scythians, and Medes, the conquerors destroyed the capital and carried off into slavery the inhabitants they didn't kill outright. The conquerors did not spare the great library of Ashurbanipal, with its record of Assyrian civilization stored in the form of cuneiform writing on some 20,000 clay tablets. They burned the library down.

In a way, explained Tikva Frymer-Kensky, it was the best thing the conquering armies could have done, from our point of view — an inadvertent exercise in what would now be known as "cultural resources management." Under ordinary circumstances the clay tablets, each about the size of a bar of soap, would have turned to dust in a few centuries, if not a few generations. But the conflagration fired the tablets, turning them into durable ceramic. "We used to joke at Yale," she said, thinking back to her days as a young Assyriologist-in-training, "that if, God forbid, the Sterling Memorial Library burned down, the only thing left would be the cuneiform tablets. They would just get harder."

Frymer-Kensky had been talking, actually, about other things — the role of goddesses in polytheism; the revolutionary implications, for people in general and for women in particular, of monotheism; the emergence of such feminine biblical imagery as the figure of Lady Wisdom — when the discussion veered off in the direction of writing and historical serendipity. This turned out to be not quite the tangent it might have seemed.

Frymer-Kensky is an Assyriologist and a Sumerologist who has focused her interest in questions of gender in antiquity as much on the Hebrew Bible as on the literature of the great Mesopotamian civilizations. She was until 1996 the director of biblical studies for the Reconstructionist Rabbinical College in Philadelphia, where she lives, and she has been and remains a professor of Hebrew Bible at the University of Chicago, to which she commutes. She has recently begun a sabbatical at the Center for Judaic Studies in Philadelphia. Frymer-Kensky has won wide recognition for a cross-cultural study titled *In the Wake of the Goddesses: Women, Culture, and the Biblical Transformation of Pagan Myth* (1992), a work that attempts to take the goddesses of polytheism seriously as theological constructs and social reflections but at the same time disdains the wish-fulfilling popularizations of "the Goddess," a romantically conceived being who now seems to sustain vast territories of certain bookstores and gift shops.

Frymer-Kensky understands why some women have turned to the "earth-centered, immanent Goddess of contemporary neo-paganism" as "a refuge from, and counterbalance to, what many consider the remote and punitive God of western religions."[1] But do these devotees and theorists understand that the societies which actually possessed goddesses were deeply patriarchal and would have had no patience for their New Age conceits? Do they appreciate the larger ideological dynamic of monotheism and, in some respects, its potentially positive implications? The presumption that anyone can speak sensibly about ancient goddesses on the basis of a heartfelt emotional outpouring rather than painstakingly acquired knowledge drives Frymer-Kensky to exasperation.

Frymer-Kensky does not conceal exasperation, or her opinions on this or any other subject. She is by her own admission a talker — "wake me up at four in the morning, and I'm ready to go" — who speaks directly and plainly, with considerable humor and without overmuch compunction: an amiably formidable presence. While forthright in stating a belief that some feminists' depictions of the past "come right out of their own psyches," she is also sensitive to the demands of psychic want. She is the mother of two children and recently published *Motherprayer*, a compilation of spiritual readings on pregnancy, childbirth, and motherhood, some of them new but most of them ancient prayers translated from Sumerian, Akkadian, Hebrew, Aramaic, and Latin. The book grew out of her own need for such a resource and the apparent lack of one during her first pregnancy, an unusually dangerous and difficult experience, two decades ago.

In the course of a long conversation at the Center for Judaic Studies, overlooking the colonial greensward of Independence Park, Frymer-Kensky recalled how the circumstances of that pregnancy deflected what had been the vector of her career. She grew up in Forest Hills, in Queens, the daughter of Polish Jewish émigrés who were actively leftist in their politics and devoutly Conservative in their religion. Judaism imbued her upbringing. From an early age she was also drawn to the physical sciences, for which she showed a strong aptitude. Her early ambition was to become a chemical engineer, but she found herself thwarted again and again by high school teachers — this was in the late 1950s — who deemed her scientific interests to be inappropriate for a woman and turned her away from formative opportunities. "I was insulted at every turn," she recalls. "I was manipulated. At one point they called in my mother and tried to get me to change." She was understandably embittered by this experience and in retrospect derives an important personal insight from it: "It explains why, although I became and am a very strong feminist, I never had the rage against religion that many of my colleagues did, because I always suffered more out in the nonreligious world" — suffered more, that is to say, from the heirs of the Enlightenment, the modern men of science.

Frymer eventually abandoned any thought of a scientific career and, as an undergraduate studying jointly at City College of New York and the Jewish Theological Seminary, took up instead the study of the ancient world, the philosophy of religion, and the Talmud. (At the seminary, she became the first woman ever to be accepted into the program for the teaching of Talmud.) She went on to pursue graduate work at Yale, acquiring a quiver of dead languages and undertaking a doctoral dissertation on certain legal issues in ancient Assyria. During the years at Yale she encountered two women, Judith Plaskow and Carol P. Christ, who played a significant role in shaping the field of feminist biblical studies, though their work had little direct relevance to Frymer's at the time. Plaskow today is best known for her book *Standing Again at Sinai* (1990), an exploration of the possibility of a feminist Judaism, which has never been out of print. She teaches in the department of religion at Manhattan College in New York. Carol P. Christ, the author of a book on goddesses and goddess rituals titled *The Laughter of Aphrodite*, has abandoned academe altogether. She is today the director of an organization called the Ariadne Institute for the Study of Myth and Ritual and among other things conducts goddess-oriented tours to the Aegean.

Frymer completed her dissertation, "The Judicial Ordeal in the Ancient Near East," and was awarded a doctorate in 1977. By then she was married, and she and her husband, Allan Kensky, a rabbi, were planning a family. When unexpected problems arose in the late stages of pregnancy and she had to rush to the hospital for a cesarean section, Frymer-Kensky grabbed some things to read: a few novels, a *TV Guide*, and a sheaf of Babylonian birth incantations that just happened to be lying around, left over from her dissertation. In the end, the Babylonian incantations occupied her attention.

> *Let the one which is sealed up be released.*
> *Let the being come out*
> *as an independent being.*
> *Let it come out quickly*
> *so that it may see the light of the sun.*[2]

Awaiting the birth of her daughter, Meira, amid the antiseptic silence, Frymer-Kensky became perhaps the first woman in three thousand years to speak those ancient Babylonian words in the context for which they had been composed.

Afterwards, when she woke up — "ten months later" — Frymer-Kensky began to wonder, with some asperity, why there was no literary material in the Jewish or Christian tradition comparable to what existed in the Babylonian tradition. She continued to publish scholarly work in her original field ("The Tribulations of Marduk: The So-Called 'Marduk Ordeal Text'"; "Unusual Legal Procedures in Elam and Nuzi") even as her attention turned increasingly to the new question she had posed.

To begin with, Frymer-Kensky explains by way of an answer, the Bible just isn't that kind of book. It is a public document serving a public purpose; it does not preserve very much in the way of private writings, the outstanding exception being perhaps the Song of Songs. The Bible does not even preserve a wedding ceremony. To find birth incantations in the Bible would be like finding excerpts from a Lamaze pamphlet in the *Congressional Record*.

Second, most of the writings from ancient Israel have simply been lost. Wedding ceremonies did, of course, take place among the Israelites. In all likelihood, chants and prayers for a difficult labor existed. But these things have not come down to us because the Israelites were, in a sense, too advanced. We have practically nothing in terms of texts, in effect because the Israelites had an alphabet. "You wouldn't want to write with an alphabet on clay, unless it was a cuneiform alphabet," Frymer-Kensky says. "Cuneiform, those funny marks, are representations made by sticking the wedge of a reed against the clay — you make the triangular head and the shaft with one quick tick. But once linear script got developed, you couldn't write on clay — it would take too long to draw the wedge through it." The Israelites wrote fluidly with their new alphabet on parchment and papyrus, materials that are easy to transport and easy to store. Unfortunately, they also disintegrate with age. And they are *not* preserved by fire.

So much writing survives on clay tablets from the Mesopotamian civilizations — literature, tax records, legal codes, schoolchildren's copybooks — that vast amounts of it still await translation. And the corpus remains "open": new tablets turn up all the time. Indeed, the sanctions-hobbled government of Iraq, which controls most of the important Mesopotamian archaeological sites, has in recent years quietly been selling off freshly exhumed tablets to the West in exchange for hard currency.

In contrast, the corpus of Israelite literature is essentially "closed," limited to the canonical books of the Bible and a few other texts that have been passed along, copied and recopied, from age to age. The Bible makes reference to other major works that once existed but now are lost. For example, the Book of Numbers (21:14–15) refers to the *Book of the Wars of Yahweh*, but the few lines quoted are all that survive. Missing too are the *Chronicle of Solomon*, the *Chronicles of the Kings of Israel*, and the *Chronicles of the Kings of Judah*. A few ancillary fragments of writing have survived, but only because they were written on pottery, potsherds, or amulets.

If this had not been the case — if the surviving corpus were large and diverse — would any significant amount of it have reflected a woman's voice? What forms can that voice take? Can it come only from a woman? Each question begets others, and the answers lead off into the imponderable. Theoretically, though, we can imagine a woman's voice surviving in at least three ways. One is overt and direct: by means of passages actually written by women. A second is indirect: by passages that preserve, through explicit or implicit quotation, the words of women in actual social contexts. The third way is more ineffable but perhaps the most compelling of all: through the complex mechanisms of psychology and spirituality, which may under various guises both draw on and demand a feminine presence.

To take the first of these: a subject as basic as the extent of literacy in ancient Israel and whether literacy was accessible to women can be approached through only a handful of clues and is largely a matter of speculation. So little is known about so many aspects of literacy in ancient times that scholars are still debating about how prevalent the practice of reading to oneself, as opposed to reading aloud, was — or was it done at all? But the acts of reading and writing do come up directly in the Bible, and there are instances when women are involved.

They make an unlikely pair, Jezebel and Esther.

Jezebel is the princess of Tyre and worshiper of Baal who marries the Israelite king Ahab, encourages him to build altars to the false Phoenician gods, and in general, according to the first Book of Kings (16:30), induces him to do "evil in the sight of the Lord more than all that were before him." In Hebrew, Jezebel's name means "Where is the prince?" The reference is to Baal, but the name is also a pun, because the consonants can be fleshed out with alternative vowels to acquire the meaning "dung." Jezebel's idolatry (from the Israelite point of view), her greed, and her scheming aggressiveness fatally complement parallel qualities in her husband and earn a curse from the prophet Elijah, who foresees that Jezebel's corpse will be eaten by dogs. And so indeed it comes to pass, when Jezebel, after the defeat and death of Ahab, is thrown from a window by her retainers: "But when they went to bury her they found no more of her than the skull, and the feet, and the palms of her hands" (2 Kings 9:35). Her name, of course, lives on in the eponymous word meaning "a wicked, shameless woman." Bette Davis won an Oscar for playing such a woman, a spiteful southern belle, in the 1938 film *Jezebel*.

Esther presents a contrast. She is the descendant of Jews who have been carried off to the court of the Persian kings after the fall of Jerusalem and the destruction of the First Temple at the beginning of the sixth century B.C. However, her identity as a Jew is kept hidden, and Esther is raised at court, where fortuitous events conspire to make her the wife of King Ahasuerus. She becomes aware of a plot to destroy the Jews of Persia, which she foils, leading to the execution of its mastermind, the evil Haman, and the inauguration of a feast to commemorate the deliverance of the Jews from persecution. The Book of Esther is read every year at the festival of Purim, which supposedly has its origins in the events the book describes. (The Hebrew *pur* means "lot"; the day chosen by Haman for the destruction of the Jews was selected by lot.)

If we think of Jezebel and Esther as historical characters, they are separated by some three hundred years of actual history. The books in which they appear were composed centuries apart. The characteristic the women share is a form of education: they are the only women in the Hebrew Bible who are depicted as being able to read and write.[3]

In its account of Jezebel's lethal expropriation of Naboth's vineyard, the Bible has this to say: "So she wrote letters in Ahab's name and sealed them with his seal, and she sent them to the elders and the nobles who dwelt with Naboth in his city." (One of Jezebel's royal seals was in fact recently discovered by archaeologists.)[4] The story of Esther ends with her promulgation of a directive to the Jews of Persia: "Queen Esther, the daughter of Abihail, and Mordecai the Jew, gave full written authority, confirming this second letter about Purim. Letters were sent to all the Jews."

Should it be surprising that of all the women mentioned in the Bible, only two should be depicted as literate? Should it be surprising, rather, that there are this many? Was literacy common, or at least not out of the ordinary, among women of royal rank, as Jezebel and Esther were? Did it ever extend to the lower classes? These are all questions without reliable answers for the period covered by the Hebrew Bible — without reliable answers when the subject is literacy among men, let alone among women. "I do think that Jezebel could probably read and write," Frymer-Kensky says, "but Jezebel was raised a king's daughter. And we really don't know. The Bible says that Jezebel writes a letter. Of course, documents say that Charlemagne also wrote, but what Charlemagne actually did was dictate."

A picture of literacy even in postbiblical times and other Mediterranean cultures, about which in general we know much more, remains difficult to retrieve. A recent exhibit at the Yale University Art Galleries, titled "I, Claudia: Women in Ancient Rome," displayed a number of wooden writing tablets, or *tabulae*, of the kind that women are sometimes seen holding in Roman portraits — for instance, in the well-known portrait from Pompeii of a husband and wife. But in these instances, it seems clear, literacy is being paraded as an exceptional virtue rather than a routine adornment. The earliest Latin document anywhere that is *known* to be in a female hand comes relatively late: it is a Roman letter from about A.D. 100, found near Hadrian's Wall in Great Britain, inviting the recipient to a birthday party.[5]

At one recent meeting of the Society of Biblical Literature, a member gave a paper on the subject of female scribes in the Roman Empire. The author, Kim Haines-Eitzen, who now teaches at Cornell University, persuasively made the case that female scribes, or *librariae*, were not uncommon in the service of affluent mistresses. The evidence is often indirect, embedded as a passing reference in something else. Juvenal, for example, remarks in the sixth of his *Satires* that if a husband spurns his wife's sexual overtures, the wife's *libraria* will be the one to bear the brunt of the spurned woman's temper. *Libraria* in this passage has usually been read and interpreted as *lani pendia*, meaning "wool-worker," thereby disguising the fact that a scribe — a female scribe — is being referred to. The underlying reason for the mistranslation in this case, as apparently in others, was a form of circular reasoning: how could the word possibly be *libraria* when we know that women lacked the skills for that job?[6]

In other instances, female literacy has been simply suppressed. A letter of Eusebius, for instance, reveals that women figured among the scribes he supplied to the theologian Origen; but Jerome, quoting this letter at a later date, makes no mention of the female scribes. One significant manuscript from late antiquity — the fifth-century *Codex Alexandrinus*, which contains both the Hebrew Bible and the New Testament — actually displayed that great rarity, a scribe's name, in this case the name of a woman: Thecla. The possibility that a woman was responsible for the codex was nonetheless contested by scholars for centuries, with the notable exception of one eighteenth-century investigator, who accepted the attribution on the grounds that there were so many mistakes in the manuscript.[7]

The issue of female literacy in antiquity, or indeed at any time, is of course of interest for its own sake — for what it reveals about the social status and attainments of women and about the structure and evolution of societies. And it is hardly surprising that some scholars have been picking over scriptural texts, even if some of their colleagues find the endeavor faintly amusing. (At the lecture on female scribes in the Roman Empire, the first question during the discussion afterward came from one of the few men in attendance, who asked, "So did women have better handwriting than men?")

But another, and by far the more prominent, motivation for investigations of literacy has to do with the question of authorship. This is a nagging question that hangs over the Bible generally, issues of gender aside. As the biblical scholar Richard Elliott Friedman has written, the Bible "is at the heart of Christianity and Judaism. Ministers, priests, and rabbis preach it. Scholars spend their lives studying and teaching it in universities and seminaries. People read it, study it, admire it, disdain it, write about it, and love it. People have lived by it and died for it. And we do not know who wrote it."[8]

Could parts of the Bible have been written by a woman, or by a number of women? Even if they were not literally penned by women, in the sense that a woman composed a full narrative and applied an ink-laden quill to papyrus or parchment, can any texts or passages be said to reflect women's authentic voices, relatively unmediated by a male editorial hand? There can be no conclusive answer. There has, however, been a great deal of circumstantial speculation.

The speculation that has received the most widespread attention, as well as a great deal of criticism by academic specialists, is the proposition put forward by the Yale University literary critic Harold Bloom, in *The Book of J* (1990), that one of the chief strands of text in the first five books of the Bible, which scholars have given the name J, was the work of a woman. *Newsweek* gave its report about Bloom's suggestion the headline "The Woman Who Invented God." *Time* magazine, pithier, ran its account under the headline "Ms. Moses." Bloom contends not only that J was a woman but that she was a descendant of King David, that she lived at the court of King Solomon's son, Rehoboam, and that she in fact had little or no religious motivation at all.

To understand the basis of Bloom's contention is to accept the general outline that biblical scholars have crafted over the years to describe how the Bible was compiled. This outline would not be accepted by the most orthodox of Jews or by the most fundamentalist of Christians, whose interpretation of a belief in the Bible's divine origin extends to particulars of composition. (Orthodox Jews, for instance, believe that the first five books of the Bible, the so-called five books of Moses, are the actual product of Moses' hand.) Biblical scholars of a more humanistic bent see the books of the Hebrew Scriptures as encompassing a vast diversity of materials — historical tales, poems, law codes, liturgical invocations, war songs, chronicles, festive chants — whose origins in some cases stretch back to oral traditions rooted in Israel's prehistory and in other cases are as recent as the second century B.C.

The task of molding literary material into the preliminary forms of the first five books of the Bible was begun during the First Temple period, but the most intensive era of biblical formation, according to the scholarly consensus, occurred just afterward, during the half-century of the Babylonian exile, beginning in 587 B.C., when the Jewish elite and much of the Israelite population endured transplantation to the enemy capital. During this time these five books took final shape, as did the books that constitute the so-called Deuteronomistic history. Much of the rest of the Hebrew Bible's content was fashioned after the Jews returned to Jerusalem, during what has come to be called the Second Temple period. Final agreement on what would constitute the canon, the officially sanctioned corpus of the Hebrew Bible, was reached late in the first century or early in the second century A.D.[9]

Back to J: whatever the ultimate sources of its content — Canaanite myth, Israelite folk tradition, divine inspiration — the Book of Genesis has long been seen by scholars as embodying a number of distinct literary threads. As early as the seventeenth century, a French cleric, Richard Simon, suggested that Genesis was the product of interwoven sources. In the eighteenth century, a number of investigators looking into the phenomenon of doublets — the fact that key stories such as the accounts of the Creation, the Flood, and so on, are typically told twice, in differing versions — noticed a distinctive pattern. In one group of doublets, the designation used for God is the Hebrew word *El,* and in the other the word used is the Hebrew tetragrammaton *YHWH.* Scholars gave the name E to the first source and J to the second source; as scholarship has become more refined, Genesis has also acquired a P (for priestly) source and an R (for redactor, or editor) source. Depending on what paths we follow, we may encounter further refinements, such as J1, J2, and J3.

Harold Bloom's focus is on J, the Yahwistic writer, the author of what would seem to be the oldest strand of Genesis. The J he discerns is a woman who was writing primarily for women and who conceived of Yahweh as essentially a literary character rather than as a god to be worshiped and prayed to. Bloom surmises further that J was a close friend of the so-called Court Historian, the author of most of the second book of Samuel, and he emphasizes the particular attention J paid to women. About six times more text is devoted to Eve than to Adam, and whereas J's treatment of major male figures (Abraham, Jacob, Moses) is mixed, the treatment of female characters (Sarah, Rachel) is on the whole positive. "I think it accurate to observe that J had no heroes, only heroines," Bloom writes.[10]

Bloom contends, more than a little disingenuously, that "in proposing that J was a woman, at least I will not be furthering the interests of any religious or ideological group."[11] In truth, his proposition about the gender of J (which he came to regret having mentioned at all, according to one interview, because it distracted from his larger contemplation of the meaning and significance of J's work, whoever J happened to be) predictably found favor in certain religious and ideological camps even as it elicited widespread skepticism (or, at best, deep agnosticism) among biblical scholars. Besides pointing out what they saw as inadequacies in the translation Bloom was working with, the skeptics questioned many of his guiding assumptions, including the idea that a characteristically "female" form of writing that is objectively discernible exists. "It must be said," the eminent biblical scholar Robert Alter observed, "that the evidence offered for J's female identity is rather tenuous. We are repeatedly told, often with engaging wit, that J in Genesis exercises an extraordinary degree of imaginative sympathy for the plight of women and the viewpoint of female characters. But this is also true of the authors of Judges and Samuel — note the instance of the rape of Tamar — not to speak of later books like Ruth and Esther." By the same reasoning, Alter added, "one could easily conclude that *Anna Karenina*, with its splendidly realized if doomed heroine and its large gallery of repulsive, feckless, or clumsy men, must have been written by a woman."[12]

As a writer and a critic, Bloom is a commanding presence, and a playfully seductive one, whose works always merit attention and usually give pleasure. If his speculations about J's gender garner objections, it is for reasons other than inherent implausibility. Richard Elliott Friedman has noted that whereas it is virtually impossible to imagine the source E coming from a female hand, partly because E is so closely connected with the priestly class, which historically was exclusively male, J does in fact present more interesting possibilities, partly because of its origin in Judean court circles, where women might have enjoyed unprecedented opportunities. Friedman concludes: "The weight of evidence is still that the scribal profession in ancient Israel was male, true, but that does not exclude the possibility that a woman might have composed a work that came to be loved and valued in Israel."[13]

It may be that *The Book of J* does a disservice in a number of ways. The gleeful outrageousness of its tone only makes sense if the idea of women's high cultural achievement in ancient Israel is in fact nearly preposterous. But as Carol Meyers has noted, "It is an open question as to whether women were deemed inferior, secondary, and otherwise incapable of high art in Israelite antiquity. Most likely such stances are largely post-biblical."[14] Moreover, by emphasizing one authorial possibility, Bloom sweeps off into the shadows many points that might be pertinent to the issue of biblical sources and gender. Even if we discount entirely the notion that women had any kind of hand in the Bible's textual formation, there remains a body of material that may ultimately have originated among women — for instance, various utterances that come from the lips of female prophets, such as the Song of Deborah and the Song of Miriam. Beyond texts such as these, whose female origin is not only plausible but in the view of some even likely, are texts of more indeterminate status, which can be spoken of as female not in authorship but in genre.

One of the most dramatic episodes of Israel's modern history is the series of airlifts that began soon after the country became independent in 1948 and brought Jews from neighboring Islamic regions to the new Jewish homeland. Among those coming to Israel were rural Jews from Yemen, who at one point in late 1948, under the program known as Operation Magic Carpet, arrived at the rate of a thousand a week, airlifted to Tel Aviv aboard DC-4 Skymasters.[15] Most of the Yemeni immigrants were peasants from small villages. Their way of life had been unchanged for centuries and preserved social patterns of presumably great antiquity.

In all, some 45,000 Yemeni Jews were brought to Israel in the course of little more than a year. Not surprisingly, they attracted the attention of scholars of various kinds, in particular of S. D. Goitein, a Hebraic and Arabic scholar who undertook a close ethnographic study of the Magic Carpet immigrants soon after their arrival. Among the issues he explored were the social and religious roles of men and women, which he found to be sharply distinguished. But certain features of Yemeni Jewish society made a deep impression on him. As he wrote in an article published in Israel in 1957 but not translated into English for several decades,

> The detail which made the greatest impression on the present writer, turning his attention to women's poetry in the Bible and giving him great insight into it, was this: the Yemenite woman, despite her lowly and limited social position, expressed in her poetry public opinion on the events of the day. Her simple verses filled the function which the editorial in a daily newspaper fills in a modern society. Verses of this sort were devoted to great political events — such as the murder of the Imam Yahya in the spring of 1948 and the suppression of the subsequent revolt, or the bombing of Yemenite villages by British planes — as well as to people and happenings in the neighboring Muslim villages and also, of course, to the Jewish community.[16]

It is not hard to see why Goitein discerned strong parallels between modern-day Yemenite women and many of the women in the Bible, whose taunts and laments, warnings and advice, prayers and prophecies, likewise serve as a gloss on the great events in the lives of the Israelites and their neighbors. Women did not necessarily write the biblical stories in which these words and commentaries appear — indeed, they almost certainly did not — but is it far-fetched to see such stories as transmitting a memory of women's voices or women's authority? Goitein used the image of feminine "remnants" in oral literature that leave "a recognizable impression" in the stories as they come down to us. He also used the image of these remnants being poured over time "from one vessel to another."[17]

Scholars sympathetic to this idea focus not on identifying or speculating about male and female authors but on identifying male and female *genres*. In their book *On Gendering Texts*, the Hebrew Bible scholars Athalya Brenner and the late Fokkelien van Dijk-Hemmes designate these genres "M" and "F," hoping that the very abstraction of such minimalist terminology will shift thoughts away from the gender of scribes bent over their work and toward the idea of "textualized women's traditions."[18]

One genre to look at is that of the so-called naming speech — the formal bestowal of a name upon a newborn child, typically embedded within a larger explanation of the meaning of that name. The birth of each of the children of Leah, the unloved wife of Jacob, is followed by a naming speech in which the child's name is derived from a Hebrew pun. For instance: "And Leah conceived and bore a son, and she called his name Reuben, for she said, 'Because the Lord has looked upon my affliction; surely now my husband will love me'" (Genesis 29:32). The name Reuben not only means "Behold, a son" but also mimics the Hebrew words meaning "looked upon misery." Jacob will never love her, but Leah will continue bearing sons. Upon the birth of her fifth, she says, "'This time I will praise the Lord'; therefore she called his name Judah" (Genesis 29:35), the name Judah embodying the expression of thanks to the Lord.[19]

In the Hebrew Bible as a whole there are forty-one instances in which children are formally named in the context of a naming speech, and in two thirds of these cases the person doing the naming is a woman. In a number of other cases — notably, that of the birth of Esau and Jacob to Rebekah — the use of the passive voice conceals the identity of the name-giver, although we can assume that it must be a woman, since the naming occurs immediately after childbirth, when only women would have been present. "The act of naming is significant," the commentator Savina Teubal has written, "because it places the name-*giver* in authority over the name-*bearer*." She goes on to observe, "In biblical times, it seems, children were named the moment they were born — by mothers and midwives who chose names appropriate to the conditions, or their perceptions of the birth itself."[20] (Of course, one of the most prominent instances of name-giving does not involve a newborn child at all but rather the new creature woman, to whom Adam gives the name Eve, meaning "mother of all living." As you might imagine, a considerable number of feminist scholars have examined this episode in every conceivable light.)

Other genres of F texts, as Brenner and Hemmes classify them, include birth songs, like the Song of Hannah (1 Samuel 2:1–10), with its strong echo in the "Magnificat" of the New Testament, and the famous songs of victory, including Deborah's and Miriam's and those of the nameless women who come forward dancing with tambourines after success in battle.

Biblical passages give evidence, even when not quoting women directly, of occasions when women's speech of a formal and public kind was an accepted aspect of social drama. From the mouths of women must have come words of ritual goading, taunting, and mockery, and also words of soothsaying and of prophecy. Five women are explicitly given the title "prophet" — Miriam, Deborah, Huldah, Noadiah, and the wife of Isaiah; the unremarkable manner in which the Bible mentions the status of these women suggests that the role of prophet was an established one.

Although the words women customarily used are not preserved, many references, such as the following one from Jeremiah (9:17), indicate that women were central to expressions of mourning and lamentation: "Call for the mourning women to come; send for the skillful women to come. Let them make haste and raise a wailing over us, that our eyes may run down with tears." In the Book of Lamentations, which records the final destruction of the Israelite kingdom and the beginnings of exile, the fallen city of Jerusalem is depicted as a woman mourner, a dirge singer, and her words (1:16) perhaps capture some of the language that such a singer might have employed on an ordinary occasion in ordinary times: "For these things I weep; my eyes flow with tears; for a comforter is far from me, one to revive my courage."

Imagine many of these functions bound up into one person, and what emerges is a tentative sketch of the "wise woman" who appears from time to time in the Bible — a woman whose familiarity and prominence in the ordinary life of the people, a number of scholars suggest, may have helped give rise to one of the most powerfully attractive feminine images in the Bible, the figure of Wisdom. Goitein wrote about the wise women he encountered among the Yemeni immigrants, offering a composite portrait:

> This is a woman who keeps a watchful eye on her fellow villagers from the day of their coming forth into the light of the world until their death. It is she who helps during childbirth; she who knows the remedies and other treatments . . . required in case of illness; she who assists in matchmaking and, when necessary, who makes peace between husband and wife. Her advice is sought not just by her family but by her whole village. It is she who is most proficient at whatever craft is practiced in the district, and she, too, who is the poet who "declaims" before the women at weddings and other festive occasions and in mourning as well.[21]

A wise woman from Tekoah (2 Samuel 14) speaks eloquently before King David, urging him to make peace with his son Absalom. A wise woman from Abel-Beth-Maacah (2 Samuel 20) negotiates on behalf of her city and saves it from destruction. The idea of "wisdom" — *hokma*, a word of feminine gender — in the Hebrew Bible, as Carol Meyers has pointed out, cannot be neatly encapsulated; it can apply to a mother's nurturing, to the teaching of household and cultural tasks, to a knowledge of folkways, to the skilled wielding of technology, to the astute perception of what constitutes a righteous path.[22] In the Book of Proverbs, wisdom is personified not only as a woman but as a divine consort:

> *The Lord created me the first of his works*
> *long ago, before all else that he made . . .*
> *Then I was at his side each day,*
> *his darling and delight.*

Lurking within this exalted figure of Wisdom, conceived of specifically as a woman, is surely the wise woman of ordinary communal life.[23] These organic origins aside, some scholars also point to the psychological significance of Wisdom's full emergence only in the writings of the postexilic period, when the public focus provided by the Davidic monarchy was forever gone. And as still other scholars suggest, it is important to see Lady Wisdom in the context of monotheism itself — to see her as a powerful expression not only of the divine feminine, an obvious role, but even more significantly as a means of intercession. As Frymer-Kensky (among others) has pointed out, in the transition from polytheism to monotheism it is of course significant that God is now only male, but the greater significance is simply that God is singular: "In the absence of other divine beings, God's audience, partners, foils, and competitors are all human beings, and it is on their interaction with God that the world depends."[24]

The place known in Arabic as Kuntillet Ajrûd, or "Solitary Hill of the Wells," can be found in the northeastern region of the Sinai Peninsula, at a place where important caravan routes once intersected, including the north-south route from Gaza, on the Mediterranean coast, to Eilat, on the Gulf of Aqaba. Beginning in 1975, a team of archaeologists from Tel Aviv University undertook excavations at this site, unearthing the foundations of structures dating back to the ninth century B.C., when this territory would have been under Israelite control. Among the discoveries were two *pithoi*, or standing stone monoliths, and on one of them had been drawn some images of men and women and also words in Hebrew that some interpreters ventured to read as "by Yahweh, our guardian, and his Asherah."

For two decades the finds at Kuntillet Ajrûd have been a source of debate.[25] To begin with, is the translation correct? If so, is "Asherah" meant to designate the Canaanite goddess of fertility, the consort of the chief male god, El? Are we to suppose, then, that Yahweh too had a consort, and that the monotheistic Israelites made room for a goddess, "his Asherah"? Was Kuntillet Ajrûd their shrine? Or was it just a caravanserai, abounding in the graffiti of travelers? And might "Asherah" refer not to the Canaanite goddess specifically but merely to the Israelite cult-image of the same name, a sacred tree or symbolic wooden pole planted near stone altars?

These are questions that elicit both narrow academic inquiry and, among some feminists with an interest in religion, a broader emotional resonance. The Israelite worldview, which offered a revolutionary vision centered on a single deity, came into being amid a cultural context of polytheism. All of the Israelites' powerful neighbors — the Canaanites, the Assyrians, the Egyptians — had sophisticated religious systems that featured a pantheon of goddesses as well as gods, with the functional responsibilities of cosmic governance and earthly development divided among them. The Israelites, not surprisingly, were hardly immune to the attractions of these systems. Atavistic references to them appear in many places in the Hebrew Bible. And of course the explicit embrace of foreign gods by the Israelites causes frequent breaches in the covenant with Yahweh. The fall of Jerusalem to the Babylonians is precipitated in part by King Manasseh's installation of a shrine to Asherah in the Temple. The Lord vows (2 Kings 21:13) in response: "I will wipe Jerusalem as one wipes a dish, wiping it and turning it upside down."

The broader emotional response occurs on a different plane. It is only natural to wonder if women must inevitably suffer disadvantages in a religious system that lacks powerful goddesses, or indeed goddesses of any kind — one in which goddesses may in fact have been suppressed. And it is only natural to wonder about the theological and psychological consequences of a system in which the one god there is comes across as a male.

Tikva Frymer-Kensky understands such complaints. At the same time, she sees polytheism and monotheism in a considerably different light from the one that is typically trained on either subject. She writes in *In the Wake of the Goddesses*, "If you could discover all you needed to know about the Goddess from inside your soul and your mind, why should anyone study Sumerian and Akkadian?"[26]

Superficially, elements of polytheism undeniably hold a certain appeal. In a culture such as ours, with all its talk about affirmative action and minority set-asides and all the public invocation of the importance of role models, the presence of women in an ancient pantheon can strike a reassuring note of progress. In the pantheons of Mesopotamia, vital natural and social functions such as the growing of grain, the brewing of beer, the making of pottery, and the turning of wool into cloth are associated with women who enjoy divine status. In the Sumerian pantheon, the goddess Nisaba watches over the storage rooms, among other duties, storage rooms perhaps being a cultural analogue of the womb. Nisaba is also responsible for another form of storage: writing, the warehouse of memory. And, of course, goddesses are generally associated with fertility and sexual pleasure. But male gods fulfill most of the important roles. They control the earth and the skies and the elements — the power structure of the universe — and they dominate the female gods. The religions of ancient Mesopotamia do not by any means constitute "women's religion." Moreover, the whole system presupposes — and legitimates — the division of heaven and earth, of thought and theology, along gender lines. In the end, the goddesses provide little in the way of succor. Frymer-Kensky writes, "The existence and power of a goddess, particularly of Ishtar, is no indication or guarantee of a high status for human women. In Assyria, where Ishtar was so prominent, women were not. The texts rarely mention any individual women, and, according to the Middle Assyrian laws, married women had to be veiled, had no rights to their husband's property, . . . and could be struck by their husbands at will."[27]

Monotheism, the chief characteristic of Western religion, represents a revolutionary theological departure. All the functions and characteristics of those male and female divinities must now be rolled into the being of the one God; "God plays all the roles," Frymer-Kensky writes, "for God is creator and sustainer, provider and destroyer." In the Bible, God brings forth the rain and snow and sun, induces fertility in man and beast and field, serves as midwife, heals the sick. The complex dynamic of shifting power relationships among the divinities themselves and their mortal clients — the jealousies, the couplings, the wars — is replaced by a single all-important relationship: that between the one God and the apogee of God's creation, human beings.[28]

God in the Bible is not devoid of gender. God is described most often with male imagery, a circumstance that prompts a good deal of literal-mindedness even now. "O'Connor Rips Radical Feminists: God Is a Man" was the front-page headline on the *New York Post* when John

Cardinal O'Connor of New York used a 1991 Father's Day sermon to criticize feminist reconceptualizations of the divine.[29] When the director of the York Mystery Plays in England announced in 1996 that the role of God was to be played by a woman at the next staging of the six-hundred-year-old event, the archdeacon of York condemned the proposal as tantamount to "paganism." He observed, "We are made in God's image, and not the other way around."[30]

Yet the God of Israel, unlike the gods of Israel's neighbors, is not a sexual being, possesses no sexual organs, and is never depicted, as Frymer-Kensky memorably puts it, "below the waist."[31] The God of Israel creates the world not by means of sexual reproduction but by an act of will. Depending on circumstance, feminine as well as masculine imagery may be invoked in metaphor. "Now I will cry out like a woman in travail, I will gasp and pant," says God in Isaiah (42:14). Later in the same book (49:15), God speaks to Israel in this manner: "Can a woman forget her sucking child, that she should have no compassion on the son of her womb? Even these may forget, yet I will not forget you."

Created in the image of the one God, human beings, male and female alike, partake of a single nature: "male and female he created them" (Genesis 1:27). Humanity is elevated in status and in competence. Whereas in the polytheistic religions the gods bestow technology and skills on human beings, in the Bible human beings develop cultural skills on their own, after "stealing" from the Tree of Knowledge (on a woman's initiative). The first act of Adam and Eve after eating the forbidden fruit is one that in Sumerian mythology would have been the gift of the goddess Uttu: they make clothes for themselves. Soon human beings are tilling fields, forging metal, building cities, writing books, making music. Eventually they will even be capable of biblical criticism. Civilization is in human hands.

The religious vision of what Frymer-Kensky calls "radical monotheism" represents an ideal — and the reality of biblical society did not conform to it. Women were subordinate to men in custom and in law, as they were everywhere in the ancient world. Their property rights were limited. Their sense of purpose in life was often equated with reproductive success. And yet, unlike the sacred literature of other Near Eastern cultures, "the Bible presents no characteristics of human behavior as 'female' or 'male,' no division of attributes between the poles of 'feminine' and 'masculine' . . . As far as the Bible presents humanity, gender is a matter of biology and social roles, it is not a question of basic nature or identity."[32] There is no battle of the sexes, no pursuit of "male" or "female" goals, no characteristically male or female behavior, no incipient gender-driven solidarity.

The emergence of monotheism can be traced in the texts of the Bible, as intimations of a more populous divine sphere give way to the monopoly of Yahweh. How and why does this process occur? A recent *New Yorker* cartoon shows pagan gods assembled among the clouds, one of them saying angrily to the others, "It's called monotheism, but it looks like downsizing to me" — an explanation that can take its place alongside various scholarly theories.[33] "The Marxist in me asks, how does this happen?" Frymer-Kensky says. "How does a social system where gender is important and where identity is an issue rise beyond that to a kind of universalizing system? My upbringing would like to say, 'Revelation! Revelation!' The counterquestion would be, how does Marxism arise in the context of the bourgeoisie? which is where it does arise. The answer is, I don't know *how* these things happen."

By elevating human beings, monotheism also puts an enormous strain on them, creating a profound psychological demand for intercessory figures. To whom do we entrust a dialogue with God? There are, obviously, the prophets. But the voice of compassionate intercession is frequently the voice of a woman. The Bible invokes Rachel — "Mother Rachel," wife of the patriarch Jacob, who died giving birth to Benjamin. Zion, the spirit of Jerusalem, is also invoked as a beloved woman. Perhaps reflecting in part the precarious status of women in their society, the fragile, beleaguered polity of the Israelites identifies itself as a woman in its supplications. Possibly the most memorable image is that of Lady Wisdom, who is sometimes depicted as a goddess. It is said in places that she already existed at the time of creation. She will go on to become the divine (and feminine) Sophia of Christian theology.[34]

"It's a convergence of the psychological, the historical, and the sociological," says Frymer-Kensky. "Psychologically, the mother is an enormous presence to the infant. The mother is the one who knows what to do when the child is hurt, tired, or wet. This has a deep impact. The impact is reinforced by the fact that women had responsibility for all kinds of technological wizardry that we now take for granted. The preparation of food. Turning sheep's wool into cloth. Collecting herbs and making potions. The wise women of the Bible may be older women who have done these things all their lives. Women are seen to have arcane knowledge. They are the child's first teachers. There is also a sense of women as being in touch with the divine agenda, which is partly, but only partly, because it is women who give birth. Women gain perspective from being pushed off to the margins of the public world, the margins of the political world. There is always something dangerous and also numinous about the margins."

This experience may also explain, Frymer-Kensky says, why there are so many stories in the Bible about women, period. If Wisdom shows women exalted, many other stories appear to use women the way Dickens used poor children, as a kind of index of social pathology. Perhaps it is only optimism, but Frymer-Kensky sees a recurring tension in the Bible on the issue of gender. On the one hand, she says, the authors are conscious of gender and of the fact that the social position of women is inferior to that of men, and on the other hand, the authors recognize that women and men are innately equal and that they are in exactly the same position with respect to God. "When I'm reading with a hermeneutic of benevolence," she said, "I call the Bible gender-neutral. When I'm reading with a hermeneutic of suspicion, I call it gender-blind."

Chapter Six

·····························

THE WANDERING ROCK

*And I found more bitter than death the woman whose heart is snares
and nets, and whose hands are fetters; he who pleases God
escapes her, but the sinner is taken by her.*
— Ecclesiastes 7:26

*Texts trigger readings; that is what they are:
the occasion of a reaction.*
— Mieke Bal

IT MAY BE GOING too far to say that the music of Tom Jones is inappropriate for any occasion, but the endless loop of his song "Delilah," intended as an inviting introduction to the papers being presented at an academic meeting not long ago, quickly became an annoyance. I listened for a fourth and fifth time as the singer summoned up the image of the shadows playing in his unfaithful lover's window, and for a fourth and fifth time was made aware of his reaction: "As she deceived me I watched and went out of my mind."

Usually the problem on such occasions is that the sound system doesn't work. Here, in a dark and windowless meeting room in New Orleans, the audience of several hundred people tried to ignore the cloying choruses (*"Why, why, why, Delilah?"*) and trumpet flourishes as they waited for a session to begin on the subject of "Women Who Kill," with presentations focusing not only on Delilah but also on Jael, Esther, Judith, and Salome. When the session finally did begin, the lights were dimmed even further, and amid sounds of settled relief the people turned their attention to a video screen, where a clip from Cecil B. De Mille's 1949 swords-and-sandals epic *Samson and Delilah* was about to be shown.

This is the version of the story with Victor Mature as Samson and Hedy Lamarr as Delilah. Its reputation has by now stabilized into one of camp respectability. The screen flickered for a moment, and then Mature and Lamarr appeared, he in a leather loincloth, she in a slinky Philistine evening gown. It was the moment when Delilah tricks Samson into drinking a sleeping draught so that she can cut his hair and deprive him of his strength. The dialogue is noncanonical:

SAMSON: You called?

DELILAH: The wine of parting is bitter, Samson.

S: Not as bitter as blood.

D: You cannot wipe away such blood as I have given you without even a farewell.

S: I have a new debt to pay the Philistines, but I'll come to you in Egypt.

D: No, Samson, I've lost you. Drain this cup, as you have drained my heart. [*Samson switches the cups, out of suspicion — as Delilah has anticipated that he will.*] You always doubt me, don't you?

S: And always love you. I'll find you, Delilah, wherever you go.

D: No, Samson, you belong to Miriam. She's the good in you. I'm the weakness, the love that would enslave you.

S: I'll never be free of you, Delilah.

[*Samson collapses.*]

The story of Samson (Judges 13–16), one of the last of Israel's judges, and of Samson's fateful dalliance with Delilah, a Philistine woman, is in its basic outlines widely familiar. Samson was born through divine intervention to an unnamed woman, identified (typically) only as the wife of Manoah, who was barren and had produced no child; the angel who announces Samson's miraculous conception warns that "no razor shall come upon his head, for the boy shall be a Nazirite to God from birth." Samson grows strong, invincible, and willful, a man of violence and appetites. He kills and dismembers a lion. He takes a Philistine woman as his wife, transgressing the desires of his family; she goes on to deceive him. Later he engages a prostitute in Gaza. In the meantime he kills many Philistines and lays waste to much property. After Samson falls in love with Delilah, the Philistines bribe her to discover the secret of his strength, which, after Samson's repeated dissimulations, she does. "She made him sleep on her knees, and she called a man and had him shave the seven locks of his head. Then she began to torment him, and his strength left him." Samson is captured and blinded by the Philistines, but when his hair grows back his strength returns. In the end, standing between the pillars of a temple, he pulls the pillars out of place, bringing death down upon himself and upon thousands of Philistines who are making merry at a pagan feast.

Was Delilah among the victims? The Bible does not say. The story of her deed certainly survived, to become a staple of high and low art, of cathedral windows and children's books, of popular song and vulgar verse. Samson, with his brute strength, his heedless libido, and his perfunctory intelligence, may be the heroic central character of these chapters from Judges, but the sly, persistent Delilah has been perceived as the dangerously appealing one, the epitome at once of betrayal, deceit, and allure. In *The Phantom of the Opera*, the phantom hurls the charge "Delilah!" at his beloved. Delilah is the name of the prostitute in the Clint Eastwood movie *Unforgiven*. Delilah has been an object of censorious commentary for millennia.

For all that, however, it may be possible to see Delilah in a somewhat different light — or to render the story in a more explanatory context. Such, at least, was the intention of some of those who spoke at the session on "Women Who Kill." One person saw the Samson and Delilah story as centering psychologically not on Delilah's deceit but on the (presumably) male authors' fears of castration. The suggestion is not implausible. Hair has famously erotic overtones, and the dangling knot that Hedy Lamarr slices from Samson — and here the video clip served as a triumphant visual aid — embodies them unmistakably. Another person took aim at one of the story's core ironies: looking at it from the Philistines' point of view, isn't Delilah really a patriot? How in essence does her behavior differ from that of Judith, the Israelite heroine who employs seduction to lure the Assyrian general Holofernes to his doom? Indeed, one school of thought among biblical scholars holds that the Samson and Delilah story was originally a Philistine fable, taken over and adapted by the Israelites. A woman seated next to me turned and whispered, "So if I'd been a Philistine, I would have been a Delilah." Her name tag, I saw, read "Judith."

Only about 10 percent of the roughly 1,400 individuals who are given names in the Hebrew Bible are women, but the stories of those women are among the most memorable in Scripture. Feminist scholars devote a great deal of attention to broad thematic inquiries — for instance, into women and the Israelite legal system, or women and economic life, or women as religious and community leaders, or women as personifications of the divine — but the character and circumstances of prominent individual women in the Bible remain a formidable source of popular attraction. The emerging feminist scholarship and criticism focused on such figures as Judith and Esther, Ruth and Naomi, Susanna and Bathsheba has by now become substantial. It joins an enormous existing corpus of art and literature that has long shown the stories of women in the Bible to be irresistible. Among feminists, the named women command attention for a variety of reasons, and often for several reasons at once, quite apart from the inherently compelling quality of the stories in which they figure.

One natural impetus to scholarly attention is quasi-historical: gaining access to glimmerings of the self-conception of a particular people at a particular time. Thus, the stories of Israel's matriarchs — Sarah, Rebekah, Rachel, Leah — can be off-putting for the seeming arrogance of their disregard for women's personal interests and feelings, but the overriding concern of *everyone* in them for the production of children, and consequently for building up the house of Israel, certainly comes through. The stories of Esther, Judith, and Susanna, for their part, are sometimes viewed together not only because of commonalities of chronology (they are all "late" stories) and ostensible subject matter (beautiful women in grave danger) but also because each can be seen as an allegory of and thus a possible source of insight into Jewish communities that existed at the sufferance of powerful Gentile forces. Of course, from the point of view of women, the meanings we carry away from such stories can be distinctly variable.

Susanna, for instance, is presented as a faithful wife and mother who, together with her wealthy and prominent husband, is a member of the

Jewish community in Babylon. A woman of leisure, she is spied upon in her bath by two lustful old men who desire to have sex with her and who falsely accuse her of adultery when she spurns their advances. Susanna, whom family and friends supinely desert, is saved from death only by the clever courtroom tactics of the prophet Daniel. With its interweaving of the sacred and the erotic, this story inspired a favorite image of medieval and Renaissance painters. (Perhaps for the same reason, the erotically charged Song of Songs was the most frequently read book of the Bible in medieval monasteries.) As Amy-Jill Levine, of Vanderbilt University, has pointed out, the story also opens up some contentious questions: "What may be celebrated from one perspective may be condemned from another. Susanna's freedom from domestic responsibilities may indicate to some the economic success of the diaspora community; to others it signals complacency and indolence. For some she is a heroine whose righteousness is recognized by heaven; for others she is a weak figure unable or unwilling to protest her own innocence in the public sphere until seemingly too late."[1]

As this statement suggests, the Bible's most vivid stories about women often raise issues that are at heart ideological: they have to do with recovering, or perhaps uncovering, the larger thematic purpose of the biblical message. Again, from the point of view of women, the meanings we carry away can be variable. Take a theme as apparently straightforward as deception. Deception, dissembling, trickery, subterfuge — as any thematic census will reveal, these are among the chief functional roles played by women in the Bible. In Genesis 27, for instance, Rebekah devises a plan whereby her favorite, the younger son, Jacob, secures the blessing of his father, Isaac, in place of the elder and rightful son, Esau. ("Now therefore, my son, obey my word as I command you.") In Genesis 39, Potiphar's wife uses the evidence of Joseph's loincloth, lost when Joseph flees her seductions, to support her false accusations. ("As soon as I lifted up my voice and cried, he left his garment with me.") In 1 Kings 21, Jezebel uses deceit to gain the vineyard of Naboth. ("Set two base fellows opposite him, and let them bring a charge against him, saying, 'You have cursed God and the King.' Then take him out and stone him to death.") In Judith, the eponymous central character, an esteemed and pious widow, adorns herself seductively like an obviously available woman in order to entrap Holofernes, whose head she eventually cuts off. ("By the deceit of my lips," Judith prays, "strike down the slave with the prince and the prince with his servant; crush their arrogance by the hand of a woman.")

What are we to make of women's wiles in such stories? In the opinion of one feminist commentator, Esther Fuchs, of the University of Arizona, who avowedly has little use for the Bible, deceptiveness "is a motif that runs through most [biblical] narratives involving women, both condemnatory and laudatory ones." In a study titled "Who Is Hiding the Truth?" Fuchs goes on: "From Eve to Esther, from Rebekah to Ruth, the characterization of women presents deceptiveness as an almost inescapable feature of femininity."[2] Of course, men too are shown as duplicitous, Fuchs acknowledges. But a double, perhaps even a triple standard has been routinely applied. Jezebel is eaten by dogs for her crimes; in contrast, King David, whose deception of the loyal Uriah (in the furtherance of his adultery with Bathsheba) ends in Uriah's death, is given a chance to repent. In other cases, deceptions fomented by men achieve a kind of exoneration through explanation. Fuchs points out finally that in those instances when women's deceptions are deemed to have been all to the good, the result of their actions is merely to reinforce the patriarchal status quo. To give one example, in Fuchs's view Ruth is held up as a figure of admiration not so much because she returns to the land of Judah with her mother-in-law, or because of her enterprising and intrepid nature, "but for her success in finding and marrying a direct relative of Elimelech, her father-in-law, and giving birth to children who would carry on the patrilineage of her deceased husband."[3] In any event, Fuchs writes, the broad-brush depiction of women as deceivers works insidiously on the reader at another, more general level: "This discriminatory treatment produces female portraits intended, among other things, to validate the suspicion that women's apparent impotence is nothing but a deceptive disguise, that underneath their vulnerable coyness lurks a dangerously calculating mind."[4]

That is one view of the situation. Toni Craven, a professor of Hebrew Bible at the Brite Divinity School at Texas Christian University, would endorse it up to a point. But in an essay on "Women Who Lied for the Faith," she explains why she finds an interpretation such as Fuchs's on the whole too extreme. Craven takes up a dozen or so well-known episodes of female deception. There is the case of Miriam, the sister of Moses, whose deception (Exodus 2) saves the life of the infant Moses when he is discovered by Pharaoh's daughter. ("At this the sister approached Pharaoh's daughter: 'Shall I go and call you a nurse from the Hebrew women to nurse the child?' When Pharaoh's daughter told her to do so, she went and called the baby's mother.") There is the case of Rahab (Joshua 2), who lies to conceal the Israelite spies in Jericho, and of Jael (Judges 4), who deceives the Canaanite general Sisera and drives a tent peg through his head when he nods off to sleep. There is the woman of Tekoa (2 Samuel 14), whose false testimony induces King David to act wisely. And (again) there is the celebrated widow Judith. These stories, Craven argues, are about women as "convention breakers," women who "lied to men, inside or outside the family of faith, for the sake of shaping their own and the next generation in ways that they judged appropriate." And the theology of the Bible presents these stories for approval. The stories are not prescriptive in a narrow sense; "surely not all are called to lie." They are, however, Craven writes, "exemplary stories of radical faithfulness that finds ways of overcoming oppression."[5]

Susan Niditch, who has written on many biblical subjects, from war to folklore, likewise emphasizes the ambivalence of underdog and trickster tales. Trickster women, she writes in an essay on Esther, "toy with the establishment and when uncovered escape, elude authority, and trick again." But at the same time these women often "seek to become a part of the system that threatened them."[6]

There is yet another way to read the biblical stories about women, one that involves history or ideology scarcely at all: it is to read them simply as stories, as fables, as tales. To read stories *as stories* — as narratives ripped from their settings — means to treat the text not as evidence to be chewed over for what it can "tell us" about past events or past states of mind, or about divine purpose, but rather for what it can reveal about the nature of the present-day interaction between text and reader. It leads, in other words, into the realm of purely literary readings. One of the most prominent practitioners of this form of reading is the Dutch literary critic Mieke Bal.

"Don't make this into a mother thing!"

Mieke Bal's good-natured but insistent reaction was in response to a question about the dedication of her book *Lethal Love* to her mother, whom she described in the dedicatory note as "the keenest of readers." I had simply asked whether she received from her mother any special insights into the act of reading, which is at the core of Bal's professional life. No, Bal went on: her mother, although a feminist who is interested in the Bible, was not a particular influence in this respect at all. Thinking back on her life's path, Bal explained that her family was more or less a Catholic one and that Catholics are well known for being traditionally the least assiduous Bible readers in all of Christendom. As a child she did, of course, absorb a selection of Bible stories, their plots already distilled into the stylized secondary form in which most of us know (or think we know) so many of them. The story of Samson and Delilah was one that she remembers hearing, and she remembers also her initial reaction to it: "I didn't like that it had to do with Delilah getting all the blame."

Mostly, the young Mieke Bal was not thinking about such questions. She was, however, developing into an intensive reader. Growing up in Heemstede, west of Amsterdam, she would read a book while walking to school. Her desk at school had a lid, and by raising it slightly she could read a book opened up inside while classes about something else were going on. She read, by her estimate, two books a day for many years. Reading represented a vast enlargement of her world — a fairly common experience. Less typical for a child, though, was her sense of the text as in effect another person, as something that a reader cannot fully appropriate, something that might offer resistance when probed, "something that can talk back." Bal went on to study literature at university and eventually obtained a doctorate in French literature, with a heavy grounding in modern critical theory. She became deeply interested in the idea and structure of narrative, because, as she has written in a brief intellectual memoir, narrative "is alive and active as a cultural force, not just a kind of literature," because narrative "enables us to make meaning out of the chaotic world and the incomprehensible events in it," and because "it can be used to manipulate."[7]

That Bal turned her attention to the Bible at all was more or less an accident. A friend who was a biblical scholar, Fokkelien van Dijk-Hemmes, invited her to join a study group with other women who were discussing various biblical stories from a feminist perspective. Bal found the discussions absorbing and was struck by the tension between the stories as she remembered them and the stories as revealed in the text. She began to read them more closely. With the help of her friend, she also took up the study of Hebrew.

I had not known quite what to expect of Mieke Bal. Her reputation as a feminist literary critic is formidable. Her curriculum vitae, presented in very small type, runs to fifty-five pages. She is currently the director of the Amsterdam School of Cultural Analysis, and since 1991 she has also been a professor of literature at the University of Amsterdam, one of relatively few tenured women (only about 4 percent of the total tenured population, as compared with about 25 percent in the United States) in the university system of the Netherlands. Before that she was for several years the Susan B. Anthony Professor of Women's Studies at the University of Rochester in New York. In print, Bal displays a penchant for dense methodological discussions, which for many readers must represent impassable obstacles set amid an already forbidding Sahara of poststructuralist theory. From time to time you encounter a sentence such as "If it is possible to define a temporal figure as analepsis-on-paralepsis, there is no reason not to include the paralepsis within the analysis of order, and to assume the possibility of the specification *paralepsis-on-analepsis*."[8] The temptation is just to sprawl in the sand and wait for help.

Yet over breakfast one morning, just a block from the site in Washington, D.C., where Susan B. Anthony mounted her futile defense of Elizabeth Cady Stanton, Bal gave the impression of warm-blooded vitality. Tall and elegantly dressed, with close-cropped white hair, she seemed an unlikely candidate for the large plate of eggs Benedict that in fact she ordered. She talked about her two grown children. She talked about feminist mystery writers such as Anne Perry, Elizabeth George, and Karen Kijewski and how she is mildly addicted to their books, from which she demands violence and multiple murders. She speculated frankly about possible connections between her interest in the Samson and Delilah story and her experience with certain kinds of men.

The story of Samson and Delilah, by coincidence, was under discussion the first time Bal attended the Bible study group. It is one of five biblical episodes that Bal takes up in *Lethal Love*, the others being the stories of Adam and Eve, David and Bathsheba, Ruth and Boaz, and Tamar and Judah. In order to obtain a kind of interpretive lens, she matches each of these stories to a form of "reception" — that is, she plays off the biblical story against one of the nonbiblical genres in which versions of the story have also been transmitted. In her recent essay "Throw Them to the Lions, Sire," about biblical narratives as rendered by Hollywood, Alice Bach, of Stanford University, notes that "in our postmodern image culture, readers are also spectators. The basic components of 'reading,' even of a biblical text, need to acknowledge that our impressions come from films, paintings, TV, ads — all of which . . . influence our interpretations of biblical literary figures."[9] Thus, Bal explores the story of Ruth and Boaz alongside the versions of that story presented in painting and poetry. She looks at the story of Adam and Eve alongside the versions that have flowered in Christian mythology, and the story of Samson and Delilah alongside the versions that appear in Bibles for children and young adults. Her insights can be wonderfully provocative. Consider the figure Eve (who is mentioned by name only twice in the Hebrew Bible). Is there really any such person as "Eve" in Genesis? Bal asks. That is, do we encounter a character who has from the outset any semblance of dimensionality or stability? Or do we create this character only after her appearances have come to an end and then project her back on a handful of disparate sequences, deluding ourselves into believing that she must have been there all along?

As noted, it is hard, maybe impossible, to find anyone in feminist biblical studies who has not read Phyllis Trible's book *God and the Rhetoric of Sexuality*. It is nearly as hard to find someone who is not familiar with *Lethal Love*. The two books could almost serve as bookends, holding in place a shelf of works whose gradations encompass a wide spectrum of concerns and methodologies. Seen side by side, though, the differences between the two books would reveal themselves as stark. Both are literary studies, yes. Both venture deeply into a selected group of Bible stories. But whereas Trible is concerned with the theological intention of these stories and remains personally committed to the idea that the Bible can serve as a spiritual resource, Bal is interested in none of that. She represents, on the contrary, the much-publicized and much-caricatured tendency in modern academic criticism to deny the validity of any one intended meaning in a text and to subvert the domination in a text of any one accepted interpretation.

"I do not claim the Bible to be either a feminist resource or a sexist manifesto," she writes in *Lethal Love*. "That kind of assumption can be an issue only for those who attribute moral, religious, or political authority to these texts, which is precisely the opposite of what I am interested in." Bal said to me at one point, in explaining why she felt aloof from a great deal of feminist biblical scholarship, "I can smell dogma a mile away." Still, as someone who is committed to "the arbitrariness of all readings," she cannot help but be disturbed whenever literary readings begin to congeal around a certain orthodoxy and develop a hardened crust, and as she points out, readings of Bible stories have hardened in a way that is for the most part misogynist. She is therefore interested in cracking and breaking through that crust. "The point of literary analysis is that there is no truth," she writes. "And when the truth is absent, women can creep in." Bal emphasizes, however, that "the alternative readings I will propose should not be considered as yet another, superior interpretation that overthrows all the others."[10] The aim, rather, is to show how other readings are possible.

This really is the bedrock of her appeal: Bal is an adroit and ruthless reader, a picker-apart of texts, whose manner of close investigation rubs off to some degree on anyone who samples her work. One purpose of presenting the Samson and Delilah story through the lens of Bibles for children and young adults is to remind readers of the stripped-down plot lines they carry around in their heads — and to remind readers, conversely, of elements of the story that flourish in the popular consciousness but not in the biblical text itself. For instance, the stripped-down version of Samson's marriage in popular storybooks gives little hint of what the Bible makes plain: that Samson, in seeking his own individual happiness, brings to a head a larger and irreconcilable conflict between tribes and social systems, the intensity and course of which are determined at every level of the story not by women but by men (and Samson himself falls victim to this conflict).

A converse instance: in the popular accounts, Delilah is variously described as "beautiful," "incapable of love," "false," "a cheat," "a hypocrite," and "greedy," as a woman who has had "many lovers" and "been engaged to many men." All of these are interpolations from outside the text, designed to foster an interpretation that has achieved an independent life (Samson as righteous but human hero, Delilah as malign and potent seductress). The Bible, in contrast, has only this to say about Delilah: "After this he loved a woman in the valley of Sorek, whose name was Delilah." The reader is told nothing further about her character, background, or motivations and nothing more about the nature of Samson and Delilah's personal relationship.

In the very next verse Delilah accepts a bribe to learn Samson's secret, an act, as Bal notes, that in popular accounts "gives evidence of Delilah's wickedness, and consequently of women's unreliability."[11] But Delilah, of course, is merely a Philistine woman acting at the behest of Philistine men, and in the Bible it is the men who are the prime movers of the action: "The lords of the Philistines came up to her and said to her, 'Entice him, and see wherein his great strength lies, and by what means we may overpower him, that we may bind him to subdue him.'"

What we see in these few examples, Bal explained when we spoke, is the high degree of tension between the original version and the received versions of the story. Once we perceive *that*, we begin to understand the possibilities open to us as readers. "So to a reader who wanted to see Samson and Delilah in a different way," Bal said, "one thing I would say is, look at how this story is determined by struggles among men, and how women are only instruments and don't have a choice about anything. A second thing I would say is, this story is not about what you think. It's about issues studied more by anthropologists than by biblical scholars —

issues of how people live, of how marriage structures work, and so on. Samson is caught up between two systems, he is in a civil war — it's a mess! Which makes *nobody* in fact the culprit." A third thing she would say, as she in fact did a few moments later, is that any reader can pry open any text by remembering to ask just a few basic questions of it, and to ask them continually: "Who is speaking? Who is seeing? Who is acting? And who is not doing any of those things?"

Lethal Love became the first volume of Bal's biblical trilogy. The second volume, *Murder and Difference*, takes up the contrasting versions of the story of Sisera's murder by Jael, as told first in Judges 4, a prose narrative, and immediately afterward in Judges 5, the so-called Song of Deborah, a far older version of the same event. The tension between the two accounts is acute. The prose narrative is a stark exposition of Jael's efficient duplicity toward Sisera: "Turn aside to me, my lord, turn aside to me; have no fear." It is a dark text, not a celebratory one. The Song of Deborah, in contrast, exults in the murder of Sisera and calls Jael "most blessed of women." In *Lethal Love*, Bal's aim was to show biblical scholars how literary scholarship could prove helpful in cracking a text apart. In *Murder and Difference*, she used the story of Jael and Sisera as a wedge, or perhaps a tent peg, to explore the analytical techniques of biblical scholarship itself. History, anthropology, theology, literary criticism — how do the rules and conventions of these various disciplines, or "codes," as Bal calls them, close off meaning as well as open it?[12]

In the last volume of the trilogy, *Death and Dissymmetry*, Bal's subject is the Book of Judges as a whole, and her focus is on violence in the book as it is bound up with issues of gender. Judges is a surpassingly violent book. It "openly celebrates murder," Bal observes. "And murder, in this text, is related to gender. Men kill women, and women kill men. And men kill men. The man-man murders are, with one exception, collective murders: wars. The woman-man murders are derived from that primary political kind of murder: women kill heroes and military leaders. The man-woman murders are different. Men, mighty men, kill innocent young daughters."[13]

These events, these killings, are usually viewed against the larger backdrop of the story told by Judges, which concerns the conquest of the land of Canaan by the Israelites. Bal asks instead, "What if?" What if we use a different backdrop, one that draws attention to issues of marriage and social relations? "The impression of extreme violence that the book makes," Bal writes, "is due less to the political struggle that seems to be at stake — the conquest — than to a social revolution" in which control over a given woman is shifting domestically "from her father, the 'natural' owner, to the husband, the arbitrarily chosen 'cultural' owner."[14]

The story (Judges 11) of Jephthah's daughter, who is never given a name, is one of the most disturbing in the Bible. It is also a special case of "transfer of ownership": in this case, from Jephthah, the Israelite general, who has promised (in return for battlefield victory) to make a sacrifice of his daughter, to God. Feminist critics have long contrasted this story angrily with that of Abraham and Isaac, noting that God stayed Abraham's hand before Isaac, a son, could be sacrificed. Where was God when a daughter's life was at stake? Bal's interest in this story, though, is drawn sharply to the issue of virginity, which is the biological state of Jephthah's daughter when she meets her fate.[15]

As Bal looks more closely at the terminology involved, in this story and elsewhere, she notices that the English words "virgin" and "virginity" camouflage the fact that two different concepts are being deployed. Jephthah says that his daughter is a virgin by using the Hebrew words for "one who has known not man," whereas the daughter describes herself with the simple word *bethulah*, which is translated as meaning the same thing. But *are* they the same thing? Bal thinks not. She argues that *bethulah* was originally female language for a condition akin to ripeness or nubility, a meaning that eventually became conflated with or absorbed into sexual language connoting "inviolate." The male compilers of the Bible may even have lost sight of the original meaning themselves. Yet the distinction calls out quietly for attention in remnants of intact oral tradition (the quoted words of Jephthah's daughter) and in such awkward, seemingly redundant locutions as "four hundred young virgins (*bethulim*) who had not known man" (Judges 21:12).

Bal's foray into philology produces a memorable image. She compares the survival of words and phrases with a special female meaning to "those wandering rocks, glacial tilts that travelled with the ice toward a new and alien world where they were put to a use foreign to their origin."[16] The phrase has itself become a wandering rock, turning up frequently now in feminist writing about the Bible. Bal no longer remembers precisely how and when the image occurred to her, except that it was during a period she spent in rock-strewn New England, teaching at Harvard Divinity School (which has itself been home to not a few glacial erratics).

"The wandering rock was a useful image," Bal says now. "If you accept the fact that the biblical text is not coherent, that the text is a patchwork, that it has fragments in it of older texts, of older situations, then there is no limit to the possibilities of interpretation. To me, this is the only way to make an argument for the Bible as having an interest for women: that the Bible does not just have one voice. Of course, it would be ridiculous to maintain that the Bible actually does have only one voice — no scholar would say that this is the case. But effectively, one sees interpretations in the culture all tending toward a single voice.

"The wandering rock is not attached to a particular setting. The rock itself embodies resistance — a rock cannot be destroyed. And the rock keeps wandering. We come across these wandering rocks even today, and get something out of them."

Chapter Seven

....

WAS JESUS A
FEMINIST?

*Just then his disciples came. They marveled
that he was talking with a woman.*
— John 4:27

*Each successive epoch of theology found its own thoughts
in Jesus . . . But it was not only each epoch that found its
reflection in Jesus; each individual created Him
in accordance with his own character.*
— Albert Schweitzer

JUST SOUTH of the Old City of Jerusalem the road from Jericho climbs
up from the Kidron Valley and toward the City of David and Mount
Zion, passing below one side of the massive retaining wall built by King
Herod in the first century B.C. to encompass and define the Temple
Mount — the elevated enclosure, 35 acres in extent, where the Jewish
temple once stood, and whose most striking structures today are the
Al-Aqsa Mosque and the Dome of the Rock. Between the road and the
wall the ground has been opened in many places for archaeological excavations, and the innards invite curiosity, but it is the wall itself that
commands predominant attention. The smooth, pale structure is impressive even to a modern eye jaded by monumental architecture. Some
of the limestone blocks with which the wall is built are more than forty
feet long and ten feet high and wide. They have been estimated to weigh
as much as a hundred tons.

The feature that stands out among all the others in this southern
elevation is the ghost of a triple-arched gateway, to which the remnant of
a long, low rise of limestone steps still gives access. In the last century of
the Second Temple period, this entrance would have provided ordinary

people with entry to the Temple precincts above, and these are the steps on which they would have trodden. Because it is recorded that Jesus visited the Temple on many occasions ("After three days they found him in the temple, sitting among the teachers, listening to them and asking them questions" — Luke 2:46), we can say with a considerable degree of certainty that if there is anywhere in Jerusalem that Jesus literally set foot on, it is these limestone steps.

I remember thinking, when the steps were first pointed out to me by a friend, how rare a thing such certainty is when contemplating the life of Jesus and the world from which he emerged. History has been generous with texts about Jesus — far more generous than with texts about many historical figures who were his contemporaries and who were incomparably his superior in power and status. Yet these texts — the books of the New Testament — are not straightforward eyewitness accounts. They are not historical works as we understand that term. There is very little about Jesus and his circumstances, the scholars seem to have concluded, about which we can unequivocally say, "It was *thus.*"

The centuries bracketing the life of Jesus were an especially volatile time in an especially volatile part of the world. In the course of a few hundred years, the areas encompassed by biblical Israel were ruled by Persians, by Greeks, and finally, after Pompey's conquest in 63 B.C., by Romans — although "ruled" implies an organizational-chart form of clarity belied by the ad hoc, decentralized, impermanently dynastic arrangements that frequently governed in what was then called Asia Minor. The wars and intrigues among greater and lesser potentates, not to mention within prominent families, constitute a confused record that even specialists can be forgiven for not committing to memory.

Below the level of political events, where most of day-to-day life is lived, the economic, cultural, and spiritual currents in Palestine at the time of Jesus are equally hard to sort out. For many Jews, Israelite religion remained centered on the Temple and the priesthood, but other Jews inhabited thriving communities throughout the Roman Empire — in Alexandria, in Athens, in Rome itself. Among these Jews, in the Diaspora, different forms of religious practice were already beginning to evolve. In the Jewish homeland, apocalyptic and nationalist movements were a palpable and growing presence, one that sometimes only bloody confrontation and reprisal could suppress. Jerusalem remained primarily an ethnically Jewish city, but it was now only one among several large cities in Palestine. Urban life, in modern cities with Jewish and non-Jewish aspects, could be found in all parts of the region, never farther from a typical country dweller than a journey of several days.

The cities for the most part had a distinct Hellenic character; Alexander the Great's conquering armies had ushered in two and a half centuries of rule by the Seleucid monarchs, and the stamp of Greek culture and language was deeply imprinted. Although ordinary people from Babylon in the east to the Mediterranean in the west spoke Aramaic and other Semitic languages in their everyday life, Greek enjoyed high status for centuries as the language of power and learning. It was in many cases the language of Jews in the Diaspora, and it was the first language into which the Hebrew Bible was translated, forming the Greek text known as the Septuagint (the text of the Hebrew Bible familiar to early Christian writers). Galilee, the predominantly rural and predominantly Jewish region where Jesus grew up, may have been somewhat more isolated and less cosmopolitan than other regions, but the social, economic, cultural, and religious forces found in the rest of Palestine also had a presence there.[1]

This is the world, whatever the precise details of its construction, into which Jesus was born and within which the Gospels and the other New Testament texts were composed. Making sense of it would no doubt be difficult even if source materials were abundant and relatively easy to interpret. They are neither. Secular materials bearing directly either on the Jesus movement or on the period of formative Judaism are few and often biased, although scholars have become increasingly ingenious about drawing out information from the evidence that does exist. Still, imagine if the bulk of what people knew eons hence about late twentieth-century America were limited to what they could derive from some history textbooks written by foreigners, a few thousand tombstones, a handful of Supreme Court decisions, and a random collection of personal documents.

As for the overtly religious materials, these can be difficult to assess.

On Jewish aspects of life at this time, for instance, it is likely that the early Mishnaic and Midrashic literature — that is, the rabbinic legal and interpretive writings, which began to be compiled late in the first century A.D. — will have some legitimate bearing. But how widely and how much? Other writings, such as the later books of the Hebrew Bible and also books such as 1 and 2 Maccabees and Judith and Ecclesiasticus, collectively known as the Apocrypha (which did not become a part of the Hebrew Bible but were composed at roughly this time), are also relevant. But precisely what relevance they have remains, again, a vexing question.

Similar issues afflict the Christian Gospels and the other New Testament texts, which are the products of believing communities and were written decades or longer after the events they purport to describe and were assembled or edited with particular theological purposes in mind. Determining the interrelationships among the earliest Christian documents and attempting to recover and reconstruct the earliest and purest versions has been a small industry for more than a century, and in recent decades it has shown signs of becoming a large one. Most scholars agree on certain broad propositions — for instance, that the Gospel of Mark is the earliest Gospel, and that Luke and Matthew both made use of Mark and also of a separate "sayings source," to which scholars have given the name Q (from the German *Quelle*, meaning "source") and of which Mark wasn't aware. But there is no unanimity on many issues, and as a result there has been endless fussing over matters big and small.

Distilling the presumptively original version of Q occupies part of the attention of scores of scholars, many of whom have also been active in the Jesus Seminar, a self-selecting group (the lineup changes over time) that has sought to establish with certitude which parts of the New Testament reflect true "Jesus material" and which parts are subsequent elaborations. The Jesus Seminar has received considerable attention over the years, owing in part to its procedures, which include casting votes with colored beads or colored ballots to determine the seminar's official view of gospel passages. In the balloting, according to the seminar's book *The Five Gospels*, red officially means "Jesus undoubtedly said this or something very like it"; pink means "Jesus probably said something like this"; gray means "Jesus did not say this, but the ideas contained in it are close to his own"; and black means "Jesus did not say this; it represents the perspective or content of later or different tradition." This voting procedure has been attacked for its hubris, for its naiveté, and for its zesty populism. (The seminar has provided an alternate legend for its red-through-black code that goes as follows: "That's Jesus!"; "Sure sounds like Jesus"; "Well, maybe"; "There's been some mistake.")[2] Eyebrows have been raised by the presence among the seminar's membership of the director Paul Verhoeven, whose movies have included *Robocop, Total Recall,* and *Basic Instinct.* In truth, of course, the seminar's scholars, like everyone else in the New Testament field, appreciate the complexity of the subject, the paucity of what we today would consider facts, and the opacity of the primary sources. The Pauline phrase about perceiving "as in a glass darkly" is one that gets applied frequently to this branch of scholarly inquiry.[3]

And then there is the matter of what the interpreter herself may bring to the discussion. "What we live in is not an objectified reality," as Elisabeth Schüssler Fiorenza has written, "but an intellectual universe that we create socially and imaginatively. Our ideas, values, social institutions, belief systems, and theological convictions together produce a sense of life and reality, a perception of the way things are."[4]

It was Elisabeth Schüssler Fiorenza's work — most notably her book *In Memory of Her* (1983), to which I was introduced in the course of research on a related subject — that initially drew me into the world of women whose academic lives revolve around the central texts of the Jewish and Christian traditions. Schüssler Fiorenza is the Krister Stendahl Professor of Divinity at the Harvard Divinity School, the first occupant of a chair named for the renowned preacher and biblical scholar who was for a decade also the divinity school's dean. (Her husband, the theologian Francis Schüssler Fiorenza, is the Stillman Professor of Roman Catholic Theological Studies, also at the divinity school; this is the chair once held by the medievalist and church historian Christopher Dawson.) Elisabeth Schüssler Fiorenza is a cofounder and coeditor, with Judith Plaskow, of the *Journal of Feminist Studies in Religion,* the first and arguably the most important of several academic journals in the field. She has written a half-dozen books and has edited an eclectic survey titled *Searching the Scriptures: A Feminist Introduction*, a collection of articles by an assortment of colleagues. She is almost a mandatory presence at any conclave that has women and religion as its subject matter. Her manner is quiet, or at least has been when I have been able to observe it, and the pronounced strains of German in her accent come across as soft. She let slip into one of her theological papers that she was a longtime fan of the television show *Murder, She Wrote*, and I can just about imagine a somewhat younger Angela Lansbury, with silver hair, playing Schüssler Fiorenza, though I do have a little trouble imagining Lansbury typing out phrases like "the paradigm of emancipatory praxis" and "the *wissenschaftlich* hermeneutic-methodological discussion."[5]

Schüssler Fiorenza, though, is fully capable of such things and more, and not only in print. I remember being chided one afternoon, in her book-lined eyrie under the rafters of the Gothic building that houses the Harvard Divinity School, for apparently assuming that more could be known with absolute certainty about the past than was ever strictly possible. In a tone of patient disappointment, Schüssler Fiorenza voiced her suspicion that I possessed a "Rankean view of history," the reference being to Leopold von Ranke, the nineteenth-century German historian who both formulated and epitomized the view (now widely regarded as unattainable or at least obsolete) that the job of historians was to discover "*wie es eigentlich gewesen*," or, as the phrase is usually rendered in English, "what actually happened."

Against a backdrop of such conversations and the imposing edifice of her prose, Schüssler Fiorenza's moments of whimsy stand out. As the headnote for an article titled "Feminist Theology as a Critical Theology of Liberation," her first important contribution to the flagship journal *Theological Studies*, Schüssler Fiorenza wanted to use an old suffragist rhyme, which the editor prevailed upon her to remove. It went like this:

> "*Mother, what is a feminist?*"
> "*A feminist, my daughter,*
> *Is any woman now who cares*
> *To think about her own affairs*
> *As men don't think she oughter.*"[6]

Bearing in mind that *wie es eigentlich gewesen* is not fully capturable, we can nonetheless note that Elisabeth Schüssler Fiorenza vividly remembers her family's flight from Romania through Hungary and Austria to southern Germany in the closing months of 1944, as World War II swept once again through the border town of Tăşnad, where she had been born and had spent the first six years of her life. "I remember as we fled there was street fighting, and the dead were lying all along the road," she says. "If I had been five or ten years older, I might have been damaged for life. But I remember being excited. Where I came from was very, very flat, all the way to the horizon, like a plate, and I used to think that heaven came down to meet the earth. And I was excited because now I thought we would get to that place, at the end of the world. I think this memory has been theologically significant for me, because I learned that narrow horizons were an illusion, and I learned not to be constrained by them."

Like so many of the towns in the Banat region of Romania's northwest, Tăşnad was a multiethnic and polyglot place whose constituent communities — Germans, Serbs, Hungarians, Romanians, Gypsies — maintained great cohesion. The land was a vast expanse of plain and marsh extending to the Carpathian Mountains. Tăşnad was a bishopric, dating back at least to the time when Romans built a fortification on the site. Attila the Hun was born nearby, and Béla Bartók. Elisabeth Schüssler's ancestors were ethnically German, probably from Swabia, and had in all likelihood arrived in Romania in the eighteenth century, during the reign of Maria Theresa, queen of Austria and Bohemia and empress of the Holy Roman Empire, who had encouraged such migration within her vast domain to foster the Germanization of its hinter regions. This movement of people, following a sizable German influx half a millennium earlier, created a large German-speaking minority in Romania. Its numbers declined sharply only with the end of World War II and the voluntary or forced departure of ethnic Germans in an atmosphere poisoned by animosity and charges of widespread collaboration by the Romanian Germans with the Nazis. The process of German depopulation was more or less completed soon after the end of the Cold War, when most of the ethnic Germans remaining in Romania sought to start their lives anew in a united Germany, which offered them a home.[7]

Schüssler Fiorenza's cultural grounding in a German Catholic community has left a legacy. "For me," she explains, "Catholicism was not an immigrant Catholicism, a minority culture, as it is for most Americans. For them, Catholic teaching and the teaching of the pope are the same thing. For me growing up, that was not the case at all. For me, a Catholic culture was not a Roman culture. The whole historical tension between the Germanic empire and the papacy makes for quite a different understanding of Catholicism, I think. For me, Catholicism is part of a culture, not just of a religious confession. This has made a big difference in terms of my theological thinking, because it has given me a kind of identity that does not need to be defended all the time, does not need to set boundaries all the time in order to be sure of itself." Her formative experiences of Catholicism also left her with a respect for its intellectual traditions, however maddening. "When I went from Notre Dame to Episcopal Divinity School," she recalls, "someone said to me, 'Elisabeth, you have to learn one thing. Catholics may hate their intellectuals, but they still respect them, whereas the Episcopalians couldn't care less. They're only interested in whether you know how to use the right fork.'"

When the end of the war in Europe finally came, in May 1945, the Schüssler family was living with many other families in a barn near Munich. "When I could not sleep," Schüssler Fiorenza recalls, relating an oddly personal detail that stands out for its relative rarity in her work and talk, "I listened to the digestive noises of the cows mixed with the sound of human snoring." (I was reminded somehow of the unexpected rhetorical intrusion of bovine sound into 1 Samuel 6:12: "And the cows went straight on the road, on the road to Beth-Shemesh, on a single highroad, lowing as they went, veering neither left nor right.") The Schüsslers eventually settled near Frankfurt, and Elisabeth resumed her education in German schools.

It is at once pointless and compelling to contemplate the decisions that fate has made for us all by proxy. What grim future might have awaited Elisabeth Schüssler in postwar Romania? Of course, Germany too offered a selection of dead ends for a woman bent on certain careers.

For a woman who was seeking to pursue advanced academic work in the 1950s and 1960s, the obstacles were considerable, as they in fact remain to this day, especially in religion.

The social structure of academic work in Germany is in essence that of the medieval guild, where the relationship of one's academic mentor, or *Doctorvater*, to his students is that of a master to his apprentices. The *Doctorvater* picks the student's dissertation topic, and he or she writes on what has been assigned. Unlike in the United States, where the decision to undertake doctoral work and the choice of topic involve elements of free will, in Germany the process bears more of a resemblance to divine selection. Its autocratic, medieval character aside, the social structure of academic work in Germany is also exceedingly masculine in its values, its ethos, and its assumptions. Though the situation has improved slightly, it is perhaps not too much of an exaggeration to say, as one alumna of the system does, that male professors in Germany are in the business of replicating themselves and their own sensibilities. The obstacles to women in the field of theology, where the needs and demands of the various churches obtain and where the major churches control the relevant portion of the curriculum at public institutions, have proved even more daunting than in the rest of academe.

Elisabeth Schüssler negotiated this regime through gymnasium, or secondary school, in Frankfurt, and through six years of studying religion at the University of Würzburg. Ultimately she obtained a doctorate in theology from the University of Munster, although she was denied a scholarship in support of her doctoral work; as one of her professors put it, "As a woman, you have no future possibilities for becoming a professor of theology," so to award her a scholarship would be to waste resources that could usefully be given to someone else. Analyzed in its best possible light, this reasoning might be seen simply as a concession to realpolitik, an acknowledgment of prevailing circumstances: there *was* no future possibility of becoming a professor of theology, at least in Germany.

Schüssler Fiorenza's doctoral thesis concerned the role of women historically in various church ministries, and it was published in Germany in 1964 with the title *Der vergessene Partner*, or *The Forgotten Partner*. (Although the title is meant to refer to women, the publisher matter-of-factly used a grammatically masculine form, an irony that did not sufficiently register with Schüssler Fiorenza at the time.) The book has never been translated into English, but it inspired the young Mary Daly when she was studying in Fribourg.

In 1967 Schüssler married Francis Fiorenza, an American theologian studying in Germany, and in 1970 the Schüssler Fiorenzas, as both of them are now called, came to the United States, having accepted teaching positions at the University of Notre Dame. She remembers asking a distinguished German professor a few years later, during a visit to Germany, whether a woman was yet serving as a member of an established Roman Catholic theology faculty, and his reply seemed to imply that one might just as soon contemplate hiring a talking dog: "He turned to his housekeeper and asked sarcastically, 'Do you want to be my successor?'"

The United States marked a turning point in Schüssler Fiorenza's experience, as she is quick to point out. America at the time offered what Germany emphatically did not: an emerging feminist movement in the realm of religion and a university system whose faculties — crucially, whose theology department faculties — were at least partly open to women. Women's caucuses, with various levels of intensity and support, were becoming almost de rigueur at academic meetings. Within specific disciplines, women were gathering informally to compare notes and plot strategy. During an early sabbatical at Union Theological Seminary, Schüssler Fiorenza joined the living room discussions of a group called the New York Feminist Scholars in Religion, whose members included Carol Christ, Beverly Harrison, Judith Plaskow, Nelle Morton, and others. "Students often ask me, 'With whom did you study feminist theology?'" Schüssler Fiorenza says, "and I always say, 'Look, it didn't exist. We had to invent it.'" In her own words, she "began doing theology consciously as a woman and for women." Much of her writing has focused on women during the conception, birth, and infancy of Christianity.

Historical reconstruction of the Jesus movement is risky and fraught. Piercing the veil of the sources and discerning what we reasonably can of social and religious reality in a distant era may involve textual scholarship — training attention on vocabulary, rhetorical style, and whatever can be inferred about the editing process. It may involve the disciplines of archaeology and anthropology, coming at early Jewish and Christian life from the outside and looking at what the physical record has to say. All this work presupposes a broad grounding in some obscure aspects of history. It can be frustrating in the extreme. The materials available are often meager, and the conclusions drawn are sometimes precarious and insubstantial. Among other things, as Schüssler Fiorenza put it during one of a number of discussions we have had over the years, "Within both Judaism and Christianity the patriarchal side won," thereby determining (if we accept her premise) the lens through which interpretation has to look. We must approach the texts with a "hermeneutics of suspicion," to use a phrase of Schüssler Fiorenza's that is now a widely used and almost involuntary trope in feminist biblical studies. The references to women that do exist in Christian works, Schüssler Fiorenza says, surely represent only a remnant; the rest has been lost to historical memory.

But we do have some significant material to work with, if only we are not blind to it. Jesus' message consisted in part of a radical attack on the traditional social structures of the Greco-Roman world — structures that limited the participation of women in the public sphere and that some segments of the Jesus movement sought to replace with what Schüssler Fiorenza calls "a discipleship of equals."[8] Exegetes can and do argue over whether this or that phrase really goes back to the time of Jesus, or to his very lips — Is it a red? Is it a black? Are the words what scholars used to call the *ipsissima verba?* — and over what form each phrase might originally have taken, but among the themes that emerge too frequently and too widely to discount in the gospel message is that of the reversal: the dismantling of established conceptions of power. The idea that those on the bottom are to be exalted may be expressed most hauntingly in the Beatitudes (Luke 6:20–22) —

> *Blessed are you poor,*
> *for yours is the kingdom of God.*
> *Blessed are you that hunger now,*
> *for you shall be satisfied.*
> *Blessed are you that weep now,*
> *for you shall laugh*

— but the same idea comes through in the numerous parables whose message is that the first shall be last and the last shall be first. Together, these sayings and stories discount social hierarchies and emphasize that those who follow Jesus should all be as slaves or all be as children — in any event, all be as equals. Jesus cautions the disciples (Matthew 23:8), saying, "But you are not to be called rabbi, for you have one teacher, and you are all brethren."

The Gospels are unequivocal in placing women prominently among the marginalized people — to quote Schüssler Fiorenza, "Sinners, prostitutes, beggars, tax collectors, the ritually polluted, the crippled, and the impoverished; in short, the scum of Palestinian society" — who made up so much of Jesus' circle. As a practical matter, Luke suggests (8:1–3), some of these women proved themselves essential: "The twelve were with him, and also some women who had been healed of evil spirits and infirmities: Mary, called Magdalene, from whom seven demons had gone out, and Joanna, the wife of Chuza, Herod's steward, and Susanna, and many others, *who provided for them out of their means.*" The recurring image used by Jesus to characterize God's kingdom, Schüssler Fiorenza points out, is that of the feast, and it is a feast to which *all* are invited, not from which some are excluded for reasons of ritual purity or gender. The parable of the lost sheep begins with these words (Luke 15:3–7): "Now the tax collectors and sinners were all drawing near to hear him. And the Pharisees and the scribes murmured, saying, 'This man receives sinners and eats with them.'" The moral of the story — that the shepherd cares about all of his flock and indeed will go out of his way especially on behalf of the missing — is amplified immediately after the telling by a second parable (Luke 15:8–10), the story of the woman and the lost coin, in which the woman proceeds to "light a lamp and sweep the house and seek diligently until she finds it." It is a story that on one level uses the image of a woman to convey a conception of God. On another level it reminds us of the disproportionately precarious economic status of women, then as now.[9]

Women are shown as having been instrumental in opening up the Jesus community to Jews outside the mainstream Jewish community and also to non-Jews — a source of tension even, apparently, while Jesus was alive, and a major issue within the Jesus movement in the years immediately after his death, as Gentiles sought inclusion. The story of Jesus and the Samaritan woman (John 4:1–42) is remarkable in several ways at once. It has deep historical resonance, as it takes place in a city called Sychar, which is the Hebrew Bible's Shechem, capital of the Northern Kingdom, and later known as Neapolis. It is today called Nablus. Shechem is the first place Jacob came to in the land of Canaan (Genesis 33:18–19) and the first place the Israelites and Canaanites came to blows. It is here, at a well, that Jesus approaches a woman who is unknown to him. This in itself would have been deemed a provocative action, and was regarded with raised eyebrows by Jesus' disciples. (In the words of John: "They marveled that he was talking with a woman, but no one said 'What do you want?' or 'Why are you talking with her?'") Even more discomfiting was the fact that the woman was a Samaritan, a group with which the Jews of Palestine had undeniable ethnic and religious links but that was also reviled as alien and inhospitable (and a sect whose few hundred remaining members in Israel live apart to this day). The Samaritan woman of the gospel story has had five husbands and is living with a man to whom she is not married. She is memorable for her ready tongue and the unyielding nature of her side of the colloquy. This woman reports her impressions of Jesus to others among her people with ingenuous exuberance — "Come and see a man who told me everything I have ever done! He cannot be the Messiah, can he?" — and the result is that the Samaritans turn out to hear him.[10]

In another story, the Syro-Phoenician woman (Mark 7:24–30), a Gentile, not only makes an argument about Jesus' message that Jesus does not refute but also comes close to delivering a rebuke. This woman has a daughter afflicted with an unclean spirit, and she begs Jesus to cast the demon out. In a reply meant to convey that the Jews ("children") have a greater claim on God's word ("bread") than the Gentiles ("dogs"), Jesus says, "Let the children be fed first, for it is not right to take the children's bread and throw it to the dogs," but he relents after hearing the woman's retort: "Lord, even the dogs under the table eat the children's crumbs."[11]

As we have seen, the figure of Wisdom in the Hebrew Bible is almost always cast in female form or invoked with female imagery, and in the Gospels, Jesus too speaks with Wisdom's voice. He looks forward (Luke

11:49) to his death explicitly through the eyes of Wisdom — "Therefore also the Wisdom of God said, 'I will send them prophets and apostles, some of whom they will kill and persecute'" — and elaborates further (Luke 13:34) in a passage with a memorable feminine simile: "O Jerusalem, Jerusalem, killing the prophets and stoning those who are sent to you. How often would I have gathered your children together as a hen gathers her brood under her wings, and you would not!" When the time of Jesus' crucifixion draws near, it is an unnamed woman at Bethany who, in the course of a meal, breaks open a jar of ointment and anoints his head, in reverent imitation of the prophetic act of anointing a king — an action whose symbolism is lost on the men in the group but that moves Jesus to say, "Wherever the good news is proclaimed in the whole world, what she has done will be told in remembrance of her." (The title of Schüssler Fiorenza's *In Memory of Her* commemorates this woman; Schüssler Fiorenza observes acidly that despite Jesus' prophetic statement, no one thought to provide the woman's name.)[12]

After the Crucifixion, the women of Galilee helped hold together the Jesus movement in Jerusalem as other disciples fled. Women were the first to discover the empty tomb and the first to experience a vision of the resurrected Jesus, as embodied in the words of the young man in the tomb (Mark 16:6–7), reported by Mary Magdalene, Mary the mother of James, and Salome: "You seek Jesus of Nazareth, who was crucified. He has risen, he is not here; see the place where they laid him. But go, tell his disciples and Peter . . ." Schüssler Fiorenza writes, "In all likelihood, the Galilean disciples fled after his arrest from Jerusalem and went back home to Galilee. Because of their visionary-ecstatic experiences, the women who remained in the capital came to the conviction that God had vindicated Jesus and his ministry. They, therefore, were empowered to continue the movement and work of Jesus."[13]

And in the decades afterward? Christianity's penumbral first centuries can be difficult to apprehend. The texts that now make up the New Testament were at this time being written, edited, and reedited, each created in the context of certain communities and to fulfill certain purposes. What emerges from Schüssler Fiorenza's reading is a Christian missionary movement that in its initial stages "allowed for the full participation and leadership of women."[14] She notes, for instance, that in the authentic letters of Paul, women are often singled out by name and given titles the same as or comparable to those held by male leaders. Prisca, a traveling missionary, is described by Paul as a peer, a "co-worker." Phoebe, in Cenchreae, is called a *diakonos*, a title Paul also gives himself.[15]

Schüssler Fiorenza argues finally that early Christianity was built around a theology of equality. The well-known passage from Paul in Galatians 3:28 — "There is neither Jew nor Greek, there is neither slave nor free, there is neither male nor female; for you are all one in Christ Jesus" — probably embodies an ancient baptismal formula. It represents not merely a radical and temporary breakthrough in Paul's thinking but an expression of broad and ordinary Christian belief. As Schüssler Fiorenza points out, Galatians 3:28 has been seen by some as "the magna carta of Christian feminism."[16]

I asked Schüssler Fiorenza if she believes that this magna carta will ever in fact enjoy the primacy that she would give it. She replied, "Yes, when I'm an optimist. When I'm a pessimist, I worry that what will happen to us, to the feminist movement, is what happened in the last century. When I look back at the last century, I'm always surprised at how many questions, how many issues, were raised that we did not think about again until a few years ago. Today, perhaps, with the democratization of the media, what has been done will not be lost.

"And yet people can study and get degrees without knowing anything about women's or feminist studies — and I am not just talking about biblical studies. Even though there has been a lot done in feminist literature and history and so on, it often does not make a dent in the way ideas are taught, the way ideas are transmitted."

Elisabeth Schüssler Fiorenza is a theologian, and she has an explicitly theological agenda. In her approach to Scripture she aims, among other things, to highlight themes of unfolding liberation and emancipation, and her work has had a profound influence not only among feminists in academe but also among certain slivers of the public. The subject of Jesus and women, however, is sometimes presented in popular accounts as if some sort of rough consensus had emerged among biblical feminists, when in fact no such consensus exists and indeed a certain amount of division is evident on a number of fronts. The divisions fall into two broad camps.

The first is occasioned by your approach to the question, Was Jesus *really* a "feminist"? Even if he comes across that way, did he know he was a feminist or consciously intend to be one? The second arises from the question, How much of a departure, if any, did Jesus *really* represent from other elements of Jewish life in his time? To what extent does the presumption of a departure — the presumption that what he had to offer was "better" — in fact reflect not so much history as a continuation of tensions, perhaps unconsciously or unwittingly manifested, between Jews and Christians?

The person who embodies an unapologetic "Jesus was a feminist" position more than any other is a man named Leonard Swidler. Swidler occupies an anomalous position. By training he is not a biblical scholar at all but a theologian and a historian of religion, and he teaches today, as he has for three decades, in the religion department at Philadelphia's Temple University, an urban school in a marginal neighborhood. His office is not in a comfortable replica of a Gothic monastery, with hushed hallways colored by sunlit streaks of stained glass, but in the kind of heavily trafficked, pervasively smudged academic high-rise that quickly begins to fray and peel. Swidler looks somewhat like the former Speaker of the House Jim Wright, with bushy eyebrows and a lanky frame. He has engaged in Catholic activism all his life and has promoted conversation among the world's faiths. He is the editor of the *Journal of Ecumenical Studies*. Since the 1960s, Swidler has worked closely on various projects with the Catholic theologian Hans Küng, who was removed by the Vatican from his position in the theology department at the University of Tübingen, in Germany, in 1979 for his views on Church authority, and he has spent an ample amount of time teaching at Tübingen. Swidler was instrumental in getting anti-Semitic language and costuming removed from the graphic reenactment of the Passion and Crucifixion of Jesus performed every year in the German town of Oberammergau, and in fostering a new and positive emphasis in the play on the Jewishness of Jesus.

Swidler and his wife, Arlene, who for many years was also a Catholic activist and a mainstay of the women's rights organization St. Joan's Alliance and who now has been incapacitated by Alzheimer's disease, first took up the issue of women and the Bible in the context of the debate within the Catholic Church over the ordination of women — a debate that in its modern phase, with a growing base of clerical and lay support in Western countries, dates back to the 1950s. The names Leonard and Arlene Swidler can almost always be found in the proceedings of the workshops and conferences devoted to this subject. For the Swidlers, the willingness of the Church to reduce women to permanent second-class status became a source of great frustration and pain. They saw it too as a disturbing example of institutional shortsightedness. More than that, the case against women in the ordained ministry seemed inexplicable to them in terms of doctrine — they couldn't see how anything they read in the Bible justified existing arrangements.

In 1971 Swidler published an article titled "Jesus Was a Feminist" in the avowedly Catholic but independent newspaper *Catholic World*. From the vantage point of a quarter of a century later, it may be difficult to appreciate how provocative and challenging an attitude that title struck, at a time when the word "feminist" had only lately reemerged from obscurity and when the most public exponents of feminism constituted to some an exotic and dangerous class of people. "To prove the thesis," Swidler's article began, "it must be demonstrated that, so far as we can tell, Jesus neither said nor did anything which would indicate that he advocated treating women as intrinsically inferior to men, but that on the contrary he said and did things which indicated that he thought of women as the equals of men, and that in the process he willingly violated pertinent social mores."[17] Swidler's article, which made many of the same points that we still hear about Jesus and his female followers, provoked angry retorts from traditionalists and resulted in several months of intramural controversy.

A few years later, in 1976, Swidler published his book *Women in Judaism: The Status of Women in Formative Judaism*, a study of the first-century Jewish background from which the Jesus movement emerged. In Swidler's reconstruction, Jewish women traditionally had no place in the leadership of religious life. They were neither expected nor permitted to study Torah. The sole legitimate locus of a woman's life was the home, and the preferred context was marriage. A male was forbidden to speak in public to a woman he did not know. Even in private life women had few rights, or their rights were severely restricted. These restrictions would have applied not only to household customs, such as not joining the men for meals, but also to such basic legal matters as marriage, divorce, the making of contracts, and inheritance. A woman's lot was further circumscribed by the laws regarding ritual purity and by her status as unclean after childbirth and during menstruation. All of this, in Swidler's reconstruction, finds prescription and justification in rabbinic sources written during the first several centuries A.D. It can also be glimpsed in the background of many gospel stories. Swidler comes to the conclusion "that in the formative period of Judaism, the status of women was not one of equality with men, but rather, severe inferiority, and that even intense misogynism was present." He argues in addition that in its attitudes toward women, "Judaism was not simply following the pattern of the societies and cultures around it" but in fact "appeared to be running quite counter to the trends" in some surrounding cultures.[18]

These themes reappeared in *Biblical Affirmations of Woman* (1979), Swidler's collection, with commentary, of female-friendly passages from both the Hebrew Bible and the New Testament, and especially in his *Yeshua: A Model for Moderns* (1988), a study of Jesus (Yeshua) with particular reference to both his Jewishness and his aggressive disregard for traditional gender categories. A telling case in point, in Swidler's view, would be the story (Luke 10:38–42) of Jesus at the home of Martha and Mary, when Martha is left to look after the household and the meal as her sister, Mary, "sat at the Lord's feet and listened to his teaching." To Martha's complaint about this state of affairs, Jesus replies, "Martha, Martha, you are anxious and troubled about many things; one thing is needful. Mary has chosen the good portion, which shall not be taken away from her." Swidler sees in this story not only an affirmation of a woman's pursuit of the intellectual life but also a challenge to contemporary practice, which did not countenance the participation of women in formal Scripture study.

Swidler's books on women, the Jesus movement, and formative Judaism don't have the dense academic apparatus found in the work of many others who have since gone over some of the same ground. Strictly speaking, his work on these topics has flourished in a parallel scholarly field. He has never presented himself as primarily a biblical scholar in the usual sense; rather, he simply attempted to grapple with issues that had not received much attention, at least when he first took them up — issues that concerned him as a scholar of religion and a devout Catholic. In fact, through his writing and teaching, he introduced a number of young scholars to problems that have continued to preoccupy them. In the 1960s, Leonard and Arlene Swidler befriended Mary Daly, whom they met at St. John's College in Collegeville, Minnesota, just after Daly returned from the University of Fribourg, and they remained close until, as Swidler puts it, Daly "disassociated herself from Catholicism, and men, and went more or less into orbit." While at Tübingen, Swidler introduced Bernadette Brooten, his student and sometime baby-sitter, to the field of biblical investigation with a feminist slant, in which she has since emerged as an outstanding contemporary figure. Swidler is admired personally even by some who disagree profoundly with many of his views, and he has invited critics to assess his work in the pages of the *Journal of Ecumenical Studies* and printed their critical reviews.

His own attitude toward his writings on Jesus and women is today curiously ambivalent. He acknowledges that this work was instrumental at least in helping to start a discussion, but he does so with a certain diffidence and surprise: "Why did it take a fourth-rate biblical scholar like me to look at what the Gospels have to say about women?" At the same time, he accepts the criticism of some of his work with a shrug of irritation: "It's like the Marshall Plan in Europe — eventually it came to be resented." That work is in any case behind him, and he has no plans to return to it. There are, he says, "plenty of women to do all that now."

However hedged with qualifications or bolstered with refinements, the basic direction of Swidler's argument is reflected in a whole wing of contemporary scholarship. One exemplar would be Ben Witherington III, who teaches at Asbury Theological Seminary in Kentucky and whose book *Women in the Ministry of Jesus* argues that "in many, though not all, regards, Jesus differed from his Jewish contemporaries," and that the teachings of Jesus "attracted women because of the new roles and equal status they were granted in the Christian community."[19] The current efflorescence of books based on a relentless peeling away of encrusted theological material includes two works that also (in different ways) portray Jesus as a radical egalitarian, John Dominic Crossan's *The Historical Jesus: The Life of a Mediterranean Jewish Peasant* and Marcus Borg's *Jesus: A New Vision*. Some version of the "Jesus was egalitarian" and the "formative Judaism was repressive" themes provides the directional bearing for entries on the subject of New Testament women in a number of standard Bible reference works.

Kathleen Corley, who teaches in the department of religious studies and anthropology at the University of Wisconsin at Oshkosh and actively participates in the work of the Jesus Seminar, is an increasingly vocal respondent from the skeptical camp on these issues. Her book, *Private Women, Public Meals*, explores what constituted "propriety" at mealtimes in the Greco-Roman world — that is, which members of what sex were present on what occasions — a form of propriety that the Jesus movement and early Christian groups regularly contravened. From time to time Corley has given a talk titled "Feminist Myths of Christian Origins," in which she critiques what she calls "the myth that the behavior and teachings of Jesus established an unprecedented and revolutionary model for the full acceptance of the personhood of women, reversing earlier and stricter Jewish codes which defined women as mere chattel."[20] The first time she gave it, she told me, "Many people were deeply disturbed. They would come up to me and they would say, 'But we really want him to be a revolutionary. How would you define him?' And I would say, 'Interesting. *Notable.* In this context, *notable.* It is a notable aspect of Jesus' movement that there are women there. There are not women everywhere. There are women in a lot of places, but they are not everywhere, and they are here, in the Jesus movement. And that is *notable.* It is a point of interest.' And they would just look at me and confess that they didn't like that.

"There is resistance," Corley went on to say, "because it's such a politically and socially useful thing to be able to say that Jesus was on the side of women in antiquity. It's usable, and in women's history there's always the struggle over finding not just the past but a usable past. A lot of women like the revolutionary/social-radical model of Jesus. And I could tell that they were uncomfortable with what I had to say, because they needed Jesus to be a social radical for their own personal faith. They were surprised that a feminist biblical scholar got up and said, 'Well, you know, maybe he wasn't. Maybe he was just a Jewish guy who had a number of women in his group, like Simon bar Gioras did, and this does not necessarily separate him in a radical way, in a tremendous way, from his Palestinian environment.' I can understand the resistance. I too wanted to find the egalitarian Jesus. I was a conservative woman driven to study biblical texts, and an egalitarian Jesus would be a tremendously helpful thing, given that I was working in a context in which people followed Paul's model that women are not to speak in church. I obviously wasn't following that model by wanting to become a biblical scholar."

As a youth in Merced, California, Kathleen Corley was an evangelical Christian and a member of a charismatic movement. She used to distribute Bible tracts on streetcorners — the sort of healthy, good-looking adolescent who makes passersby wonder what kind of environment she sprang from and in what direction she could possibly be heading. She became intimately familiar with much of the Bible, albeit in a proof-texting kind of way — that is, she was able to cite certain passages of text to "prove" an assertion, such as citing Leviticus 21:9 to underscore the impermissibility of premarital sex ("And the daughter of any priest, if she profanes herself by playing the harlot, profanes her father; she shall be burned with fire"). With some trepidation — the fear being that it might ruin her faith — she sought out higher education, enrolling at Westmont College, a highly regarded Christian school in Santa Barbara. Here, despite Westmont's reputation as a devout and conservative institution, she learned about the Bible in a new way. It had never been forcefully brought home to her, for instance, that Paul was a real person who wrote real letters to real people. She had had no reason to know that there were books which were a lot like the ones in the Bible but for some reason didn't happen to be *in* the Bible, books like the so-called Gnostic Gospels, written under such names as Thomas, James, and (most surprising of all) Mary. She took Greek, though her adviser tried to dissuade her from doing so, thinking it would be too hard. It turned out that she liked Greek and was good at it, and she sped right through it. In graduate school, at Fuller Theological Seminary, in Pasadena — another conservative institution — she continued with her Bible studies and picked up Hebrew and Coptic. Through a natural progression she became interested in the Nag Hammadi texts, a collection of early Christian documents discovered half a century ago in Egypt. Eventually she found her way to the Claremont Graduate School, where she completed her doctorate while working in various capacities for other scholars at Claremont's Institute for Antiquity and Christianity. One of her jobs at the institute was secretary to James M. Robinson, the distinguished New Testament scholar who has overseen the *Nag Hammadi Library in English* translation project since its inception in the mid-1960s.

Corley does not dispute the contention that women were intimately associated with the Jesus movement, or that they participated in inclusive meals. These characteristics are attested to in all of the gospel traditions and as "facts" are as historically reliable as anything in the Gospels can be. But are these characteristics unique to the Jesus movement? Corley points out that women had been involved in other ancient religious and philosophical movements, such as the Therapeutae, the Cynics, the Pythagoreans, the Stoics, and the Epicureans. Interestingly, some of the women who consorted with these groups were characterized by critics as "whores," the same word used in the Gospels to characterize some of the female followers of Jesus. Were they literally whores, Corley wonders, or were they instead on the receiving end of a calumny by men who disliked their public involvement in religious activity of this kind? Corley's surmise is that when Jesus is quoted as saying things like "Truly, I say to you, the tax collectors and the harlots go into the kingdom of God before you; for John [the Baptist] came to you in the way of righteousness, and you did not believe him, but the tax collectors and the harlots believed him" (Matthew 21:31–32), he is using sarcasm to throw the slander back in the faces of his critics. She has argued that "harlot" — the Greek *porne* — in this context is a usage that indeed goes back to the historical Jesus.[21]

Although the association of women with Jesus remains notable, to use Corley's word, their status as depicted even in some notable instances in the Gospels must at times give us pause. The story of Martha and Mary, for instance, is often cited approvingly for its implied suggestion that it is not improper to give a woman rabbinic instruction in matters pertaining to the law. In this story Mary is described as seated at the feet of Jesus. "Although such a pose does indicate that Mary is receiving instruction," Corley has noted, "her posture also reflects a more conservative, matronly role, and she remains silent throughout the whole scene. The more radical stance would have been to invite Mary to recline with him like an equal on a banquet couch," as a man would have been invited to do. In Corley's view, the story of the Syro-Phoenician woman whose daughter is afflicted with an unclean spirit also has disturbing undertones. Yes, it may well signal that women were among the first to bring the word of Jesus to the Gentiles. What, though, does it otherwise say about Jesus as a feminist? By the indirection of his metaphor, Jesus not only equates the woman and her daughter with dogs; the term he uses, Corley notes, as conveyed in the New Testament's Greek, should in fact be translated as "little bitches."[22]

And what about all that female imagery, Corley asks — all those images in the parables having to do with sweeping floors and baking bread? Some interpreters see this as evidence of a special solicitude for women on the part of Jesus. Corley believes it merely shows an awareness that women were in the audience. Moreover, Jesus wasn't proposing in these parables that women put aside traditional roles; rather, he was taking such roles for granted. Furthermore, Corley reminds us, the parables themselves are not "about" gender issues. They are about the kingdom of God.

Leaving aside the intrinsic nature of the Jesus movement, is it legitimate to use Jesus' first-century Jewish environment as a foil? Judith Plaskow has described the situation succinctly: "The argument that Jesus was a *feminist* — rather than simply a Jewish man who treated women like people — rests on 'the rule of antithesis,' on contrasting his behavior with his supposed Jewish background."[23] Corley, like Plaskow and others, does not accept this argument. She reviews a variety of materials, including documents from contemporary nonreligious sources such as the so-called Babatha archives (an extensive collection of personal documents found with the remains of a Jewish woman who died in the Bar Kochba revolt in A.D. 135). "New evidence," she writes,

> suggests that women in ancient Judaism in fact lived lives similar to their Gentile counterparts, and that a monolithic view of Jewish women's experience based on a few sources is impossible to maintain. Recent scholarship has in particular challenged the uncritical use of Rabbinic sources for reconstructing first-century Jewish practice . . . Some Jewish women had the right to divorce their husbands as did their Roman counterparts; some were leaders and patronesses in their synagogues; some Jewish women were educated in philosophy; some Jewish women joined men for festive and formal meals.[24]

On the matter of what might be called Christian exceptionalism, Corley describes a process of continual retreat as scholars fall back to previously prepared defensive positions in the face of new evidence. The aim is to highlight distinctions, with regard to women, between Jewish and Christian attitudes. If Jewish women in the Diaspora appear to have enjoyed a certain social latitude — more than had been thought — then the point of contrast with Christianity gets shifted, say, to Jewish women in Palestine, or if even that won't do, then to Jewish women in Galilee, or in upper Galilee, or in the countryside of upper Galilee.

"To go back to a Jewish woman's life in Judea before the destruction of the Second Temple — well, it's very hard to do. What sources do you use for this? It's hard to use the Gospels. It's hard to use Paul's Diaspora products. Josephus is tainted on his side, plus he's writing in Rome. It's not like we have a cache of letters. We have the Babatha papyri, but now we're already up to the second century. Nor can we be sure that any one life conveys information about women in general or about the society's view of gender."

The speaker was Amy-Jill Levine, the Carpenter Professor of New Testament Studies at the Divinity School at Vanderbilt University. Levine, known as AJ to just about everyone, is a scholar whose specialties include the Gospel according to Matthew and the literature of early Judaism. She is also a speaker in very high demand on issues of women and religion. And she is something of an administrator and entrepreneur, as successful academics must often be nowadays; she recently was appointed to oversee a multimillion-dollar outlay for a new program, funded by the Carpenter Foundation, in religion, gender, and sexuality.

"What is important in history depends on what people want to proclaim to be important," Levine went on. "In studying the first century, the majority of scholars tend to be Christians and therefore interested in Christian history. Jews for the most part have not looked at the first century. Learning Jewish history when you're growing up, you do the Hebrew Bible, selected portions; you do the Maccabees, so you can get Hanukah in there; you may get the destruction of the Second Temple. And then *bang*, you're up to the rabbis. Christianity is sort of bypassed. We don't talk much about the first century. That's *their* century. And hard as it is to do the history of Judaism in Judea and Galilee in the first century, how much more so is it to do the history of Jewish *women?*"

Levine grew up in North Dartmouth, a small town in coastal Massachusetts, a Jewish girl in a largely Roman Catholic neighborhood. Her father for a time ran a shoe store (Levine remembers that he sold a lot of orthopedic shoes to nuns), was successful in the stock market, and went into the scallop business. The family was not devout, but when Levine's father died, her mother decided that she was going to say Kaddish for him. There was some discussion in the local synagogue about whether as a woman she would be counted in the minyan, the minimum number of persons needed for a communal religious service to be conducted, but she simply insisted, and that was that. During Levine's years at Smith College, where she was an undergraduate, and at Duke University, where she completed her graduate work, she grew sensitive to, and impatient with, being the only Jew or one of the few Jews in a class. "The questions in my religion courses were usually, 'Miss Levine, what do the Jews think about . . . ?' And it was difficult being the spokesperson for all of Judaism and also being the spokesperson for all women. I couldn't quite manage both." When Levine got her first job, at Swarthmore College, she was both the first Jew in the religion department and the first woman on the tenure track. Unfamiliarity bred discomfort. "They didn't quite know what to do with me. One of my colleagues, every time we would come to a door together, would hesitate, because he wasn't sure whether he should open the door or not: would I be insulted one way or the other?" (Levine makes a point of lightly calling attention to the oddities of circumstance as she sees them. She gave me directions to the Divinity School at Vanderbilt by noting that it is the building, as her daughter used to say, that has what looks like a lower-case *t* prominently on top.)

Levine has always had a taste for stories and myths, and as this natural bent became entwined with interests in religion and women's issues, she gravitated toward the Gospel of Matthew and then to the writings of the Second Temple period known as the Apocrypha, which are not included in the Hebrew Bible. The Gospel of Matthew is well known as being the most Jewish of the four Gospels; it is believed to have emerged from a Christian community composed largely of Jews. Matthew frequently draws parallels between events in the life of Jesus and events in the Hebrew Bible, and he frequently quotes passages from the Hebrew Bible to support his theology. (Matthew's quotation of Isaiah 7:14 — "Therefore, the Lord himself will give you a sign. Behold, a young woman shall conceive and bear a son, and shall call his name Immanuel" — contributed to the subsequent development of the "virgin birth" interpretation, since the term "young woman" in the original Hebrew was rendered into the Greek version that Matthew would have known as *parthenos*, or "virgin.") In her book *The Social and Ethnic Dimension of Matthean Salvation History*, Levine depicts Matthew's Gospel as one in which women play active roles and are clearly part of Jesus' inclusive community, even if Jesus' (or Matthew's) agenda has little to do with gender and everything to do with Jesus' (or Matthew's) antipathy toward *all* established structures of privilege.

Levine's tone can be drily acerbic, matter-of-factly judgmental in a way that is somewhat reminiscent of commentaries in *The Woman's*

Bible. In a discussion of the healing of Peter's mother-in-law (Matthew 8:14–15), she considers the verb "to serve," noting that this is the task the mother-in-law resumes when she has been healed, a task that Jesus himself has performed. She remarks that "although instructed 'to serve,' the Twelve [that is, the disciples] are never described as doing so." She adds, "And the ultimate irony is that whereas the unnamed mother-in-law rises from her bed to serve Jesus, Peter will sleep when Jesus needs him."[25]

In recent years Levine has spent more and more time looking at the apocryphal writings and the rich and varied world of Second Temple Judaism that they help to open up. She has written about Judith, a woman "beautiful in appearance, and . . . very lovely to behold," who by a seductive masquerade entraps and then beheads the Assyrian general Holofernes, thereby delivering the people of Israel — an allegory of the challenges of fidelity in the context of the Jewish Diaspora. She has written about Tobit, a book of many parts centered on the eponymous protagonist (who has through misfortune been blinded); his niece, Sarah (who has lost seven husbands to a demon on seven successive wedding nights); and Sarah's path toward love with Tobit's son, a story that offers insights into the customs and ramifications, both legal and folk, of marriage. Levine is currently writing about Susanna, the additions to Esther, and the books of the Maccabees. A collection of essays she edited, *Women Like This: New Perspectives on Women in the Greco-Roman World*, looks at a variety of writings from the Second Temple period. (One of these essays, "Women's Authorship of Jewish and Christian Literature in the Greco-Roman Period," by Ross S. Kraemer, offers a concise survey of what is known about women and literacy in Greco-Roman times; Kraemer observes that although female literacy was probably common in some social classes, "no literary text is *known* to have been written by Jewish or Christian women" until the late fourth century A.D.)[26] All of this work calls into question the view of formative Judaism as either a homogeneous phenomenon or a social force more problematic for women than other tendencies in ancient thought.

"I don't think that first-century Judaism was all that repressive," Levine says. "I don't think it was obsessed by purity regulations. I don't think it was any more or less awful than pretty much any other society at the time. Nor do I think Jesus was a feminist. I do think, for whatever reason, whatever his message was — and this is an open question — that women resonated with it. But I don't think it was because he was directly addressing them. I look at Jesus much the same way I would look at Gandhi or Martin Luther King. I don't think they were particularly out there to address women per se, but listening to them preach and listening to what other people might find to be the heart of the message, I say yes, I should support civil rights, I should work toward social justice. Or, for Jesus, I can see value in open-table fellowship, I can appreciate a sense of renewed Judaism or revitalized Judaism. I think I can even resonate with the claim that maybe the Kingdom of God is at hand. But not because I'm a woman. Just because I'm a human being."

I asked Levine, "If there was one question you could have definitively answered about women in the first century, what would it be?" She laughed and warned me that she was the sort of person who was likely to have a different question tomorrow, or an hour from now. And then she said, "I'd like to talk to Martha and Mary. I'd like to ask, So what did you and Jesus talk about? What did you guys get out of this? What was in it for *you*?"

Chapter Eight

....

BORN OF A WOMAN

And Mary said, "Behold, I am the handmaid of the Lord;
let it be to me according to your word."
— Luke 1:38

It has come to me, then, that one must sift through
the nonsense and hostility that has characterized thought
and writing about Mary, to find some images, shards,
and fragments, glittering in the rubble.
— Mary Gordon

THE ACROPOLIS at Zippori, in the lower Galilee, is a place of strategic prominence. During Israel's war of independence, in 1948, it was a headquarters and a staging point for Palestinian attacks on nearby Jewish settlements. The Crusader citadel built there in the eleventh century has over the centuries been occupied by Knights Templar and Ottoman Turks. From this citadel in 1187, Guy de Lusignan led his army to its destruction by Saladin in the shadow of the geological protuberance nearby known as the Horns of Hittin, effectively bringing to an end the Kingdom of Jerusalem.

Saladin occupied the citadel, but at the same time he took the opportunity to tear down a structure just below the summit and to the west of it: the Church of Saint Anne and Saint Joachim. The church had been ravaged before, and it would be rebuilt again; Louis IX of France — Saint Louis — visited the shrine there in 1251, during the seventh Crusade. Today it is a shell once more, the former nave now an expanse of grass exposed to the sky. The triple apse in the eastern wall survives intact, leaving no doubt as to the structure's onetime function. A church existed at this location as early as the fourth century A.D., because Christians believed the site to mark the home of Anna (or Anne) and Joachim, whom tradition holds to be the parents of Mary, the mother of

Jesus. An early nineteenth-century visitor left this vague account: "St. Anne is supposed to have resided in this place, and there are the ruins of a Gothic church erected over the spot, which her dwelling formerly occupied."[1] The historical record is not of much help with any of this. Neither is the New Testament, which not only fails to mention Mary's birthplace but also fails to mention the names of Mary's parents.

The first account of Anna and Joachim is found not in the Gospels but in a text from the second century A.D., variously called *The Protevangelium of James* or *The Book of James*, purportedly written by the James who was the brother or the cousin of Jesus. This text tells the simple and even charming story of how a daughter is bestowed by divine intervention on an older, childless couple: "And behold an angel of the Lord came to her and said: 'Anna, Anna, the Lord has heard your prayers. You shall conceive and bear, and your offspring shall be spoken of in the whole world.'"[2] We cannot help but recall the account in 1 Samuel of the birth of the prophet Samuel to the elderly Hannah, whose name is echoed in the name Anna. In the *Protevangelium*, the childless couple's daughter, Mary, is eventually chosen by lot to marry a widower named Joseph. The rest is history (or at least Gospel).

Where the connection of Joachim and Anna with Zippori came from remains unclear. The original shrine may well have been established by Helena, the mother of the emperor Constantine, who during a lengthy sojourn in the Holy Land in the fourth century A.D. managed to link a number of biblical events to specific locales (no doubt with a certain amount of quiet local connivance). A more solid connection between Mary and Zippori failed to turn up during a search of the books and archives at the place that offered perhaps the best chance of yielding one: the Marian Library at the University of Dayton, in Ohio. The University of Dayton was founded by the Roman Catholic religious order known as the Society of Mary in 1850. The Marian Library, established in 1943 as an independent unit of the larger university library, preserves the world's most comprehensive collection of research materials on the mother of Jesus. The collection begins with some ninety thousand books — serious works on theology and history, art and literature — but it spreads almost helplessly, or perhaps fervently, into the vast realms of pious kitsch that the Christian cult of Mary has given rise to and helps to sustain.

I accompanied the library's director, the Reverend Thomas A. Thompson, on a tour of the facility one wintry afternoon, down brightly fluoresced canyons of leather bindings on tall metal shelves, catching golden glints of titles to left and right. *De laudibus B. Mariae. Le Cantique des cantiques de Salomon. Historia Deiparae Virginis Mariae.* Other kinds of items have been shoved into boxes and stored wherever they can fit. The library is a vast repository of old Christmas cards with a Madonna theme, and of Virgin Mary holy cards and mother-and-child postage stamps, and of devotional medals of many kinds. Volunteers maintain a clipping file. One long wall holds rows of statuary. A figurine depicting a pregnant Mary — an unusual genre — stands out from the others. ("Some people object," said Father Thompson. "They prefer not too much realism in religious art.") A collection of crèches from around the world, like a spreading shantytown, occupies available surfaces atop bookshelves and card catalogues in the library's main reading room — a miniature theme park, in its way, of suboptimal obstetrics.

On the library's Web site you can click on the menu option "Titles of Our Lady" and retrieve subcategories like "Mother of Sorrows," "Mother of Mercy," "Mother of Divine Consolation," "Heavenly nurse," "Help of the helpless," "Ornament of angels," "Stainless maiden," "Dispensatrix of all grace," and hundreds more. (You will search in vain, however, for the title "Our Lady of Perpetual Responsibility," the name of the Catholic church in Garrison Keillor's fictional Lake Wobegon.) Click on the menu option "Norms and Process for Judging Private Revelations," and the Web site will provide pertinent information for conducting an inquisitory tribunal into any reported appearances of Mary, phenomena that have become a reliable background feature of modern life. "Our approach is to strike a happy medium between vain credulity and sterile skepticism," the document begins. "The first norm for evaluating miraculous events is that there be moral certainty, or at least a great probability, that something miraculous has occurred." It goes on: "The second norm deals with the personal qualities of the subjects who claim to have had the apparition; they must be mentally sound, honest, sincere . . ."[3]

Mary in her symbolism evokes in many a deep ambivalence. In one of the best-known passages of *Mont-Saint-Michel and Chartres*, Henry Adams invoked the Mary of medieval art and the emotional chord she touched: "The proper study of mankind is woman and, by common agreement since the time of Adam, it is the most complex and arduous. The study of Our Lady, as shown by the art of Chartres, leads directly back to Eve, and lays bare the whole subject of sex."[4] As a focus of popular devotion for hundreds of millions of people, Mary of course has no rival in Christendom. *Life* was hardly risking a drop in newsstand sales when it made "The Mystery of Mary" its December 1996 cover story. ("Two thousand years after the Nativity," the cover type announced, "the mother of Jesus is more beloved, powerful, and controversial than ever.") Erasmus, in his book *The Praise of Folly*, felt compelled to warn believers against relying overmuch on "the Virgin Mother, to whom the common people attribute more than to the Son."[5] For Catholics and Orthodox, though not for Protestants, Mary's status, theologically, is exalted.

Whatever we make of the stories of the appearance of Mary to various individuals or groups of people around the world — at Medjugorje, in the former Yugoslavia; in Belleville, Illinois; in Hrushiw, Ukraine; in Colfax, California; in Cuapa, Nicaragua; in Bayside, Queens; in suggestive images appearing almost everywhere, it seems, on such objects as wet cocktail napkins and overheated tortillas — it can certainly be said that the number of reports of such appearances is not diminishing. Scores of newsletters are devoted exclusively to Marian apparitions, as is a full-fledged journal called *Signs of the Times* (circulation sixty thousand). The shrine to the Virgin Mary at Lourdes, France, receives more than five million visitors annually, as do the shrine at Fatima, Portugal, and the icon of the Black Madonna in Czestochowa, Poland.[6] Pope John Paul II cherishes an especially deep personal devotion to Mary, whom he credits with saving his life when he was shot by a would-be assassin in 1981. (The bullet that was removed from his abdomen now adorns the crown of the statue of Mary at Fatima.)[7]

Mary's prominence extends beyond Christianity and into Islam, which incorporates much of what the Gospels say about the life of the prophet Jesus. Mary is mentioned thirty-four times in the Koran. Although most Christians are unaware of the fact, Muslims accept the doctrine of the virgin birth.

In the course of the past several years, meanwhile, the Vatican has received some five million signatures, from nearly every country on earth, affixed to petitions calling on the pope to proclaim Mary the "Co-Redemptrix, Mediatrix of All Graces and Advocate for the People of God," a theological mouthful and a doctrinal stretch. If the idea of a theological petition drive seems faintly improbable (can there be recalls too?), we should remember that insofar as Mary is concerned, theology has filtered up as much as it has trickled down. "Nothing like this organized petition drive has ever been seen in Rome," Newsweek reported last year.[8] In truth, the present drive recalls the popular agitation a century and a half ago that prompted the Vatican, in 1854, to proclaim the doctrine of the Immaculate Conception (which holds that Mary was conceived without original sin) and the agitation a century later, including eight million signatures on petitions, that prompted the Vatican, in 1950, to proclaim the doctrine of the Assumption (which holds that after her death, or "dormition," Mary was corporeally assumed into heaven). Pope Pius XII declared on this last occasion that Mary, "when her earthly life was finished," was "taken up body and soul into the glories of heaven."[9]

At the same time, of course, the image of Mary has little or no deep significance for many people, and for others it is a source of distress and a focus of vocal anger. At some academic gatherings you might sooner hear uplifting sentiments about Jezebel or Delilah than about Mary. Protestants have endowed Mary with none of the doctrinal apparatus that Roman Catholics have and often view Mariology, as the theological study of Mary is known, with distaste, as an irrelevance, or indeed as tantamount to superstition and idolatry — as Mariolatry. Mariology, the theologian Karl Barth once observed, "is an arbitrary invention in the face of Scripture" and a "diseased construct of theological thought."[10] The Vatican's peremptory declaration of the Assumption so rankled Protestants, introducing a troublesome vibrato into ecumenical discussions of various kinds, that Catholic officials resolved to play down the subject of Mary at the Second Vatican Council (and did so).[11]

Highlighting a depiction of Mary as an essentially pliant woman who meekly acceded to the social norms of her day — "Behold, I am the handmaid of the Lord; let it be to me according to your word" — and who embodied a churchly stance toward sexuality that is in various ways both implicitly and explicitly oppressive, a number of feminist writers on religion, though by no means all of them, have given up on Mary. The abolitionist and feminist Sojourner Truth was willing to leverage the Virgin Mary to her own advantage. Confronted with the argument that women should not enjoy the same rights as men because Jesus was a man, not a woman, Truth replied, "Whar did your Christ come from? . . . From God and a woman! Man had nothin' to do wid' Him!"[12] Contemporary feminists are likely to regard the emphasis on Mary's virginity as a denigration of female sexuality and more broadly as a denigration of human nature itself. They are scarcely heartened by the affirmation of Mary as primarily "an eminent and singular exemplar of both virginity and motherhood," to quote the Vatican's 1988 apostolic letter *On the Dignity and Vocation of Women.*[13] "All generations will call me blessed," proclaims Mary in Luke 1:48, but in truth a number of commentators during the past few generations have called her other things as well. "Mary cannot be a model for the New Woman," writes Marina Warner in her book *Alone of All Her Sex: The Myth and the Cult of the Virgin Mary.* "It is more likely that, like Ishtar, the Virgin will recede into legend."[14] (For a brief period in 1997 it seemed as if the theological model for the New Woman might be Princess Diana, whose funeral demonstrated the unthinking but unshakable popular adherence to the view that nature, as Henry Adams put it, "regards the female as the essential, the male as the superfluity of her world.")[15] Mary Daly, whose positions seem to become more uniquely evolved with every new book, sees Mary being "portrayed/betrayed as Total Rape Victim — a pale derivative symbol disguising the conquered Goddess."[16]

"Mother of Irony" is not one of the titles of Mary that will show up on the Marian Library's Web site, but in the case of Mary it would not be inappropriate. Elizabeth Johnson, a Catholic nun who is among the most imaginative and also the most accessible of contemporary feminist theologians, has taken note of the modest, tenuous connection between anything that can reliably be said about Mary the actual person and "the immense sprawl of the historical phenomenon" that has existed in her name.[17] For all the sense of grievance directed at Mary from some quarters, the fact is that her image can be fashioned in almost any conceivable way. And so indeed it has been.

In the epistle to the Galatians (4:4), Paul writes that Jesus was "born of woman," and because the epistles of Paul are the earliest Christian documents, this oblique reference is chronologically the first in the New Testament to Mary. From a historical point of view, there is not much else in the text to amplify it. The Catholic theologian Karl Rahner has stated simply that "the Church does not know Mary's life story."[18]

In the Gospels, Mary appears first chronologically in the scene of the Annunciation in Luke 1:26. A virgin living in Nazareth, betrothed to a man named Joseph, she is visited by an angel who asks whether she will accept the plan that God has devised: to bring forth the Messiah. Apart from her strong central presence in the Nativity narratives of Luke and Matthew — narratives that are divergent or contradictory — she plays a role in only a handful of New Testament stories. There is the visit to Jerusalem with the adolescent Jesus at Passover (Luke 2:41), when she loses him briefly and upon finding him offers a mother's relieved rebuke: "Son, why have you treated us so? Behold, your father and I have been looking for you anxiously." There is the scene of the wedding at Cana (John 2:1), when Mary in effect pushes a seemingly reluctant Jesus into public life by prompting him to perform his first miracle. There is her attempt, apparently rejected, to see Jesus while he is teaching (Mark 3:31). Later, Mary stands below the cross when Jesus is crucified (John 19:25). She is last mentioned (Acts 1:14) as being among those who gather in Jerusalem in "the upper room" after Jesus ascends to heaven. All told, she is referred to fewer than twenty times in the New Testament (fewer times than in the Koran), and not always by name.

As a matter of historical reconstruction, the little that can be said about Mary ventures almost immediately into the speculative and generalized terrain of "would have been" (that is, of formulations like "As a

Jewish woman in rural Galilee, Mary would have been . . ."), and even this terrain constitutes a relatively narrow strip because of the sheer paucity of information about the ordinary lives of Jewish peasants in first-century Palestine. The name Mary, or Miriam, as it would have been on the lips of Mary herself, hearkens back, of course, to the sister of Moses. There were apparently siblings in the household where Jesus grew up; sisters are mentioned but are not given names, and four brothers are named — James (Jacob), Joses (Joseph), Jude (Judah), and Simon (Simeon). These names too hearken back to Israel's formative period — to the patriarchs of four of Israel's twelve tribes — as does the name of Mary's husband and Jesus' putative father, Joseph. Can we suppose, as the New Testament scholar John P. Meier has suggested in his book *A Marginal Jew,* that the family of Jesus shared an especially pronounced ethnic or national awareness as Jews in a significantly Hellenized land? From the intensity of Jesus' religious feelings in later life and his deep knowledge of Scripture, we can perhaps infer that his parents' religious commitment was strong. Mary certainly lived as a Jew, whatever that meant for her time and station.[19]

What language or languages did Mary speak? Even for Jesus, the language issue is not settled with absolute certainty, beyond the assumption that he at least spoke Aramaic (but what about Greek?). Nor do we know for certain that Jesus could read and write (the three passages that can be seen as showing him doing one or the other have a vexed quality about them, some scholars believe), much less whether he learned the alphabet at his mother's knee. Mary presumably grew up in the vicinity of Nazareth, a town of no more than a few thousand people when she knew it, and a place of little significance; the town's name does not appear even once in the Hebrew Bible. Was Mary a widow when Jesus, at about age thirty, began his public life? Joseph never makes an appearance outside the Nativity narratives in Matthew and Luke, and Mary is the only parent with whom Jesus is portrayed as having an adult relationship. The relationship at times appears strained. Passages in Mark suggest that Mary and other members of the family did not understand or approve of what Jesus was up to. In Mark 6:4, Jesus says, "A prophet is not without honor, except in his own country, and among his own kin, and in his own house," words spoken in the presence of at least some of his family and probably in his home town of Nazareth.

Since historical reclamation of Mary's biography is virtually impossible, most feminist scholars focus instead on the history of symbolism and of doctrine and on what that symbolism and that doctrine do or should mean. One obvious starting point is the proclaimed virginity of Mary at the moment of the conception of Jesus, her pregnancy being an act of divine intervention. This is the state of affairs reported independently by Matthew and Luke. "And in the sixth month," says Luke (1:26–27), "the angel Gabriel was sent from God to a city of Galilee, named Nazareth, to a virgin betrothed to a man whose name was Joseph, of the house of David; and the virgin's name was Mary." Matthew bolsters the story and the fact of Mary's presumptively virginal status with an apparently prophetic quotation from Isaiah (7:14), to the effect that "a virgin shall conceive and bear a son, and his name shall be called Emmanuel." Scholars have long been aware that the word for virgin (*parthenos*) in the Greek text of Isaiah, which Matthew would have known from the Septuagint, does not have exactly the same meaning as the original Hebrew word being translated. That word, *almah*, simply means "young woman." Even *parthenos* does not always mean "virgin"; in Genesis 34:3 of the Septuagint, Dinah, the daughter of Jacob and Leah, is referred to as *parthenos* after she has been raped by Shechem. Some thus see the idea of the virgin birth as a misunderstanding, although Matthew may be invoking Isaiah for support rather than deriving the idea of Mary's virginity from it. As noted, Luke independently asserts a belief in the virgin birth.[20]

The virgin birth is an issue, of course, largely because of the way in which it has been used, wittingly or unwittingly, to besmirch sexuality; the further presumption is that women are the embodiment of carnal temptation and thus bear responsibility for humanity's "fall" into a state of sin. This is a corollary of Mary's exaltation above all other women — an exaltation, as the one who would bear the Messiah, that became entwined in theology with the state of virginity itself. As doctrine developed, the duration of Mary's virginity lengthened: she was a virgin not only at conception but remained one through birth and ever afterward.

The brothers and sisters of Jesus, explicitly mentioned in Scripture, were explained as cousins (or, according to the *Protevangelium,* as the children of Joseph by a previous marriage). Mary's ultimate theological status as a woman free from all sin was causally linked to her freedom from all sexual relations.

Mary and her virginity also offered a contrasting, tempting, and redemptive parallel to the figure of Eve, as the theologian Irenaeus observed at the end of the second century: "For Adam had necessarily to be restored in Christ, that mortality be restored in immortality, and Eve in Mary, that a virgin, become the advocate of a virgin, should undo and destroy virginal disobedience by virginal obedience."[21]

A related element of the Nativity narratives that has received close attention from scholars interested in women has to do with the family tree of Jesus. Both Luke (3:23–38) and Matthew (1:1–17) aim to show that Jesus, as the Messiah, can claim descent from David. Both evangelists provide the appropriate genealogies, Luke's in fact going all the way back to Adam. As is typical in the Bible, the genealogies for the most part follow the male line, and they follow it through Joseph. (Though not regarded by Luke or Matthew as the biological father, Joseph was the legal father, which in Jewish law was all that mattered at the time.) But in the genealogy of Matthew the author interjects the name of four women besides Mary: Tamar (not the daughter of David, raped by Amnon, but the earlier Tamar of Genesis 38), who in pursuit of justice for herself poses as a prostitute and is impregnated by Judah, the father of the men whose successive deaths have left her a widow; Rahab, the prostitute of Jericho who hides Joshua's spies as the Israelites successfully seek to conquer the city (Joshua 2); Ruth, a widow who maneuvers herself into marriage with Boaz, a kinsman of her dead husband; and "the wife of Uriah," that is, Bathsheba, whom David takes in adultery and eventually marries (after arranging for the death of her husband), and who bears the future King Solomon (2 Samuel 11, 12).

Commentators have long surmised that these women are included in the genealogy because they have something in common or help to make a particular point, but they have not agreed on what the point or the something-in-common might be. The word that comes up most frequently in explanations is "irregularity." The irregularity could, for example, be ethnic. One interpretation focuses on the fact that Rahab, Ruth, and Uriah are all Gentiles and thus from outside the Israelite tribe. Could their inclusion be a signal of Matthew's theological interest in opening the Jesus movement to non-Jews? Amy-Jill Levine, in her study of Matthew's Gospel, does not discount this explanation but perceives a deeper purpose. The four women stand, or for some reason find themselves, outside the bounds of comfortably ordered society; sexuality is involved; all four are restored to a position or status that society would deem normal or acceptable. Operating at a distinct disadvantage in terms of social power and behaving in a manner at odds with established conventions, these women overcome exclusion through the triumph of a "higher righteousness" that advances the Lord's ulterior purpose. Mary, in this view, becomes the moral continuation of her biblical predecessors. "The feminist implications of this interpretation," Levine concludes, "are bittersweet." On the one hand, she observes, Matthew seems to be suggesting "that categories of sex as well as of race are made irrelevant by the Christ event." On the other hand, "these women were forced to use their bodies in order to write themselves into history."[22]

The most controversial interpretation of the Matthean genealogy, which encompasses and explains both the purpose of the genealogy and the assertions about the virgin birth, has been put forward most recently by the New Testament scholar Jane Schaberg in her book *The Illegitimacy of Jesus* (1987), whose title pretty well accounts for the heated nature of the debate that has surrounded it. Schaberg's contention, at once new and in a way very old, is that the infancy narratives in Matthew and Luke are formulated the way they are because the evangelists are responding to a view, prevalent among their contemporaries, that Jesus was simply an illegitimate child. Schaberg writes, "Mention of these four women [in Matthew's genealogy] is designed to lead Matthew's reader to expect another, final story of a woman who becomes a social misfit in some way; is wronged or thwarted; who is party to a sexual act that places her in great danger; and whose story has an outcome that repairs the social fabric and ensures the birth of a child who is legitimate or legitimated." She goes on: "My claim is that the texts dealing with the origin of Jesus, Matt 1:1–25 and Luke 1:20–56 and 3:23–38, originally were about an illegitimate conception and not about a miraculous virginal conception."[23]

"Now the birth of Jesus came about in this way," Matthew writes (1:18–19): "When his mother Mary had been betrothed to Joseph, before they came together she was found to be with child of the Holy Spirit; and her husband Joseph, being a just man and unwilling to put her to shame, resolved to divorce her quietly." Schaberg's investigation of this passage leads into the dimly lit crannies and wide-open emptinesses of our knowledge of Jewish law in the Second Temple period. What might — what *should* — happen to a woman in Mary's circumstances? What legal options could the betrothed man exercise, since it was the man, naturally, who enjoyed the right to exercise options?

Schaberg adduces other gospel texts as evidence for her interpretation, noting how they gain added resonance if read with the idea of Jesus' illegitimacy in mind. She sees the survival of a slur in the reference to Jesus in Mark 6:3 as the "son of Mary," with no mention made of Joseph, noting that the usual procedure would have been to identify a man by his paternity. In the Gospel of John (8:41), a debate between Jesus and "the Jews who had believed in him" brings a riposte from the Jews in these words: "*We* were not born of fornication." The implication, as Schaberg sees it, is that "*You* [Jesus] were."[24] Whatever the prevailing view of the matter in Jesus' lifetime, it is certainly true that innuendo about his paternity enjoyed currency afterward. In the middle of the third century, the theologian Origen devoted part of his polemic *Contra Celsus* to countering Celsus' charge (garnered, the pagan author said, from older Jewish sources) that the father of Jesus was a Roman soldier named Panthera (or Pantera).[25]

Schaberg's purpose in revisiting this issue is twofold. One is simply to use the subject as a historical probe, a means of investigating legal, social, and scriptural matters that turn up along the way. The other lies on an entirely different plane. Schaberg sees her reconstruction as theologically liberating. Her reading of the Nativity narratives affirms the essential concern of God for the outcasts of society. At the expense of upholding Mary's "privileged" selection as the virgin mother of Jesus,

Schaberg highlights instead the precariousness of an actual woman in Mary's actual situation. She calls into question too the Church's celebration of virginity and asceticism as requisite handmaidens of the highest female virtue, a celebration that may leave ordinary women who are leading ordinary lives with feelings of unassuageable inferiority.

As noted, there is no question that claims regarding the illegitimacy of Jesus have been widely believed at various times and places. Schaberg contends that the claims have a historical basis and that the true situation was known to Matthew and Luke. Her views elicit tough responses from some other scholars. "Schaberg's long catena of dubious interpretations makes the whole project dubious in the extreme," John Meier writes in a sharp, lengthy, and spirited footnote in A Marginal Jew. "Repeated affirmations of theory take the place of detailed arguments, rhetorical questions abound, and counterindicating data are ignored or passed over quickly in footnotes."[26]

Tough assessments from colleagues are inherent in the enterprise. Schaberg, though, has also gone through some of the difficult experiences that other feminist scholars have endured when simplistic versions (or, frankly, even when accurate versions) of their views have been given wide public exposure. Mary in particular will always touch a nerve. The magazine Bible Review reportedly received more mail in response to the 1988 article "Can Scholars Take the Virgin Birth Seriously?" than for any other article in its forty-year history.[27] In Schaberg's case, the publication in the Detroit Free Press of a series of articles about her views on Mary and the virgin birth, and also about her views on Mary Magdalene and whether she was ever really a whore, caused a number of major donors to cancel gifts to the University of Detroit-Mercy, the Catholic university where Schaberg was the chair of the religion department. It also brought a large volume of negative mail:

> "You belong to the group of women who believe they can do with their bodies what they wish. Not so."

> "Dear Heretic, Mary Magdalene may not have been a whore, but you certainly are one! I won't keep you from your work. I'm sure you have other saints to smear and unborn babies to kill. Signed, A White Male (the cause of world strife)"

"God kept Mary and Jesus pure from the revolting, shameful things you write about."

"Only an egomaniac would put themselves in the position of knowing more than the great theologians of the church."

The Reverend Adam Maida, the archbishop of Detroit, observed in a television interview that "among the many things we need to ensure is that those who teach and come to Catholic universities will somehow live out [traditional Catholic] faith. Those who teach must be faithful to the magisterium of the Church." He went on, "I don't get involved in the internal administering of the university, but if there is someone who was speaking a heresy, I would have to challenge that."[28]

A draft letter of support for Schaberg, intended to be circulated among the faculty, concluded with a statement that offers a window on perceptions of the reigning atmosphere: "We are sorry to be sending this letter to you anonymously. However, this is still life for some feminist scholars in some places." In the end, the letter was never distributed. Jane Schaberg remains a member of the faculty at the University of Detroit-Mercy. She is at work on a study of Mary Magdalene.

The day I met Jaroslav Pelikan, the Sterling Professor of History Emeritus at Yale University, was also the day on which *Newsweek* published its cover story titled "Hail, Mary," which noted, among other things, that Marian apparitions have been reported three times more frequently in the twentieth century than they were in the three previous centuries. Pelikan was not entirely surprised. "The number of these apparitions that have occurred just since my book on Mary came out has been extraordinary," he said, referring to his 1996 book *Mary Through the Centuries*. "I know, because I keep getting telephone calls and letters that ask me to comment on something that has shown up in a parking lot in Los Angeles or in a supermarket somewhere. No, thank you!"

Pelikan has been "in the Mary business," as he puts it, off and on for some forty years, ever since, as a young faculty member at the University of Chicago, he was called on by the editors of the *Encyclopaedia Britannica* to rewrite the entry for "Mary" that had been in use since the

encyclopedia's fabled eleventh edition, of 1911. The encyclopedia's coverage of certain aspects of religion had been eliciting criticism for years,
as its comfortably liberal Anglicanism had been encountered by a far
bigger and more diverse readership than had originally been the case.
For a time it was rumored that an X at the end of an entry meant that the
entry had been sent for vetting to authorities of the Catholic Church. (In
truth, it simply meant that an entry had been revised.) When the "Mary"
entry came up for an overhaul in the late 1950s, the encyclopedia's
editors found themselves commissioning draft after draft from author
after author, only to have each new entry rejected on various grounds by
one or another of the outside readers. The young Jaroslav Pelikan was
called in to make one last attempt at a unified entry; if he failed, the
editors intended to publish entries reflecting several conflicting points of
view. Pelikan somehow succeeded. The "Mary" entry in *Britannica*,
though revised over the years, remains to this day a product of Pelikan's
hand and concludes with the initials "J. J. Pn."[29]

It would be safe to say that Pelikan's considerable reputation is not
built upon a foundation of feminist scholarship. He is a historian of
Christianity whose books, when they appear (as they do with astonishing
frequency), tend to have the solidity and majesty of a geological upthrust. His five-volume work *The Christian Tradition: A History of the
Development of Doctrine*, completed in 1989, is the centerpiece of his
scholarly achievement, but Pelikan is perhaps best known among the
public for his accessible recent book *Jesus Through the Centuries*. He
holds honorary degrees from some thirty-five universities around the
world, and he has been the Jefferson Lecturer, chosen by the National
Endowment for the Humanities. For all his eminence, he has a reputation for friendliness and good humor. When I met him one morning on
the steps of Yale's Sterling Memorial Library, he introduced himself as
"Jary Pelikan," a name I found about as easy to employ as I would have
found "Augie" after making the acquaintance of the bishop of Hippo.

I had sought out Pelikan because of *Mary Through the Centuries*,
which is a companion volume to the book on Jesus. Subtitled *Her Place
in the History of Culture*, the new book briskly surveys not so much the
little that can be known about the historical Mary but rather what Mary

has been understood to stand for in the nearly two millennia since she lived and died — what she has been understood to stand for by women as well as men, by Jews and Muslims as well as Christians, by the materially and spiritually oppressed of the world as well as its artistic and intellectual elite. As we walked to Pelikan's office in a quiet brick passageway that runs beneath a clock tower in Pierson College, he commented on the construction that had strewn impediments all around the Yale campus — a consequence, he explained affably, of a university policy known as "deferred maintenance." The discussion segued naturally toward euphemism. As befits a man who could read English by the age of two and German, Greek, Hebrew, Latin, Russian, Serbian, and Slovak by the age of twenty, Pelikan seems to relish the subtleties and surprises of language. I remember an observation he made in one of his writings about the differing translations of the Christmas message from the angels to the shepherds in Luke 2:14: is it "peace and good will to all men" or "peace to men of good will"? The observation pithily pointed up the divergence in views of God's grace and predestination. In an aside in *Mary Through the Centuries*, Pelikan observes that the noun "bead" (as in the beads on a rosary, indicating the saying of the "Hail Mary") and ultimately the verb "to bid" come from a Germanic word meaning "to pray."[30] Even his own name gives him a certain delight, perhaps in part because the pelican has long been an important Christian symbol. Pelikan has assembled a collection of statues of these birds, and he sends out notes on cards bearing a small, elegant pelican image in gold, which he calls "pelikards." A large wooden pelican perched silently on his desk as we spoke.

Pelikan began by addressing the issue of Mary's somewhat anomalous status among feminists. Although many feminist scholars have gone to great lengths to investigate and "reclaim" the lives of women whose role in Scripture is in some cases quite modest or has been suppressed altogether, they have shown comparatively limited interest in Mary, even though among biblical women she is rivaled only by Eve as a presence in the modern world (and Eve is really a distant second). Whereas some feminists celebrate images of motherhood and childbirth in the Bible, especially when that imagery seems to have been officially discouraged, in the case of Mary they have tended not to make very much of such imagery, or to treat it with suspicion, precisely because it has been officially celebrated. When the subject of Mary does come up, the focus is often less on positive features of her religious symbolism than on irritation and impatience with any negative ones.

"Some of the explanation of both phenomena, I think," Pelikan said, "is a certain tone-deafness among many secularist scholars to the accents of religious faith, and also a kind of reductionism which cannot come to terms with the religiousness of religious faith. Another part of the explanation has to do with the tension between Mary as a valiant woman who crushed the head of the serpent and Mary as a model of humility and submission — a tension that has been resolved in a considerable part of the Church's literature in the direction of submission. Mary has been used as a club to beat down women's aspirations — 'Holy Mary, meek and mild,' that sort of thing. And so the antipietist tendency of many historians, which I share, ends up in some of them relegating Mary somewhat peremptorily to the side of the instruments of oppression. It overlooks the subtlety of her position."

The subtlety of her position? Yes, Pelikan went on. Philosophically, he explained, it has been more or less the mainline consensus in the history of thought that discipline and freedom, responsibility and privilege, are somehow linked. Behind this question lurks the larger theological one of how human autonomy can be asserted, maintained, and exercised in a cosmos where the power and authority of God are absolute. The prophet Isaiah asked, "Shall the clay say to him that fashioned it, What makest thou?" Mary offers an entry point into this discussion. To be sure, Pelikan noted, there has always been the "cramped" theological tradition that sees in Mary's consenting statement "Behold, I am the handmaid of the Lord" an acquiescent and powerless young woman who has no choice but to submit to the will of God (and why would she want to refuse?). But the more dynamic theological tradition sees Mary's statement differently: not as a passive ratification but as an act of willed assent that could have been withheld, an act whose free expression was necessary before God's will would be done. And "if that was true of the most shattering intervention into human life and history ever launched by

God," Pelikan writes in *Mary Through the Centuries*, summarizing the arguments of many early Christian thinkers, "it had to be true of how the grace of God always operated, respecting human freedom and integrity."[31] To put it another way, as Pelikan did when we spoke, "God doesn't rape. He woos."

They might not frame the matter in quite the same way, surely, but those feminist writers who are reluctant to discard Mary altogether do look at her precisely as a paradigm of courageous and active free will. The theologian Rosemary Radford Ruether is a prominent case in point. Commenting on Mary's decision to participate in the unfolding of God's design and to bear the child, Ruether writes, "Indeed, it puts her under danger as someone who has been making her own choices about her body and sexuality without regard for her future husband. She may be accused of being a prostitute or a 'loose woman' and 'put away.' In Luke, the decision to have the redemptive child is between her and God . . . Luke goes out of his way to stress that Mary's motherhood is a free choice."[32]

In *Mary Through the Centuries*, Pelikan pursues essentially two parallel evolutionary strands. One is the theological strand. How does this poor, probably unlettered Galilean girl become a sophisticated intellectual construct, personified by such names as *Mater Gloriosa* and *Sedes Sapientiae*, and the object of violent polemics at Church councils? The impetus begins, of course, with theological speculation about the nature of Jesus. Was he fully divine *and* fully human? Did he just *appear* to be human? The literal motherhood of Mary is a crucial element in the assertion of the full, literal humanity of Jesus. The phrase "born of woman," which appears in canon and creed in various formulations, is not mere throat-clearing. It is a way of saying about Jesus, in effect, "This is no phantom, this is no mere shade or specter. Look — there's the bloody afterbirth to prove it."

If Jesus in his humanity looks back at Mary, as if for confirmation, his divinity too has consequences that ripple backward. If Mary is the mother of the human Jesus, is she also the mother of the divine Jesus? If she is indeed the "mother of God," what consequences must this have for her own nature and her own person, and for the very condition of her soul? Early and medieval theologians pursued such questions with a logic and a relentlessness that is almost touching, and the result is an intricate scaffolding of speculation and surmise, the struts of supposition tightly lashed by reason. "Concerning no other merely human being," Pelikan writes, "none of the prophets or apostles or saints, has there been even a small fraction of the profound theological reflection that has been called forth by the person of the Blessed Virgin."[33]

The second strand of Pelikan's work is cultural. Whether the subject is political oppression or the ideal of the feminine or racial prejudice, the person of Mary, he contends, has somehow entered into it. He observes that Mary has had far more impact on definitions of the feminine (make of such definitions what we will) than her son has had on definitions of the masculine. She is a bridge to Islam. In the Koran only one of the 114 suras, or chapters, is given the name of a woman, and the name of that sura is "Maryam: Mary." The character of Mary in the Koran is more memorably drawn than that of Jesus or of Muhammed himself. As "the last figure of the Old Testament" and someone whose name commemorates Miriam the prophetess, the sister of Moses, Mary is also a bridge to Judaism — "the unbreakable link between Jewish and Christian history."[34] Indeed, the metaphors and allusions that hover about the Mary of Christianity are drawn at least as much from the Hebrew Bible as from the New Testament. She is Eve and she is Wisdom. She is the woman of valor of Proverbs. Pelikan summons forth an image of the "multicultural Mary" as embodied in countless artistic depictions of the Black Madonna, and this too comes from the Hebrew Bible. The image originates in the association of Mary with the bride in the Song of Songs, who proclaims, "Black am I, and beautiful" (1:5). The famous icon of the Black Madonna at Czestochowa may owe its complexion to soot, but this is not so for the acculturated Marys of Asia, Africa, and Latin America — for instance, for Mexico's richly complected Lady of Guadalupe, *la Morenita*, as she is known, or "Little Darkling."[35]

The most powerful women in an age of powerful men — the great abbesses of the medieval West, whose story, Pelikan believes, most feminists have mysteriously ignored — drew their inspiration explicitly from Mary. For many of those same reasons, Mary is invoked today by people engaged in struggles for social justice around the world. Despite all the attempts by various authorities over the years to set boundaries on Mary, to define her in certain ways for certain purposes, she has resisted such efforts, or eluded them, and so remained at large, perpetually beyond official control.

"The language of the Magnificat," Pelikan went on — and here he shifted rhetorical tone, putting himself into oratorical mode as he quoted the words:

> *He has put down the mighty from their thrones*
> *and exalted those of low degree;*
> *he has filled the hungry with good things,*
> *and the rich he has sent empty away*

— "that's pretty potent stuff. And it has led to a rehabilitation of Mary in the minds of many current activists — for instance, among Third World liberation theologians — as it did for somebody like Dorothy Day.

"I don't mean to sound programmatic. You can't tell from my book where I stand on the issues of 1997, which for me is a compliment, not a complaint. Because issues such as the ordination of women are as hotly discussed as they are, it is clear that some people were disappointed that all this ammunition had been collected and then not exploded. What other people want to do with it is their business, not mine."

He went on a moment later. "I've often said, when asked to comment about the events of the past few days or the past few weeks, that everybody is an expert on the twentieth century. My role is to file a minority report on behalf of all the other centuries, a minority report on behalf of the dead. It's a kind of cure for amnesia."

Chapter Nine

·····················

PROMINENT AMONG
THE APOSTLES?

*And it shall come to pass afterward that I will pour out my
spirit on all flesh; your sons and your daughters shall prophesy
. . . Even upon the menservants and maidservants in
those days, I will pour out my spirit.*
— Joel 2:28–29

*For if a man does not know how to manage his own
household, how can he care for God's church?*
— 1 Timothy 3:5

THE COMMENTARY in the guidebooks is terse. "A banquet scene on
the apse arch," one of them says simply, "includes the figure of a
woman." Another observes, "Besides some stucco decoration it has well-
preserved frescoes, including one behind the altar that may represent an
early Christian *agape*, or ritual feast."

The subject is a wall painting, and the location is a catacomb in
Rome. The Via Salaria is the old salt road, which from the earliest days
of the city carried trade between Rome and the neighboring people
known as the Sabines, who occupied the mountainous region of central
Italy just south of present-day Umbria. The Via Salaria runs due north,
cutting through the Aurelian walls not far from the Borghese Gardens,
and after a mile or so it jogs to the northeast, where it effectively becomes part of the boundary of the Villa Ada, a public park and embassy
compound. This northern suburb includes the fashionable, if somewhat
dull, Roman neighborhood known as Parioli. Beneath the winding roads
and the villas with their lush walled gardens and spindles of umbrella
pine lie extensive networks of catacombs, layer upon layer, most of them
accessible only through private land and therefore closed to the public.

But out on the Via Salaria, adjacent to the Villa Ada, are the Catacombs of Priscilla. The entrance can be found on the property of a convent at Via Salaria 430, and for a small fee you can take a tour of its chambers, guided by one of the nuns.

The Priscilla of these catacombs is not the Priscilla, or Prisca, praised by Paul in his letter to the Romans ("Greet Prisca and Aquila, my fellow workers in Christ Jesus, who risked their necks for my life, to whom not only I but all the churches of the Gentiles give thanks") and indeed mentioned by him six times. This Priscilla is from a later time (perhaps two centuries later) and from a senatorial family, the Acilli, whose estates included the surrounding domain. Parts of the catacombs' upper structure were in all likelihood elements of the family's villa. And in one of these elements, called the Cappella Greca, archaeologists a hundred years ago discovered a fresco that was given the name *fractio panis*, or "the breaking of the bread." The image is unmistakable: seven figures are arrayed around a table in a celebration of what appears to be the Eucharist. Bread lies before them, and the figure on the far left holds a loaf, as if about to break and bless it — the consummate act of Christian priesthood. What is remarkable about the fresco is that all seven of the figures are depicted as women.[1]

Were these women what today we would call priests? Whatever they were called, did they perform priestly functions? If they were and if they did, then how could this be so, when the weight of tradition for nearly two millennia has insisted that the reality was otherwise — that women were from the very beginning unwelcome in and barred from priestly roles?

"I greet you all most cordially, women throughout the world!" Thus began Pope John Paul II's formal "Letter to Women," released by the Holy See on the eve of the Fourth World Conference on Women, which was sponsored by the United Nations and was held in Beijing in 1995. In the letter, which was drafted within eyeshot of the Catacombs of Priscilla, John Paul addressed women in their capacities as mothers, wives, daughters, and sisters, as workers, as members of religious orders. He condemned the long history of sexual violence against women. He called for "equal pay for equal work, protection for working mothers, fairness in career advancement, [and] equality of spouses with regard to family rights." He noted that women's contributions to society had been largely overlooked in the archives of conventional history and acknowledged that social "conditioning" had been "an obstacle to the progress of women." To the extent that the Catholic Church deserved blame for any of the historical ills he cited, the pope confessed, "For this I am truly sorry."[2]

The pope's letter was a powerful apologia, but on the issue of whether women might be allowed to serve in the priesthood his demeanor remained unyielding: this departure from traditional practice was not to be. That the pope would not be altering his position was first signaled in this document by a telltale choice of introductory wording, a seemingly vague yet weighty reference to the two sexes performing "a certain diversity of roles," which heralded a presentation of the now familiar line of argument that starts with the observation that Jesus bestowed the status of apostle only on men.[3]

In truth, no one had really expected that this line of argument would shift. John Paul's bubble-topped "pope-mobile" was never an inviting candidate for a bumper sticker you sometimes see: "Ordain Women, or Don't Baptize Them." In 1976 the Vatican had addressed the issue of women's ordination comprehensively, from its point of view, in its "Declaration on the Question of Admitting Women to the Priesthood."[4] In 1994 the pope had declared that the issue of women's ordination was no longer "still open to debate," that the Church had "no authority whatsoever" to confer such ordination, and that the declaration against admitting women to the priesthood "is to be definitively held by all the Church's faithful."[5]

This 1994 letter was titled "On Reserving Priestly Ordination to Men Alone." It was published three days after the Vatican released the English-language edition of the new Catholic catechism, which had been a subject of considerable argument over the issue of whether gender-neutral language would be employed (for instance, using the word "humanity" instead of the word "man"), as an international team of translators had proposed in a draft document. In the end, gender-neutral language was not employed.

The Catholic Church has not, of course, been alone in its resistance to the ordination of women, and it does not account for all the headlines when a religious gender crisis momentarily erupts in America or elsewhere in the world: "Women in Pulpit Divide Baptists"; "Furor in Germany Over Female Rabbi"; "Cleric Hard-Liners Crack Down on Revealing Women's Eyes"; "Mormon Woman Faces Discipline for Feminist Essay."[6] Some liberal denominations and many Pentecostal and Holiness denominations have permitted women to enter the ministry since the nineteenth century. The Quakers do not have a clergy, but women were accepted from the very outset as equals in all matters. Among major denominations, the important early landmarks in the renewal of interest in women's ordination during the past fifty years include the embrace of women's ministry by the African Methodist Episcopal Church in 1948 (the AME church today has more female clergy than any other denomination in America) and by the Methodists and Presbyterians in 1956.[7]

Within the eighty-plus Christian denominations that today countenance women's ordination, the debate prior to ultimate acceptance was in many cases divisive and bitter and provided a showcase of sharply etched views. As the Church of England grappled in the 1970s with the issue, one Anglican minister commented, "It is clear that a woman's character and her endowments centre much more normally and obviously upon home and family and she has those quick emotions which enable her to care for and cherish children and make the home happy, although this is not to say that she could never go beyond it." A bishop stated, "The Incarnation was in a male and I believe that it was left to our Lord to represent God."[8] Another cleric professed the view that "a woman offering up the communion offers the sight, the sound, and the smell of perversion."[9] The Church of England, the mother of the worldwide Anglican communion, remains deeply split over women's acceptance into the priesthood, even though the doctrinal matter was formally settled, by two votes in the annual synod, in favor of women's ordination in 1992.

"Biblical feminists," one evangelical theologian, Clark H. Pinnock, has urged, "must stop depicting the traditional view in such dark colors. If it should turn out to be true that God did intend males to exhibit strength in leadership roles and females to excel more as the guardians of society's emotional resources, why would this be viewed ipso facto as an evil arrangement?"[10] The arguments that have been advanced against women's leadership, or at least against such a role as manifested through ordination, have included the fact that Jesus chose only men to be among the Twelve and the contention that because Jesus himself was a man, a male in the priestly role is an "iconic" necessity. The arguments have also included the assertion that for these reasons, the apostles and their successors did not elevate women to an equal ecclesial status, thus instituting a male priesthood "by constant and universal tradition."[11]

A further argument against women in the priesthood comes from an entirely different quarter and theological outlook. An influential group of feminists within Catholicism, including Elisabeth Schüssler Fiorenza, maintains that accepting women as priests and bishops would only reinforce the clerical structures and institutional authoritarianism they detest. In other words, why invest in a fight for the leadership of what Schüssler Fiorenza has called "an elite, male-dominated, sacred, pyramidical order of domination" when the real goal must be to recreate Christianity along radically new lines?[12]

Leaving that particular question aside, we can certainly ask just how constant and universal the tradition of a male-only priesthood has in fact been. In his book *The Ministry of Women in the Early Church*, the Jesuit historian Jean Daneliou states that "there has never been any mention of women filling strictly sacerdotal offices" and goes on to say that "the argument from Scripture and Tradition has an impressive solidity about it."[13] In a book with the same title as Daneliou's another cleric and historian, Roger Gryson, concludes that "there is no evidence . . . that [women in the early church] exercised leadership positions in the community." He adds, "The only duty with which women have been invested is the diaconate."[14]

The copy of Gryson's book that I have read, which came from the Andover-Harvard Theological Library at the Harvard Divinity School, where it can be expected to have received bristling scrutiny, had the words "No! No! No!" scribbled frequently in the margin, and at one point the comment "This is hermeneutics by Gryson, not by Paul." On the title page, in the same hand, as if marking the doorway to indicate the presence of evil spirits, appears the cautionary adjectival cluster "patriarchal/sexist/androcentric."

Gryson seems to be a scholar of painstaking habit and mild-mannered sensibility, not an angry ideologue, but as a number of feminist scholars point out, evidence has existed all along which plainly indicates that the facts about women in the Christian ministry are different from what has long been widely supposed or officially maintained. Elisabeth Schüssler Fiorenza, whatever her views on modern ordination, is one of these scholars. An exponent from a younger generation, as we will see, is Karen Jo Torjesen. In some places and some times, the ecclesial status of at least some women was deemed to be equal to that of even the most exalted men. Evidence for this is to be found, for instance, in some of the letters of Paul, which are the very earliest Christian texts that have come down to us, and in the Acts of the Apostles, attributed to Luke, which purports to describe the Jesus movement during the first years after Jesus' crucifixion. Evidence is also to be found in other ancient documents and in the revelations of archaeology. Additional evidence comes in a peculiarly double-reverse fashion, in the form of official protestations about and condemnations of certain kinds of activities, which merely underscore the fact that such activities were occurring.

Paul mentions many women by name in his epistles. In the epistle to the Romans alone he speaks of Julia, Junia, Mary, Persis, Phoebe, Prisca, Tryphaena, and Tryphosa, and of women identified only as "the mother of Rufus" and "the sister of Nereus." The early Christians, in order to distinguish their activities and offices from those of pagan religions, did not use the standard Latin or Greek terms for "priest" when referring to people who performed priestly responsibilities, and in any event a priesthood with a formal definition and a set of defined procedures for entry did not become established until the third century. However, a number of terms other than "priest" were used to designate the status of various church leaders, and all of these terms are applied to women as well as men. In Romans 16:1–2, Paul writes, employing the same functional title, *diakonos*, that he applies to himself, "I commend to you our sister Phoebe, a deacon of the church at Cenchreae, so that you may receive her in the Lord as befits the saints, and help her in whatever she may require from you, for she has been a helper of many and of myself as well." A little later on in the same passage he writes of a husband and wife, each of whom he designates as "apostle," insisting that the designation is prior to his own: "Greet Andronicus and Junia, my kinsmen and my fellow prisoners; they were prominent among the apostles, and they were in Christ before me." Some missionary pairings, one study suggests, consisted not of a married couple, but of a team of women (Tryphaena and Tryphosa? Martha and Mary?).

It is not that churchmen and exegetes have failed to notice figures such as Phoebe and Junia, Tryphaena and Tryphosa, during all the past centuries of biblical commentary. But the significance of these women has typically been skewed toward irrelevance — "recut," as Mary Rose D'Angelo observes, "by both the writers and the interpreters of the New Testament to fit their ideas about the role and place of women."[15] Sometimes commentators have argued that the titles the women are given simply don't have the meaning they would seem to have, or the meaning they have when applied to men. Perhaps more insidiously, sometimes commentators have argued that while a titular designation is accurate, the person being referred to is not a woman after all.

Phoebe of Cenchreae, whom Elisabeth Schüssler Fiorenza discusses in an article titled "The 'Quilting' of Women's History," fell afoul of the first type of argument. On Paul's behalf, Phoebe carried to Rome the letter that is today called the epistle to the Romans. Some of what is known about her can be derived from what Paul did *not* say about her: remarkably for a woman of this period, as Schüssler Fiorenza points out, she is not defined by association with a husband (if she had one, he is not mentioned) or otherwise by means of gender, such as with the word "virgin" or "widow." The one role that is mentioned is an ecclesial one; as noted, Paul refers to her as *diakonos*, which is not only the same title he gives himself but also the one he gives his intimate coworker, Timothy, and another man, Apollos, mentioned in the same epistle. He also uses it to describe a man named Tychikos, mentioned in the epistle to the Colossians. In all cases save that of Phoebe — in other words, whenever it applies to men — interpreters have seen the title as designating formal ecclesial leadership. Phoebe in addition is referred to as *prostatis*, a benefactor, a word that likewise indicates a position of leadership or patronage in both religious and secular contexts when men are being referred to.

But Phoebe's position has been diminished by male interpreters. Schüssler Fiorenza quotes the words of one scholar who characterized Phoebe as "an apparently well-to-do and charitable lady who because of her feminine virtues worked in the service of the poor and of the sick as well as assisted at the baptism of women." Rather than reading *diakonos* as an indication of parity with that other *diakonos*, Paul, interpreters have read back into it the diminished sense of "deaconess," derived from the separate ecclesial office for women that developed many centuries later. Rather than reading *prostatis* as indicating parity with the functions of bishop and elder, as it does for men in 1 Thessalonians, interpreters have tended to see it very differently when it comes to women. As one of them concludes in his assessment of Phoebe of Cenchreae's status, "There is no reference, then, to a 'patroness.' Women could not take on legal functions, and according to Revelation only in heretical circles do prophetesses seem to have had official ecclesiastical powers of leadership . . . The idea is that of personal care which Paul and others have received at the hand of the deaconess."[16]

The woman named Junia has faced a very different sort of problem — gender theft.[17] Junia was a common female name in the ancient world. Several ancient religious commentators, such as Origen of Alexandria and John Chrysostom — men who would not be held up as protofeminists — assumed as a matter of course that the Junia mentioned in Romans was a woman. ("Indeed," John Chrysostom wrote, "how great the wisdom of this woman must have been that she was even deemed worthy of the title of apostle.") The assumption of Junia's womanhood prevailed until the Middle Ages.

Then a reaction set in. Paul had reserved the title "apostle" for persons of great authority — people who had served as missionaries and had founded churches. To a medieval mind, such people had to have been men; accordingly, Junia underwent a change of sex. Later, Martin Luther popularized a reinterpretation of Junia as Junias, an apparently masculine name — the diminutive, perhaps, as scholars later speculated, of Junianius or Junilius. One problem, though, is that the name Junias cannot be found in antiquity — not in documents, whether secular or religious, and not in inscriptions. One of the great contributions that computers have made to biblical scholarship is the availability on databases of vast quantities of the Latin, Greek, and Hebrew writing that survives from ancient times, including poems and plays, graffiti, gravestone renderings, even grocery lists on papyrus. A search through these sources reveals that Junias does not exist as a name, diminutive or otherwise. All we have is Junia — in this case, the name of a woman "prominent among the apostles."

Yet, the evidence notwithstanding, the editors of a revised volume of the standard Greek text of the New Testament have deleted any reference to the feminine "Junia." The name is not even listed as a variant, to indicate that Junia is an established reading of the original text, regardless of what the editors think of it. "Junias" stands as definitive.[18]

Outside of Scripture, other information suggests a revised picture of clerical reality in the early church. A striking ninth-century mosaic depicting four women can be seen above the doorway to the Zeno Chapel in the Basilica of St. Praxedis in Rome. The Virgin Mary and the saints Pudentiana and Praxedis are three of the women. The fourth, whose square halo is meant to indicate that she was still alive when the mosaic was made, bears the title *episcopa*, meaning bishop, and the name running down the side is Theodora. Actually, the *R* and the *A* in the name have been obliterated, as if someone were trying to disguise the name's feminine character, but the word *episcopa* itself betrays a feminine form, and the person depicted is without question a woman. Was she indeed a bishop? The suggestion has been made that at a time when clerical celibacy was by no means universal, Theodora was the wife of a bishop, but the nature of her head covering suggests that she was unmarried.[19]

There is compelling material from other sources. Recently a translation of an article by an Italian scholar, Giorgio Otranto, titled "Notes on the Female Priesthood in Antiquity," appeared in the *Journal of Feminist Studies in Religion*. Otranto is the director of the Institute of Classical and Christian Studies in Bari, and his article, translated and with a commentary by Mary Ann Rossi, is an analysis of a long letter sent by Pope Gelasius I in A.D. 494 to a number of dioceses in Italy concerning a variety of administrative, organizational, and judicial matters that needed urgent attention. One passage contains a condemnation indicating that, as Otranto shows, the practice of admitting women to the priesthood in these dioceses had become locally unexceptional. Gelasius writes, "Nevertheless we have heard to our annoyance that divine affairs have come to such a low state that women are encouraged to officiate at the sacred altars, and to take part in all matters imputed to the offices of the male sex, to which they do not belong." Otranto concludes, on the basis of a close linguistic investigation and a comparison of the language of this letter with that of other papal documents, that Gelasius is not referring to women's participation in some non-Eucharistic service or to an isolated incident. "In sum," Otranto writes, "we may infer from an analysis of Gelasius's epistle that at the end of the fifth century, some women, having been ordained by bishops, were exercising a true and proper ministerial priesthood in a vast area of southern Italy, as well as perhaps in other unnamed regions of Italy."[20]

Otranto does not stop there. Having established these circumstances to his satisfaction, he reopens the debate over the meaning of the word *presbytera*, the feminine form of *presbyter*, a noun that in the masculine form has always been seen as referring to someone who exercises sacerdotal functions. *Presbytera* is found, for example, on an inscription from the tomb of a woman named Leta in southern Italy, dating to the same time period as the Gelasian epistle, and has hitherto been interpreted as referring to the wife of a *presbyter*, even though the inscription, which mentions the husband, who built the tomb, gives him no such title — an unprecedented omission if he was truly a presbyter. Surely there are now grounds, Otranto argues, for seeing Leta as a *presbytera* in her own right, and grounds too for reevaluating the function of all the other women who have been given the designation *presbytera* in ancient sources.

Otranto jumps ahead to ninth- and tenth-century Italy and a letter written by a bishop named Atto, in Vercelli. The letter reveals that a priest named Ambrose has come to Atto with this question: how should the words *presbytera* and *diacona*, which the priest has come across in ancient church writings and knows to have a feminine connotation, be understood? As Otranto notes, Atto's response "leaves no room for doubt." His reply, in part, goes as follows:

> Hence since your wisdom has determined that we ought to decide whether to understand "priestess" or "deaconness" in the canons, it seems to me that since in the primitive Church, according to the holy word, "many are the crops and few the laborers," for the helping of men even religious women were ordained caretakers in the holy Church. This is something that blessed Paul points out in his epistle to the Romans when he says, "I commend to you my sister Phoebe, who is in the ministry of the church that is in Cenchreae." One understands this because then not only men, but also women were in charge of the Churches . . . This practice c. 11 of the Laodicean Council later prohibits when it says that it is not allowed for those women who are called "priests" or "those presiding" to be ordained in the Churches.[21]

Many of the issues involving women and the Christian ministry are taken up by Karen Jo Torjesen in her book *When Women Were Priests* (1993). I spent an afternoon with Torjesen one autumn day at her home in Claremont, California, in the shadow of the San Gabriel Mountains, and in her nearby office at the Institute for Antiquity and Christianity, on the Claremont Graduate University campus. The institute is lodged in a handsome mansion of whitewashed brick, inconspicuous among Claremont's other tidy outposts set within a broad landscape of manicured serenity. In the front hallway a breakfront holds ancient ceramics — an amphora and some bowls, a spray of potsherds — and a complete set of the *Nag Hammadi Library in English*. On some of the walls hang lugubrious sepia portraits of bearded old men, eminent theologians and biblical scholars of the past. They present a startling contrast with Karen Torjesen herself, who is youthful and athletic and in full color, with a southern Californian cast to her features.

Torjesen today is the Margo L. Goldsmith Professor of Women's Studies and Religion at Claremont, a chair that was created and endowed by the eponymous benefactor, a wealthy real-estate executive, to support the first master's degree program in women's studies and religion. Torjesen's pathway into her field of study is in some ways highly unusual and in other ways completely ordinary.

The unusual part has been Torjesen's lifelong openness to varieties of religious and social experience. Her childhood was not typical of childhood in postwar America. As an experiment in what today would be called alternative lifestyle, Torjesen's parents moved the family to Central America for several years, beginning in the early 1950s. The formative religious influence in Torjesen's life was her mother, and as a girl she was deeply involved with a conservative Baptist church. In high school in Elk Grove, California, she became active with the Nazarenes, another conservative denomination (though one of the first to ordain women). In college she associated with the charismatics, and afterward in Germany with the Lutherans. Subsequently she became involved with the Episcopalians; after that with various strains of house-church worship, and then with experiments in gendercentric religion that would fall under the broad rubric Woman-Church, which refers to feminist faith communities that may or may not have links with established religious bodies.

Torjesen's career aspirations have been equally peripatetic. She earned her undergraduate degree from evangelical Wheaton College in Illinois, where she majored in chemistry with the intention of becoming a doctor and a medical missionary. That plan was deflected (permanently, it turned out) by her husband's educational commitments. Torjesen found herself in Claremont, where eventually she undertook graduate work in the history of the early church, studying with (among others) James M. Robinson, the man who has guided the Nag Hammadi project. Her initial motivation was the conceit that the further back one goes in church history — "right to the precipice of the origins," as she once described to me the destination of her ambitions — the closer one might get to some sort of pure, distilled version of Christianity. In truth, she found, as others too have found, that the further back one goes, the more confusing and diverse the picture actually becomes.

Torjesen's expectation on finishing her doctorate was not to pursue a university career per se; the competition for jobs was simply too intense. She hoped instead to secure a position at a place like the school of theology at the Melodyland Christian Center in Anaheim, California, an evangelical worship complex founded by the charismatic preacher Ralph Wilkerson. It was at this moment that a *deus ex machina* entered her life, in the form of Ekkehard Muhlenberg, a professor of religion at Claremont, who was about to return to Germany after a ten-year academic sojourn in California to take up a chair at the University of Göttingen. Muhlenberg invited Torjesen to become his assistant, and Torjesen found the offer impossible to refuse. For all its institutionalized misogyny, German scholarship has long been a source of new thinking and a cause of continual ferment on religious issues (recall Wilfrid Sheed's memorable image: "Another theologian comes grunting out of the Black Forest"). Five years in the university culture of Germany gave Torjesen a solid academic pedigree and placed her in an entirely new scholarly trajectory.

There was as yet no detectable feminist element in her work, although Torjesen even then would unequivocally have described herself as a feminist in a personal sense, if you had asked. When she returned from Germany, she took an academic position at Mary Washington College in Fredericksburg, Virginia — a position that became open owing to the serendipitous departure of a professor named Elizabeth Clark, who was among the first wave of religion scholars to write on feminist themes. Clark, who was moving to Duke University (where she remains), had been teaching a course called "Women's Sexuality and the Western Religious Tradition," which ran from the ancient Greeks up through the Vatican's 1976 statement on women's ordination. Torjesen inherited this course.

"It was at this point that my research began to shift," Torjesen says. "I had taught a course in Germany on the church orders, which are manuals for regulating church office and discipline, covering about five centuries. In the first paper I did after coming back from Germany, I looked at women as they appeared across these texts. I was aware, having just come back into the States, of the debate on women's ordination in the American context, and in those debates often the contents of the church orders were being pointed to, which made me realize that I had a research base from which to enter into the discussion." Fredericksburg is not far from Washington, D.C., and Torjesen traveled once a week to Dumbarton Oaks for its collection of early Christian materials and for the irenic glory of its architectural and botanical environment.

Following her husband back to southern California, Torjesen then found herself, somewhat improbably, at the very conservative Fuller Theological Seminary in Pasadena, which was being urged by some of its more liberal denominational constituents, such as the Presbyterians and Methodists, to bring more women onto the faculty. Although the full story scarcely bears repeating, there ensued the sort of episode that gives academe a reputation for pettiness and vindictiveness; its elements included Torjesen's dismissal, an ensuing period of protracted contention, and an eventual apology to Torjesen from the seminary. By then, through James Robinson, Torjesen had become reaffiliated with Claremont. Soon afterward, Margo L. Goldsmith, who had planned to endow a chair in women's studies at Fuller, decided to endow one at Claremont instead. "By the end of that experience," Torjesen says now, "I felt pretty broken and bloody. I identify my becoming a political feminist from that time — it was a very radicalizing experience. Feminism then became not only my research agenda but also a political agenda."

Torjesen's book *When Women Were Priests* is very much a work of careful scholarship, but it also unfurls a banner under which the committed can march. A handsome color reproduction of the "Theodora Episcopa" mosaic adorns its cover. The book is at once academically solid and persistently assertive in its outlook; it reminds you at times of a nineteenth-century reformer's brief, with its implicit confidence in what calm reason and straightforward truth can accomplish. Even so, it does not shy away from discussions of "the goddess" or the use of phrases like "the construction of gender." Torjesen herself seems to embody a conviction in the omnicompatibility of ameliorating zeal; "All reform is interdependent," as Elizabeth Cady Stanton observed. *When Women Were Priests* strikes an interdependent note in the six-point type on the copyright page, which states that "Harper San Francisco and the author, in association with the Rainforest Action Network, will facilitate the planting of two trees for every one tree used in the manufacture of this book."

In her book Torjesen makes a number of points about women in the formative years of Christianity that have been amplified and confirmed by others. She notes that the Christians, like the Jews, saw the role of prophet as heedless of gender lines. In Acts 2:17–18, Peter quotes the prophet Joel: "I will pour out my Spirit upon all flesh, and your sons and your daughters shall prophesy . . . And on my servants and my maidservants in those days I will pour out my Spirit; and they shall prophesy." The New Testament texts contain a number of allusions to prophetic speech by women. Women were extraordinarily active and assertive in the early Christian community at Corinth, to judge from Paul's two letters addressed to it, and in fact disputes arose over the proper comportment of women. The precise nature of this contention, along with its broader sociological and theological setting, is a subject that has been examined in detail by many scholars, notably Antoinette Clark Wire in *The Corinthian Women Prophets.* The reconstruction and interpretation of the developments in Corinth is itself a contentious matter, opening up as it does a complicated discussion about the sexual worldview and the whole pattern of gender relations in the ancient world. It is important to note that although Paul in 1 Corinthians clearly states that women should wear veils when prophesying (a position for which he provides chaotic supporting arguments), he nowhere attempts to suppress women's prophesying, and he nowhere questions its legitimacy. One way to understand the Corinthian situation is simply as follows: the social mores of the Greco-Roman world may demand certain proprieties, but a higher law confers privileges that transcend gender and that must be affirmed.[22]

Furthermore, Torjesen writes, it was not at all unusual in the ancient world for women to assume the leadership of voluntary, civic, even religious institutions; therefore, the role of *patrona* in the Christian community should not be surprising. As Torjesen notes, "The church took its cue from society's leadership models."[23] In the role of patron, women in the Roman world often wielded power in a public sphere, beyond the household realm where their authority was established and where it was in many respects confined. Livia, the wife of the emperor Augustus, might be an extreme example, given the opportunities afforded by her exalted status and great wealth, but many women of far lesser means enjoyed a public influence made possible by their active support of diverse activities (helping to secure citizenship and appointments; providing dowries; endowing civic and religious organizations). Torjesen, the Margo L. Goldsmith Professor of Women's Studies, needs no lesson on the uses or value of patronage, or on the manner in which patronage can facilitate opportunities for women where none previously existed. The dedication in her book reads: "For Margo L. Goldsmith, a patron of women, a friend of scholars, a founder of the Women's Studies in Religion program at Claremont." Torjesen herself comments somewhat drily, when asked about the subject of patronage and her career, "I was learning about patronage while I was writing about it."

As we have seen, a degree of egalitarianism in the area of gender, at least as compared with the dominant mores of significant segments of the larger society, was characteristic of the Jesus movement. The earliest Christian worship communities were also gathered together by particular households, where they assembled for prayer and liturgy, and it was within the individual household that women in both the Judaic and the Greco-Roman world exercised the most power. At Capernaum, on the northern shore of the Sea of Galilee, excavated remains are visible under a hideous modern church of flying-saucer design. These remains are those of the primitive chapel that grew organically out of a one-room place of worship inside the house of Peter — a classic house-church.[24] Lydia of Thyatira, who was converted by Paul in the city of Philippi, is described in Acts 16:14–15 as having been baptized together with her household, "household" meaning her servants and slaves and perhaps also, because Acts describes her as "a seller of purple goods," her employees. Lydia puts her domain at Paul's disposal — "'If you have judged me to be faithful to the Lord, come to my house and stay.' And she prevailed upon us" — and it becomes, surely, the nucleus of a house-church community.

The figure of Lydia offers another useful example of an "information tel," a seemingly unprepossessing site until someone actually digs into it. The scriptural references to Lydia are fleeting, yet they contain clues to a story that can be greatly elaborated if you have the determination to probe beneath the surface features. The Brazilian feminist scholar Ivoni Richter Reimer has done just this for Lydia and a number of other women whose circumstances she attempts to reconstruct in her book *Women in the Acts of the Apostles.* The setting of the passage in Acts (16:13–15) is the city of Philippi, in Macedonia, and the text reads as follows:

> We remained in this city some days; and on the sabbath day we went outside the gate to the riverside, where we supposed there was a place of prayer; and we sat down and spoke to the women who had come together. One who heard us was a woman named Lydia, from the city of Thyatira, a seller of purple goods, who was a worshipper of God. The Lord opened her heart to give heed to what was said by Paul. And when she was baptized, with her household, she besought us, saying, "If you have judged me to be faithful to the Lord, come to my house and stay." And she prevailed upon us.

What might we say of this Lydia? Her name, to begin with, is the type known as an ethnicon, a name denoting an ethnic origin — in this case a person from Lydia, an area of what is now western Turkey and famous in ancient times for its dense commercial activity. (The Lydians are credited with having invented coinage.) Having an ethnicon for a name probably means that at some point in her life Lydia had been a slave and that her name had been bestowed impersonally, on the basis of a characteristic. Lydia, we are told, comes from Thyatira, a city that was well known for its textile industry. A considerable literature survives about the trade in purple goods, in which she was involved. The description of Lydia as a "worshipper of God" connects her also with the group of people known as the "God-fearers," designating Gentiles who were attracted to Jewish religion. The God-fearers were predominantly women.[25]

Where is the action of the story taking place? The word used for "place of prayer," Reimer establishes, means a synagogue whenever it is used in a Jewish context — in communities throughout Asia Minor —

and the synagogue would in all likelihood have been a focal point of community life in general. It would appear, then, that the women who had "come together" for prayer were participating matter-of-factly in the regular Sabbath synagogue service — a point of some importance, because scholars long took it for granted that women did not routinely participate in such services at this time. The synagogue is described as lying "outside the gate" and along "the riverside," facts that not only tell us where the Jews may have lived but also strengthen the link to the purple trade, since the cloth-dying business was dirty work that produced foul odors and required large amounts of water.

In attempting to flesh out Lydia of Thyatira and her circumstances, Reimer draws on a variety of literary and inscriptional evidence that is independent of Scripture. For example, in attempting to assess the social role of a synagogue in the Jewish community's broader life, she examines some water bills on papyrus for the Egyptian city of Arsinoë from the end of the second century B.C. These bills indicate that the synagogue was paying more for water than the local baths were, and prompt Reimer's surmise that the synagogue fountains served as the main water source for the entire Jewish community. When Schüssler Fiorenza used the word "quilting" in the title of her article about Phoebe of Cenchreae, she was referring to the fact that history, especially women's history, often amounts to a patchwork fashioned from whatever unlikely materials happen to be available. Lydia's story, like Phoebe's, must be quilted together.

"We are moving beyond the monopoly of text, of sacred text, as the only source of knowledge," Torjesen says. "We can use other documentary sources. We can use art and architecture. More and more scholars are willing to use a wide variety of materials. A second thing that is happening is methodological — the development of gender analysis, which relies on sociology and anthropology and critical theory. That kind of perspective is emerging because we are increasingly aware of living in a multicultural world. We can no longer refer everything to one central, dominant culture. We have to be able to articulate each culture in terms of its internal dynamics and coherence."

I asked Torjesen whether any of her peers — men and women with her training and status, with her interest in ancient religion — still entertain real doubts that women were exercising leadership roles, including clerical roles, in early Christian times.

"There are scholars with very conservative religious commitments who probably still resist," Torjesen replied. "One encounters it more in the form of private reservations than of real scholarly discussions. I'm sure a minority viewpoint could be articulated. But there isn't anyone that I know of who has, in writing, addressed this vast new body of literature — the research that has built up over the past ten years or so. There isn't anybody that I know of who has argued a counterposition."

Karen Torjesen's spacious and airy second-floor office at the Institute for Antiquity and Christianity was formerly occupied by a scholar named Bernadette Brooten, who after several years of teaching at Claremont went on to the Harvard Divinity School and from there moved to a full professorship at Brandeis University. Brooten was once a student, at Tübingen, of the "Jesus Was a Feminist" author Leonard Swidler, and she was also a research assistant there for the theologian Hans Küng. She is the author of the Junia study mentioned earlier. Over the years Brooten has been a mentor to many young women. The sense of a rapidly proliferating network in the field of women and religion, and extending beyond, is at once palpable and hardly surprising. It is a development that on occasion elicits dark speculation from conservative critics. "The feminist movement," writes Donna Steichen in her book *Ungodly Rage*, "has been astonishingly successful in occupying the official structures of the national churches in the West — notably in northern Europe, Canada, and the United States — like so many hermit crabs (even more like jays, who destroy the eggs and young of other birds in order to inhabit nests they did not build)."[26]

A capsule summary of the implications of Brooten's earliest research might read like this: with respect to roles played by women, there was more differentiation inside Judaism in the Greco-Roman world than many scholars acknowledge. This touches once again on a sensitive issue. Some scholars, particularly those who want a liberalization of

Christian church policies concerning women, have argued that if early Christianity fell short of an egalitarian ideal, it was in part because of the nature of the Jewish world out of which Christianity emerged. Christianity might have produced more women leaders, one argument runs, if only there had been more in Judaism. Brooten believes that the spectrum of practices deemed tolerable among Jews in ancient times was broad and diverse, just as Judaism today, like Christianity today, is far from monolithic. Indeed, she argues, we can actually be more confident that Christian women like Phoebe and Prisca and Lydia occupied positions of authority because we know that a significant number of Jewish women who were their contemporaries also did. Women leaders of the synagogue were, of course, always the exception, but, Brooten states, it is wrong to see the emergence of women leaders in Christianity, likewise a minority, as entirely unprecedented.

In her doctoral dissertation, later published in book form as *Women Leaders in the Ancient Synagogue*, Brooten considered nineteen carved inscriptions dating from as early as 27 B.C. to as late as the sixth century A.D., in which Jewish women are accorded official titles relating to the communal life of a synagogue, titles such as "head of the synagogue," "leader," "elder," "mother of the synagogue," "priest." Thus we encounter, in Crete, "Sophia of Gortyn, elder and head of the synagogue," and in Rome, "Veturia Paulla, consigned to her eternal home, . . . mother of the synagogues of Campus and Volumnius," and again in Rome, "Here lies Gaudentia, priest, aged 24 years." From a Jewish cemetery in Tell el-Yahudiyyeh, in Lower Egypt, comes this inscription: "O Marin, priest, good and a friend to all, causing pain to no one and friendly to your neighbors, farewell! [She died at the age of] approximately fifty years, in the third year of Caesar [Augustus], on the thirteenth day of Payni [= June 7, 28 B.C.]."[27]

Titles like "priest" and "head of the synagogue," when applied to women, have long been interpreted as honorific rather than functional. Consider the inscription on a marble plaque found in Smyrna, from the second century A.D.: "Rufina, a Jewess, head of the synagogue, built this tomb for her freed slaves and the slaves raised in her house." The traditional view has been that Rufina, the "head of the synagogue," or

THE WORD ACCORDING TO EVE / 192

archisynagogos, had no real functional authority and was in all likelihood merely the wife of the true *archisynagogos*.[28] Scholars regarded Rufina as having been awarded the title, Brooten wryly notes, *"honoris causa."* In dense, meticulous arguments, Brooten mounts an assault on that view. She takes up the cases of Rufina, Marin, Sophia, Veturia Paulla, Gaudentia, and other Jewish women and exposes what she sees as the flawed suppositions and tortured reasoning necessary to conclude that their titles were not functional.

In the case of one woman, a person named Jael, who is referred to in an inscription from Aphrodisias in Asia Minor as the presiding officer or patron of a synagogue, Brooten takes on the contention that the name Jael did not belong to a woman at all.[29] Jael of Aphrodisias has what might be thought of as a Junia problem. As Brooten points out, the only reason the question of gender comes up at all is that an important title is attached to the name and the name sits on top of a list of other names, all of which are male. In less politically charged circumstances, this Jael would simply have been assumed to be a woman. "Jael" was and is a well-known woman's name. Jael — the famous Jael who drives a tent peg through the head of Sisera — is prominent in Judges. But a number of contemporary scholars have hunted through Scripture and other ancient sources to see if they can find a precedent for a Jael who is a man, because it seems to them so unlikely that this Jael could have been a woman. In some manuscripts of the Book of Ezra, as it appears in the Septuagint, they have found a Jael in a list of male exiles who had married foreign women and repudiated them on their return to Israel. This identification remains highly speculative, however. The Septuagint, remember, is the Greek version of originally Hebrew texts, and the transliteration of Semitic names from Hebrew into Greek is haphazard and inconsistent. What this means, Brooten explains, is that to accept Jael as a man's name, we have to accept an example that may be nothing more than an artifact of transliteration. We have to prefer this explanation to the evident fact that Jael has historically been a woman's name and is attested to in a major book of the Bible (where the name occurs six times), where it belongs to a well-known figure whose story was probably a staple of synagogue readings.

"All of which," Brooten says, "raises several questions for me. How many women do there have to have been for there to have been *any*? And if it's part of the marginalization of women that women are very rarely leaders to begin with, then even in those circumstances in which women do occur as leaders, they may be either perceived as not being women or perceived as not being leaders." Brooten imagines a day far in the future when scholars will confront a document that lists the names of Prime Minister Margaret Thatcher and the members of one of her all-male cabinets. It would only be a matter of time, she speculates, before some scholar came along and pronounced Thatcher herself a man.

Brooten can be playful, but she readily acknowledges how thin our knowledge of ancient behavior and ways of thinking sometimes is, and how vast the gulf is between our own culture and the cultures of the ancient world that we are trying to understand. How confident can we be, I asked her once, that we are reconstructing something trustworthy about the dynamics of *then*? "That's something I think about all the time," she replied. And then she laughed. "I've often had this thought: that I'll die and go to heaven, and Rufina will meet me, and I'll greet her as *archisynagogos*. And she'll say, "*Archisynagogos*? Nah. That was just my husband's title."

Chapter Ten

....

VENUS IN
SACKCLOTH

*Jesus said to her, "Woman, why are you weeping? Whom do
you seek?" Supposing him to be the gardener, she said to him,
"Sir, if you have carried him away, tell me where you have
laid him, and I will take him away." Jesus said to her,
"Mary." She turned and said to him in Hebrew,
"Rabboni" (which means Teacher).*
— *John 20:15–16*

*Are we to turn about and all listen to her?
Did he prefer her to us?*
— *Gospel of Mary*

ONE OF THE ROUTES that Jesus would have taken when he traveled
from his home town of Nazareth to his adopted city of Capernaum, as
described in Matthew 4:12–14, led north toward the village of Cana and
then eastward across the plain of Azotis and through the Valley of the
Doves toward the Sea of Galilee. At the Sea of Galilee, the overland
route from the west met the great Via Maris, the ancient highway that
linked the civilization of Egypt with that of Mesopotamia. For a stretch
the Via Maris followed the western shore of the Sea of Galilee, and its
path defines the modern highway.

At the intersection of the overland route and the Via Maris, under the
rugged face of Mount Arbel, there once lay a fishing town called Magdala. In Aramaic the word *magdala* means "tower," and the remains of a
tower can be seen near the waterfront at Magdala today. The Greek
name for the town was Tarichaea, which means "dried fish." Magdala
was long a fishing center, and even now you can see fishermen in their
lighted boats, plying the sea at night in search of sardines and of a catch
known locally as Saint Peter's fish. The name is derived, some argue,

from a story (Matthew 17:24–27) in which Jesus advises Peter on how to find the means to pay the Temple tax: "Go to the sea and cast a hook, and take the first fish that comes up, and when you open its mouth you will find a shekel; take that and give it to them for me and yourself."[1]

Of course, the name may also have been associated with the Galilean fish simply because Peter was a fisherman in Galilee. Not far from Magdala, during the severe drought of 1986, a two-thousand-year-old fishing boat was discovered in the mud when the waters of the Sea of Galilee dramatically receded. It is today on display at Kibbutz Ginosar.[2] The boat is typical of the kind that the apostles Peter, James, and John would have used as they fished the lake. All it seems to need, you may think while contemplating the boat, is a sign saying "Zebedee & Sons."

Or perhaps the true story of the boat is a darker one. The only "naval battle" fought during the Great Revolt of the Jews against the Romans occurred off the shores of Magdala in A.D. 67, when a small Roman flotilla under the commander Titus (the same Titus who destroyed Jerusalem a few years later) pursued and destroyed a ragtag and miserably equipped assemblage of boats occupied by fleeing rebels who had no safe place to land on shore. There were no survivors. "And a terrible stink, and a very sad sight there was on the following days over that country," the chronicler Josephus wrote, "for as for the shores, they were full of shipwrecks, and of dead bodies all swelled . . . This was the upshot of the sea-fight."[3] Of the inhabitants of Magdala who were not killed, most were sent as slaves to help dig the emperor Nero's abortive canal across the Isthmus of Corinth. The synagogue was turned into a fish-pond.

When an irritable Mark Twain visited Magdala in 1867, he found a poor Arab village, "thoroughly ugly, and cramped, squalid, uncomfortable, and filthy — just the style of cities that have adorned the country since Adam's time, as all writers have labored hard to prove, and have succeeded."[4] In a tone of feigned bemusement that fails to camouflage arch disdain, Twain claimed to admire the designs formed upon the house walls with camel dung. Today a visitor will find on the site only vacation bungalows, and nearby a new Israeli farming community, somewhat inland, named Migdal.

And yet you cannot pass, or at least I could not pass, the road signs for

Migdal on Route 90 north out of Tiberias without thinking of the person whose name they conjure: Mary of Magdala, that is, Mary Magdalene, one of the most prominent followers of Jesus, who either was born in or made her home in Magdala. The Mary Magdalene of legend is one of the more remarkable female phenomena deriving from Scripture, her reputation and symbolism in subsequent ages held up by a rickety scaffolding of interpretation erected upon a meager foundation of text. Her career — follower of Jesus, witness to the crucifixion and burial of Jesus, first among the disciples to see the empty tomb, reputed prostitute, presumed rival of the apostle Peter, exemplar both of lust and of the power of repentance — comes readily to mind when feminist biblical scholars consider the fate of Scripture in the hands of men.

One place to begin looking for Mary Magdalene is in a storage room at the Yale University Art Gallery in New Haven, where the earliest extant depiction of her image has been preserved. It is a damaged fresco from the wall of an ancient house-church discovered in 1929 in the ruins of a place known as Dura Europos, a caravan center and fortified city on a bluff above the Euphrates River, amid the desert of what is now Syria. The fresco shows Mary and two other women approaching what is presumably the tomb of Jesus. Each woman holds a torch in one hand (it is early morning, before dawn) and a bowl of spices for anointing Jesus' body in the other. They are depicted, in other words, as "myrrophores," bearers of myrrh, an exotic spice that could be mixed with oil. Myrrophore is one of those wonderful occupational categories that seem to exist only in scholarly recapitulations of the biblical world. In the Yale fresco, Mary and the other myrrophores, dressed in white, emerge from a dark background, their faces illuminated by the torches.[5]

The Dura Europos painting dates back, at the latest, to the first half of the third century A.D. This can be said with certainty, because Dura Europos was destroyed by the Persians in about A.D. 256 and was never reoccupied or rebuilt. That the fresco survived as successfully as it did is owed to the fact that the city's rubble filled up many interior spaces and acted in effect as a preservative. The event being depicted is one that is described in all four of the Gospels, at greatest length and detail in the Gospel of John (20:1). "Now on the first day of the week," the account begins, "Mary Magdalene came to the tomb early, while it was still dark, and saw that the stone had been taken away from the tomb." Mary was coming with myrrh: there had been no time to prepare the body of Jesus with ointment prior to burial, because the Sabbath was drawing nigh. No description exists in any scriptural texts of the Resurrection itself; the discovery of the empty tomb by Mary and her companions thus becomes the closest that human testimony can approach to the defining moment of Christianity. From the beginning, Christians have been unable or unwilling to forget that Mary Magdalene, a woman, was the first to arrive.

After the figure of Mary the mother of Jesus, there may be no feminine New Testament image more frequently portrayed in Christian iconography than that of Mary Magdalene. The depiction that inhabits my own memory most vividly is the wooden statue by Donatello that today stands in the Museo dell'Opera del Duomo, in Florence. This is not Mary the witness to the empty tomb but Mary the ravaged slattern, her face pocked with age and hollowed by sin, her hair stringy and gnarled, her torn tunic hanging loosely from a malnourished frame, her hands about to join each other in penitent supplication. It epitomizes the fallen woman redeemed. But just across the River Arno, in the Pitti Palace, hangs a very different Mary, Titian's Mary, full-bodied and sensuous and still capable of physical love, though her red-rimmed eyes are raised to heaven and beseech forgiveness. And then we regard the Mary of Caravaggio, a complex woman, richly dressed, obviously strong, caught at a moment of transition between two lives and seemingly uncertain as to whether she truly wishes to see the error of her ways. Four centuries later, Martin Scorsese gave us, in the film *The Last Temptation of Christ*, his version of Nikos Kazantzakis's Mary, the village whore — "proud-gaited, high-rumped Magdalene, her breasts exposed, lips and cheeks covered with makeup."[6] It is for this Magdalene that the crucified Jesus, in a dream, descends from the cross, and it is to this Magdalene that, in the Scorsese film, he makes love. "The thing that fascinated me about Mary Magdalene," the actress Barbara Hershey, who played the role, once explained, "is that she represents all aspects of womanhood: she's a whore and a victim, a complete primal animal, and then she's reborn and becomes virginal and sister-like."[7]

So prominently does Mary Magdalene loom in the popular imagination that it is easy to forget that all the original information about her takes up no more than a few hundred words spread among the four Gospels, recounting only a handful of distinct episodes. In the Gospel of Mark (15:40–41), she appears for the first time in the aftermath of the Crucifixion, with these words: "There were also women looking on from afar, among whom were Mary Magdalene and Mary the mother of James the younger and of Joses, and Salome, who, when he was in Galilee, followed him, and administered to him." Later, in the so-called longer ending of Mark, whose relationship to the rest of the text remains a matter of some doubt, Jesus after his resurrection is said to appear first to Mary, although her testimony is not at first believed by the other disciples. In the Gospel of Matthew (27:55–56), Mary Magdalene is likewise present at the Crucifixion. Upon arriving at Jesus' tomb to anoint his body after the Sabbath, she finds the tomb empty. The empty-tomb tradition is also related in the Gospels of Luke and John; in John, Mary actually encounters the risen Jesus, whom she mistakes for a gardener. Apart from her presence at the Crucifixion and at the empty tomb, Mary Magdalene is mentioned in the Gospels in only one other passage, Luke 8:1–3, the important moment when she is introduced: "The twelve were with him, and also some women who had been healed of evil spirits and infirmities: Mary, called Magdalene, from whom seven demons had gone out, and Joanna, the wife of Chuza, Herod's steward, and Susanna, and many others, who provided for them out of their means."

These fragments represent everything that is indisputably revealed in the Gospels about Mary. It is not said or even intimated that Mary Magdalene is a sexual libertine or a carnal entrepreneur. How and when did this connection come about? As the New Testament scholar Jane Schaberg has put the question, how did Mary Magdalene become a whore?

There are several ways to respond. One narrow answer begins with the Gospels themselves. As noted, conceivably the first fixed image of Mary Magdalene in the Christian imagination is as the original witness, if not to the Resurrection of Jesus itself, then to the core circumstances, whatever they were, in which the Resurrection stories are embedded. In the Gospel of Matthew, Mary Magdalene and "the other Mary" come upon an angel at the tomb, who tells them that Jesus "has risen." In the shorter ending of Mark the events described are similar, with "a young man, in . . . a white robe" revealing the news to Mary Magdalene, to Mary the mother of James, and to Salome, who have come to the tomb to anoint the body; in the longer ending, the women take the news to the other disciples and at first are repeatedly disbelieved. In Luke, it is likewise Mary Magdalene and a group of other women who divulge their experience at the tomb to the male disciples, and again their story is dismissed. The same progression from female witness through female testimony to male responsorial doubt occurs in the Gospel of John; the apostle Peter, though, runs to the tomb to see for himself and, having achieved what Augustine would later call "ocular proof," deigns finally to accept what the women have told him: "Then Simon Peter came . . . and he went into the tomb; he saw the linen cloths lying, and the napkin, which had been on his head, not lying with the linen cloths but lying rolled up in a place by itself" (John 20:6–7). John adds the telling detail that when Jesus makes himself known once again in person, it is not to Peter but to Mary.

Mary Magdalene is the common element in all the Gospel accounts of the events surrounding the Resurrection. Because Mary reported the empty tomb to the disciples, she became known among some early Christian writers as *apostola apostolorum* ("apostle of the apostles"). This is the ancient Mary celebrated on the wall of the house-church at Dura Europos. Another early view of Mary is as the symbolic New Eve, for whereas the disobedience of the original Eve in the Garden of Eden, as some commentators would have it, brought about the fall, so Mary's recognition of the "gardener" as the resurrected Jesus marks the advent of redemption. The role of New Eve, however, came with an accretion of certain additional elements, for the very idea of Eve in some minds summoned up the notion of sin, and in some minds the very idea of redemption summoned up the notion of repentance.

It is not always easy when attempting to disentangle popular folkways and an official worldview to establish which serves as the vine and which as the trellis. But Mary Magdalene, as specifically articulated by name in a limited number of important Gospel references, became conflated over the years with other Gospel figures of doubtful reputation.[8]

Some of the most memorable imagery involving Mary Magdalene in the Gospels relates to her as a person who goes to anoint the body of Jesus after his death. But Mary Magdalene is not the only woman associated with the act of anointing. In Matthew 26:6–13 and in Mark 14:3–9, Jesus, not many days before his arrest and crucifixion, is given dinner at the home of Simon the Leper (rather, "Simon, a man who had leprosy," as the *Inclusive Language Lectionary* prefers it), where an unnamed woman comes to him with an alabaster jar and, causing scandal by using an expensive perfume that might have cost a typical laborer a year's wages, proceeds to anoint his head. The disciples object strenuously to this extravagance, but Jesus quiets them and explains that the anointing is in advance of and in preparation for his own burial. Not coincidentally, anointing is also biblical imagery associated with the designation of an Israelite king. That thematic echo, linking this unnamed woman's activities and Mary Magdalene's later role, is reinforced by John's version of the same story (12:1–3). Here the dinner is said to take place at the home of Lazarus, whom Jesus had raised from the dead, and the woman with the ointment is in fact given the name Mary. She anoints the feet of Jesus, not his head. Although this Mary, as clearly stated, is Mary of Bethany, the sister of Lazarus and Martha, and not Mary of Magdala, evidence from Christian writings suggests that a blurring of Mary Magdalene and the woman who performs the anointing of Jesus began at a very early date.

The association of Mary Magdalene and the act of anointing leads to an even more provocative passage. In Luke 7:36–50, Jesus is dining at the home of a Pharisee — that is, a Jew who would tend to take the demands of purity and the rituals of religious observance very seriously — and, as in John's account, a woman anoints his feet and kisses them and dries them with her hair. The woman, this time unnamed, is now identified as being from "the city" and "a sinner," and Jesus in the end forgives the woman her sins, saying that "your faith has saved you."

Nowhere is the nature of her sin specified, although a sexual aspect is unmistakably suggested. Jesus' willingness to accept the woman's ministrations, when he should have known (the Pharisee thinks to himself) "what kind of woman this is who is touching him," is meant to signal his defilement, at least in the opinion of those Pharisees present.

And, of course, it is explicitly stated that Mary Magdalene is a woman of some means — she is one of the three women who "provided for [Jesus and the disciples] out of their resources" — and that she has had seven demons cast out of her. The origin of those resources and the nature of those demons have always been a source of suggestive speculation, no less now than in the past. Jane Schaberg recalls once giving a paper on the subject of Mary Magdalene and listening afterward to a professor at the meeting comment that the woman-of-means passage points strongly toward Mary's career on the streets, because "How else could a *woman* be *wealthy?*"[9]

To the equation "Mary Magdalene equals woman-with-ointment equals prostitute" can be added two more elements: the story in John 8:1–11 of the unnamed woman caught in the act of adultery (whose life Jesus saves with the words, "Let him who is without sin among you be the first to throw a stone at her"), and the story in John 4:8–29 of the unnamed Samaritan woman who is living with a man not her husband (and who spreads a report among Samaritans of her encounter with Jesus, after proclaiming, "I know that the Messiah is coming"). It is also perhaps not irrelevant that Magdala, Mary Magdalene's town, though not in Samaria, was associated in some quarters with licentious behavior.[10]

The link connecting all these elements, establishing that from then on there would in effect be three or more persons in one Mary, was finally forged by no less an authority than the pope. A modern visitor to the great Basilica of San Clemente in Rome first enters not the imperial-era basilica but the magnificent medieval structure erected after the Norman sack of Rome in A.D. 1084. Several other levels deep beneath this church preserve, among other things, an ancient shrine to the Mithras cult and the remains of the homes of some wealthy Romans from the first century A.D., including the home of the family of Clement,

the third pope, which was turned into a house-church after Clement's
martyrdom. Directly below the present basilica lies the vast expanse of
the original one, built in the late fourth century and rediscovered in the
nineteenth. This structure is the oldest Christian basilica that still exists
in Rome in fully recognizable fashion.[11] Here, in September of 591,
Pope Gregory the Great — formerly the monk known as Hildebrand,
and the man who sent Augustine of Canterbury to Britain — delivered
himself of an opinion on the matter of Mary Magdalene that has resonated down the ages. "She whom Luke calls the sinful woman, whom
John calls Mary," Gregory said in his homily, "we believe to be the Mary
from whom seven devils were ejected according to Mark. And what did
these seven devils signify, if not all the vices? . . . It is clear, brothers, that
the woman previously used the unguent to perfume her flesh in forbidden acts. What she therefore displayed more scandalously, she was now
offering to God in a more praiseworthy manner . . . She turned the mass
of her crimes to virtues, in order to serve God entirely in penance, for as
much as she had wrongly held God in contempt."[12]

The typology of Mary Magdalene that was given official sanction by
Pope Gregory the Great has dominated the Western tradition, in art and
commentary, ever since. (For the record, and for what it is worth, the
Roman Catholic Church in 1969 officially overruled Gregory's declaration.) But a very different conception of Mary Magdalene once flourished, a conception that seems to have been suppressed. Relics of its
memory reappeared by accident beginning about a century ago, in
Egypt.

The first relic was a codex, a manuscript bound into book form, that
materialized more or less out of nowhere and was suddenly offered for
sale in Cairo in 1896. Nothing about the provenance of this codex is
known. It was bought by the German scholar Carl Schmidt and removed to Berlin, where it acquired the Latin name of the German capital and became known as the Papyrus Berolinensis 8502. The Berlin
codex, it was eventually learned, contained what was left of a text in
Coptic called the *Gospel of Mary*, the Mary of the title being Mary
Magdalene. Two other small pieces of this Gospel, in Greek, turned up

elsewhere in the ensuing years. Internal evidence of various kinds suggests that the *Gospel of Mary* may date from as early as the first half of the second century, only a generation or two away from when the canonical Gospels took final form.[13] The *Gospel of Mary* is not itself a historical text — it does not describe real events, and does not purport to — but it is evidence of a debate among and within early Christian communities on the issue of whether women could lead such communities or whether such behavior was tantamount to heresy.

The *Gospel of Mary* did not at first receive much attention. Schmidt died, and the onset of two world wars brought scholarly activity in Europe to a halt. There was also a small flood caused by burst water pipes, which destroyed the first edition. Then, just as World War II was coming to an end, an earthenware jar was accidentally discovered in Egypt, which provided much of the necessary context in which the *Gospel of Mary* needed to be seen.

We can never know why twelve ancient codices and a fragment of a thirteenth came to rest where they were found. A rugged curtain of cliffs rises above the valley of the Nile River near a village called Nag Hammadi. The time was the late fourth or early fifth century. For whatever reason, someone, perhaps a monk from the nearby monastery of St. Pachomius, took steps to preserve some fifty-two holy books, Coptic translations of works that had originally been written in Greek, works of the kind that had been denounced as heretical by the fourth-century theologian Athanasius, the archbishop of Alexandria. The words of the prophet Jeremiah (32:14–15) may have played through the mind of the person hiding the codices — "Put them in an earthenware jar, that they may last for a long time" — for it was in such a jar, hidden in a cavity under a rock at the base of the cliffs, that the papyrus manuscripts were eventually discovered.[14]

These texts have come to be called the Nag Hammadi library. By the early 1950s, after feuds and transactions of considerable complexity, including at least one murder, almost all of the Nag Hammadi collection rested in the hands of the Coptic Museum in Cairo, which for a time proved selective about whom it would allow to study the documents; two complete photographic copies were eventually made available to scholars outside Egypt. It was clear, however, that the codices, which contained forty previously unknown works, would offer unprecedented access to the world of the Gnostics, a diverse group of Christian communities, active as early as a century after the time of Jesus, that diverged sharply from the emerging Christian orthodoxy in many ways, especially with regard to the prominence both in theology and in community life of women.

Powerful feminine imagery and ideology suffuse many Gnostic texts. Some describe God as a dyad, embodying both masculine and feminine aspects. The feminine is invoked explicitly in prayers: "May She who is before all things, the incomprehensible and indescribable Grace, fill you within, and increase in you her own knowledge."[15]

The elevation of female motifs and status, at least in the written word, found parallels in Gnostic practice, which often permitted women to hold priestly office. Gnostic thought could be disorderly and fantastical and for a variety of reasons was spurned by Christian polemicists (although some elements seem to find anticipation in the Gospel of John). But the Nag Hammadi documents preserve some early Christian traditions and reflect currents important to an understanding of Christianity's unruly beginnings. Starting in the early 1960s, when facsimiles of these texts began to become available, a team of scholars working under the general direction of James M. Robinson began translating them into English and exploring the world from which they emerged. The analysis of the documents has served as a training school for two generations of New Testament scholars. The Nag Hammadi field is by and large a friendly, interconnected group, free of the rancor and jealousies that have for decades bedeviled the Dead Sea Scrolls community. One prominent figure in this field is Karen L. King.

A visitor to the campus of Occidental College in northern Los Angeles cannot help but notice several things. One is the demographic complexion of the student body: fully half of the undergraduates are black, Hispanic, or Asian, a proportion that roughly mirrors the makeup of the surrounding community, whose composition Occidental set out some years ago to reflect more accurately. A second thing is the trailers with portable dressing rooms and the trucks with lights and cameras and recording equipment. Occidental has doubled as the set for the fictional California University on the television show *Beverly Hills 90210*. The stone plinth at the main entrance that bears the name Occidental College is from time to time covered with a false front made of plywood, which proclaims its secondary identity.

I ventured out to Occidental in order to see Karen King, who not long afterward was named to a full professorship at Harvard Divinity School. King is one of a handful of women who have made Mary Magdalene an important subject of academic inquiry. Her religious interests are not exclusively antiquarian, however. She has been active in a liberal Episcopal church in Pasadena. At Occidental she taught a popular survey course on the diversity of traditional religions and new spiritual movements in the Los Angeles area, an activity that continually pointed up the way social realities can shape religious meaning and practice.

Like a number of other women and men of her generation in New Testament studies, King received much of her training through intensive work on Gnostic materials, not only those found in the Nag Hammadi library but also the *Gospel of Mary*. She ordinarily writes an easy prose of considerably less than Teutonic density, but in reading one paper she wrote about Mary Magdalene, I came across a passage whose evidence of supporting documentation, in the form of a tight corset of citational supranumerology, brought home what painstaking work — what careful blending of past surmise and ongoing inference — can lie behind even what seems like a straightforward statement of fact:

> In looking at Christianity in the first two to three centuries, it appears that in many, although not in all cases,[28] women's authority was based on prophetic experience. The Corinthian women prophets,[29] Philip's daughters,[30] Ammia of Philadelphia,[31] Philumene,[32] the visionary martyr Perpetua,[33] and several leaders in the Montanist movement (Maximilla, Priscilla or Prisca, Quintilla, and three other women who are identified as prophets in Montanist inscriptions)[34] — all these women were prophets and exercised authority in various ways.[16]

I once attended a session at the annual meeting of the American Schools of Oriental Research, an organization devoted to archaeology in the Middle East, at which an epigrapher read a paper on certain issues involving inscription fragments from ancient Palestine. When the author was finished, a ponytailed respondent with no experience of the demands of epigraphy arose to deliver a formal response, criticizing the author's paper for, among other things, what he deemed to be an excessive use of footnotes. The footnotes, he said, were "porcupine quills meant to protect an underdeveloped epistemology." Jaws dropped. A collective inhalation drew doors and windows tight. The ponytailed respondent came from outside the discipline, and his criticism was widely viewed as outrageous. In reconstructing texts and inscriptions from the ancient world, an immense amount of scholarly apparatus, reflecting a prior working-over of the same patch of ground, may be required to support what otherwise seems to be an innocuous phrase or sentence. (To give an extreme example, the reconstructed *Documenta Q* version of the Lord's Prayer, recently published by the International Q Project, contains a handful of words of original prayer followed by two hundred pages of dense footnotes.)[17]

Karen King grew up in the ranching community of Sheridan, Montana, far away from this world. She was drawn into it more or less by accident — "I stumble into things," she explains — when, as an undergraduate at the University of Montana, she happened to take a class from John D. Turner, a member of the *Nag Hammadi Library in English* project, who passed around copies of tentative translations of various Gnostic texts. The Gnostic materials circulating at the time were typically stamped with the notation "This material is for private study by assigned individuals only. Neither the text nor its translation may be reproduced or published in any form, in whole or in part."[18] This was the scholarly equivalent of "Wet Paint: Do Not Touch." King had grown up with a deep interest in religion and had at various times sampled the various denominations that Sheridan had to offer. She was drawn to the Gnostic texts and intrigued by the outlooks they expressed. After obtaining her bachelor's degree, she undertook graduate work in religious studies at Brown University and at the Free University in West Berlin. At Brown, King was for years the only female graduate student in the religion department. She was the only female graduate student anyone could clearly remember having *ever* been in the department.

While in Berlin in the early 1980s, King participated in the work of the Berlin Koptische-Gnostische Arbeitsgruppe, based at Humboldt University in what was then East Germany. The *arbeitsgruppe* has long been one of the main repositories of Nag Hammadi scholarship (the other being the Institute for Antiquity and Christianity at Claremont), and East Berlin's Egyptian Museum was also the physical home of the Papyrus Berolinensis. Once a week, at dawn on Fridays, King would cross into East Berlin at the Friedrichstrasse checkpoint, often after being closely searched by East German guards; given that the Gnostic texts themselves probably survived only because they were hidden, the experience was eerily apposite. Once in East Berlin, she would work all day with her colleagues in the *arbeitsgruppe*, most notably the New Testament historian and Egyptologist Hans-Martin Schenke, who generously set aside one day a week for this purpose. She would go back to West Berlin shortly before her visa expired at midnight.

Over the years the various texts of the Nag Hammadi library have been parceled out to scholars for translation and analysis. King began looking at various issues in such Gnostic texts as the *Apocryphon of John* and the *Gospel of Thomas*. In 1985, not long after she arrived in Los Angeles, she conceived and organized an international conference on the subject "Images of the Feminine in Gnosticism" and edited the conference papers into a book of the same name — her first major work, now a standard collection in the field. She proudly sent the book to her mentor, Schenke, only to discover that the subject matter held utterly no interest for him. He told King some years later that he had given the book to his wife, thinking that she might have some use for it. As noted, European institutions of learning, German ones in particular, have been far less open to women and feminism than American ones; the tendency there is to see the encounter of feminism and the Bible as a passing ideological whim. Those Americans!

(Karen Torjesen had a nearly identical experience with her German mentor, Ekkehard Muhlenberg. After sending him a copy of *When Women Were Priests*, she received a letter back saying, in effect, as Torjesen paraphrases it, "The cover is beautiful. The acknowledgments are deeply moving. But I'm afraid I cannot bring myself to read it.")

For more than a decade, Karen King's chief scholarly focus has been on the figure of Mary Magdalene — not the Mary Magdalene of history, about whom there is almost nothing that anyone can say beyond what has been summarized, but the Mary Magdalene who seems to have flourished in the popular Christian imagination from the very earliest days after the death of Jesus. In particular King's attention has been drawn to the *Gospel of Mary*, in whose narrative the status of Mary Magdalene, sharply contrasted with that of Peter, suggests deep divisions within Christian communities over the proper leadership role of women.

At the beginning of a long conversation one morning in her office at Occidental, King made a point that others take pains to make: how fissured an enterprise Christianity was in its first few centuries. As anyone who has been involved in contemporary Christian churches cannot help but be aware, King said, many of the faithful, and even some scholars, hold a romantic view of early Christianity, believing that into a world of unbelief there came belief, and for a time this belief burned simple and pure, and the teachings and rituals passed on by Jesus to his disciples were passed on in this simple and pure form to others. They believe further that over time the pure teachings and rituals became in places corrupted, in a variety of different ways. To these corruptions was given the name heresy. Today in the established Christian churches, in which doctrine and liturgy have obviously evolved to a point beyond anything Peter and Paul might have dreamed of, many yearn wistfully for the supposedly unadulterated Christianity that existed in the first and second centuries A.D.

In fact, as almost any New Testament scholar will patiently explain, the world of early Christianity was fragmented. Considering the circumstantial environment — the Roman Empire, with its extraordinary mixture of peoples and languages, of philosophies and religions — how could it not have been? "Christianity," said King, "did not fall from heaven as a perfectly pure and already complete done deal." There were traditions within early Christianity that the evolution of a stronger, more institutionalized tradition in time largely effaced. Acknowledging this fact has implications for our own epoch and for people who have felt excluded or even oppressed by the dominant tradition. It has implications in particular for women.

The *Gospel of Mary* offers a window onto this world. The portion that has managed to survive is relatively short, and as is often the case with texts of this kind, the task of reconstruction and translation involves picking your way across numerous lacunae. The result sometimes seems strangely like a wiretap transcript, with all its garbled and inaudible and tentatively reconstructed words and passages:

> Then he continued. He said, "This is why you get si[c]k and die: because [you love] what de[c]ei[ve]s [you]. [Anyone who] thinks should consider [these matters]!
>
> "[Ma]tter gav[e bi]rth to a passion which has no Image because it derives from what is contrary to nature."
>
> The Savior answered and said, "A person does not see with the soul or with the spirit. Rather the mind, which exists between these two, sees the vision an[d] that is w[hat] (pp. 11–14 missing)[19]

Parts of such a reconstruction will not become certain until a scholar can do what is called a final collation, which means comparing all the work thus far — that is, the translation, which has been based on an analysis of a text, which has in turn been based on a transcription, which itself has been derived from photographs — with the manuscript originals. In the case of the *Gospel of Mary*, the manuscript in Berlin is supplemented by fragments in Oxford and Manchester. (King has examined them all.) The Nag Hammadi manuscripts are preserved at the Coptic Museum in Cairo. Long ago separated from one another, each of the hundreds of delicate leaves is today pressed between sheets of hard, clear plastic, like an anatomical specimen or a tissue section, the surfaces still betraying evidence of the papyrus fronds used in the manufacture. Only by looking at the originals can a scholar tell whether a certain darkening of the papyrus was really ink from a word or letter fragment, as a photograph might suggest, or just plain discoloration, an uncommunicative age spot. By looking at the originals she or he can more easily tell if a truncated stroke seemed about to turn one way or another.

It is possible to go even further. While working on her dissertation on the Nag Hammadi text called *Allogenes*, King spent weeks at the Coptic Museum with her fragments of manuscript, bathing parts of it in ultraviolet light to bring out bits and pieces of normally invisible ink, asking herself questions like "Is this letter absolutely clear? Could it actually be one of two or three letters? Have I deluded myself into believing that it has to be a certain letter on the basis of suppositions I've made?"

The first scene in the *Gospel of Mary* occurs after the Resurrection of Jesus. Jesus, referred to throughout not by name but as "the Savior," is speaking with his disciples, among whose number is Mary Magdalene. The subject of the discourse, which takes the form of something like a Socratic exchange, is the nature of sin and the path toward salvation. Jesus then departs.

In the second scene the male disciples are extremely upset, but Mary steps in to comfort them and turns their attention to discussing the words that the Savior has left them. Peter asks her to offer some guidance, and she goes on to recount a revelation that has been imparted to her privately in the form of a vision of Jesus. Mary's words are well spoken and confidently expressed. But when she is done, squabbling breaks out among the disciples, led by Andrew and Peter. Andrew professes disbelief that the Savior could have said what Mary reports he said, and gives as the reason for his doubt that the reported teachings strike him as strange. Peter's objections take a blunter, more blustery form; he is skeptical, to put it mildly, that the Savior would have conveyed revelation through a woman when so many men were available: "Did he really speak with a woman without our knowledge [and] not openly? Are we to turn about and all listen to her? Did he prefer her to us?" After this outburst a disciple named Levi reproves Peter ("You have always been hot-tempered") and counsels the other disciples to heed Mary's revelation. Levi is given the last word. Thereupon the disciples "go forth [to] proclaim and to preach."

The *Gospel of Mary* is intriguing on a number of levels. One is simply its theological content, in which the cross and the Resurrection are submerged, far from central, the emphasis resting instead on Jesus' teachings as the crucial matter for eternal life. It rejects the whole Christian theology of sin, atonement, and judgment in favor of a process of internal spiritual development based on Jesus' teachings. The Gospel provides dramatic context and narrative tension in the confrontation between Peter and Mary Magdalene. This confrontation is deeply rooted, and makes itself apparent in what does and does not appear in various New Testament texts. Although all four Gospels describe Mary Magdalene as being among the first at the empty tomb and two of them describe her as the first person to whom a resurrected Jesus makes himself known, she is not mentioned by Paul as being one of those to whom Jesus *ever* appeared after the Resurrection. (Paul's list begins with Peter and then proceeds to include "the twelve," and then "more than five hundred brethren at one time," and ends with "last of all, as to one untimely born, he appeared to me.") Indeed, Paul doesn't refer to Mary Magdalene at all. Some ancient versions of the Gospel of Mark add material at the end in which the appearance to Mary Magdalene is described. Meanwhile, some ancient versions of the Gospel of Luke add a disputed verse (Luke 24:12) that gives Peter a role at the empty tomb: "But Peter rose and ran to the tomb; stooping and looking in, he saw the linen cloths by themselves; and he went home wondering at what had happened."

Because of his presumptive founding role in the establishment of Christianity, the figure of Peter is often used by early Christian writers, as King observes, to "authorize theological positions." But she also points out that a more complicated image of Peter emerges even in the canonical Gospels. More than any of the other disciples, it is Peter who misunderstands, who bumbles, who plays the oaf, who acts out of anger, who evinces all-too-human frailties. It is Peter whose trust in Jesus fails when, after Jesus has bid him to come and walk toward him on the water, he begins to sink (Matthew 14:28–31): "O man of little faith," Jesus says to Peter as he catches hold of him. "Why did you doubt?" When Jesus is arrested in the garden of Gethsemane, it is Peter who impulsively and unhelpfully draws his sword and slices off the ear of the high priest's slave (John 18:10). Despite having promoted himself as the most unfailingly loyal of the disciples (Mark 14:29–31), it is Peter who, when the climactic moment comes, publicly disavows any connection with Jesus on three separate occasions. After the Resurrection, Peter cannot bring himself to believe the truth of what Mary Magdalene, a woman, reports to him, even though he later comes to accept that it is true. As often as not, it is Peter who does not quite understand the meaning of whatever happens to be going on. These qualities are not altogether unappealing, and remain warm to the touch over the centuries, long after most accounts of unblemished virtue have grown cold.

The portrayal of Peter as somewhat intemperate and dim is richly elaborated on in noncanonical writings from early Christian times. Not only in the *Gospel of Mary* but also in the *Gospel of the Egyptians*, the *Gospel of Thomas*, and *Pistis Sophia*, Peter finds himself taking the losing side of an argument, and in each case losing to Mary Magdalene. In *Pistis Sophia*, Mary acknowledges her fear of Peter — "for he threatens me and he hates our race." Jesus goes so far as to validate Mary and her teachings with the observation that Mary's heart "is more directed toward the kingdom of heaven than all thy brothers."[20] The issue in the disputes between Peter and Mary always involves whether it is legitimate for a woman to prophesy and to preach.

"Peter is almost always the one who turns out to be wrong," King explains. "He is portrayed, in the Gospel of Mark in particular, as the disciple who doesn't get it. The other disciples don't get it either, but it is to Peter that Jesus says, 'Get behind me, Satan.' And Peter is the one singled out to deny Jesus three times. And yet in the canonical tradition, Peter is also the rock on which the Church was built. So there's an ambiguous portrait of him in the tradition. These Gnostic texts build on that portrait when they pit him in conflict with Mary Magdalene. The disputes between Mary and Peter seem to reflect issues that were being debated, especially in the second and third centuries of the Christian era. What are those issues? Who Jesus is and what his teachings mean for people. Who should have legitimate authority and leadership power. In the *Gospel of Mary*, those issues center almost always on male-female interactions. In Peter's eyes, Mary speaks too much, asks too many questions. But in the end, she is the one who is right."

There was, King observes, a long history, not only in Christianity but in other ancient religious traditions, of women assuming the role of prophet and of being popularly accepted as legitimate in that role. At the same time, there was also a long history of resistance in many quarters to women in a prophetic role and a tendency to besmirch the reputation of women who claimed the status of prophet by questioning their virtue. The relationship between prophecy and sexuality was sometimes seen with startling literalness. One scholar has pointed out that according to early Greek writings, women were deemed more susceptible to possession because their bodies had an additional orifice, making the entry of spirits that much easier. There was a strong correlation, King has noted, between the esteem in which a woman's prophecy was held and attendant proclamations of her virtue; conversely, to set about sullying a woman's sexual reputation was a standard method of undermining her legitimacy as a prophet. Thus, the early church commentator Tertullian writes of the prophet Philumene, with whom he violently disagrees, that she "became an enormous prostitute." Virtue, of course, is to a considerable extent a social construct, and this is especially the case with sexual virtue. If the boundaries become confining, if the social territory they encompass is pervasive, then the scope for prophecy or other forms of religious leadership will be correspondingly constricted.

"In the case of women's prophecy," King has written, "the weight of judgment about moral character fell back upon judging their conformity to established gender roles: that meant women fulfilling their roles as wives and mothers, and keeping silence in church assemblies."[21] We can see the evolution of what King calls a double bind: only a woman of conventional habit, outlook, and circumstances would be accorded the legitimacy demanded of a prophet, but such a woman by definition would shun such a public role. It was, so to speak, a self-fulfilling prophecy.

Such a self-fulfilling prophecy was not a mere abstraction. The kind of leadership displayed by the Mary Magdalene figure in texts like the *Gospel of Mary* and the *Gospel of Thomas* found real-life analogues in the activities of women in communities like those of the Montanists, the Marcionites, the Valentinians, and the Carpocratians — communities that were denounced by authorities wielding various degrees of power. As King writes, "Every prominent stream of theology and practice within early Christianity that supported women's leadership was sharply opposed, even decried as heretical."

Whatever the sources of its various strands, whatever the social and religious environment that braided them together, the legend of Mary Magdalene as it has come down to us — Mary as the holy harlot — was fully formed by the early Middle Ages. A tenth-century sermon by the abbot Odo of Cluny encapsulates most of its essentials: after an existence devoted to "sensual pleasures," Mary helps, by means of a reformed life and zealous ministration to the daily needs of Jesus, to rescue (somewhat) the female sex from the obloquy into which Eve cast it. She becomes a "Venus in sackcloth," as one writer observes.[22] Variations on this theme, and variations upon the variations, unfolded for a thousand years. The legends include those in which Mary lives out her days in the South of France and those in which she is seen as having become, literally, the bride of Christ. The fundamental ambivalence toward her is well captured by the contemporary writer Marina Warner: "The Magdalene, like Eve, was brought into existence by the powerful undertow of misogyny in Christianity, which associates women with the dangers and degradation of the flesh. For this reason, she became a prominent and beloved saint."[23]

Mary Magdalene's rendered image is widely familiar in its various genres, but one depiction stands out for the association it makes with another biblical figure whose dramatic role is likewise essential, whose reputation has likewise suffered, and whose name is likewise, in essence, Mary — the figure of Miriam, the sister of Moses. By hiding Moses in the bulrushes, Miriam effectively ensures his rebirth, enabling him one day to lead his people into the Promised Land, and yet Miriam herself is cruelly ravaged by disease and becomes a symbol of penitence.

The parallels with Mary Magdalene — witness to the rebirth of Jesus in the Resurrection, enduring penitent for unenumerated misdeeds — were plainly apparent to those who created the Mary Magdalene chapel in the Sanctuary of St. Francis at Assisi. There in the chapel, Mary and Miriam — the Miriam who led the victory song, a tambourine in one hand — are enshrined together, witnesses to a parallel twist of fate.

Chapter Eleven

....

A GLIMPSE THROUGH
THE DOOR

And when she had finished her prayer, she turned
and saw a great pit full of water, and said: "Now is the time for
me to wash." And she threw herself in,
saying: "In the name of Jesus Christ
I baptize myself on the last day!"
— Acts of Paul and Thecla 3:34

Avoid the profane tales told by old women.
Rather train yourself toward godliness.
— 1 Timothy 4:7–8

"HELLO, THIS IS Bernadette, in Cambridge." The voice was that of
a caller to Christopher Lydon's *The Connection*, a radio program on
WBUR in Boston, and the subject of the program was "Sexuality, Clerical Ministry, and Gay Spirituality." I recognized the caller's voice at
once — the pitch, the precision, the hint of humor — and admired the
way the voice's owner deftly and unobtrusively made reference to her
new book, *Love Between Women: Early Christian Responses to Female
Homoeroticism*. I had heard the caller on a number of occasions, across a
table or in a lecture hall, and could easily summon to mind a picture of
the tall woman with the striking Levantine features who went with the
voice. Her commentary continued as I pulled over to the curb to listen:
"When we look at why early Christians condemned sexual relations
between women, we realize that Paul shared some cultural assumptions
about sexuality that are alien to our world and *should* be alien to our
world. Paul and others in the Roman world believed that natural relations are relations between a subordinate woman and a man who is over
her."[1] Some of what Paul has to say about women, in other words, reflects not any systematic theology but simply the fact that he lived when
he did.

Bernadette is Bernadette Brooten, now the Robert and Myra Kraft and Jacob Hiatt Professor of Christian Studies in the department of Near Eastern and Judaic studies at Brandeis University. As noted, she has spent a great deal of time puzzling over ancient carved inscriptions and over the way women in particular are officially described or designated in them. She probably would enjoy contemplating the kinds of information and inference some scholar a millennium hence might draw from the full rendition of her own academic title. Who were these Krafts and Hiatts? What was a professor of *Christian* studies doing inside a department of *Judaic* studies? And didn't the "*-or*" suffix in an occupational title in ancient English typically designate a male?

Brooten's mind has a quirky cast to it. She is a popular teacher and a persuasive presence. I have no trouble imagining how she might cajole guards at the Vatican Library into granting her access to materials that were said to be off-limits (as I know she has done). When I have dined with her, the conversation has always taken unusual turns, navigated by her interest in unlikely manifestations from odd corners of the ancient world. Waiters, it seems, always approach just as Brooten is animatedly uttering something atypical for lunchtime conversation — for instance, "I just came across an obscure reference to selective clitoridectomy for adult women who seem to have masculine desires" — but back off, waiterly, under cover of a mumbled remark about maybe our needing more time. Brooten, heedless, is usually by then in pursuit of another subject — sexual orientation as presented in Roman astrological charts, say, or Egyptian love spells for women interested in other women, or an ancient anecdote about sexuality and dream interpretation.

Brooten is mindful of the degree to which our knowledge of women's history in antiquity remains at a profoundly primitive stage; as she has pointed out, "for women, the state of the sources is similar to that for men and women in the periods usually deemed prehistorical."[2] These sources often are not only thematically scattered but also just plain scarce. Brooten told me once about a female synagogue leader from the Roman era whose name she knows only as a result of improbable accidents of contingency. The woman's name had been carved in stone, in Greek, and had survived for fifteen hundred years in a village in Turkey.

At the turn of the century the stone was reused by peasants in a farm building, and it is now lost. Just before this happened, a Greek Orthodox scholar had by chance copied out the inscription and published it in a small Turkish journal in an article written in Karamanli, which is Turkish rendered in Greek characters. When ethnic Greeks were expelled from Turkey in the early 1920s, volumes of this journal somehow made their way with the exiles to Greece, where they were preserved and forgotten. Only in the 1980s did a Karamanli-literate Greek theologian, browsing through the journals, happen upon the reference to the female synagogue leader. By coincidence, he knew of Brooten's doctoral dissertation, on the evidence in Greco-Roman funerary inscriptions for women's leadership in the ancient synagogue, and brought the reference to her attention.

Such is the tenuousness, frequently, of the chain of evidence where women in antiquity are concerned. "The most we can hope for," Brooten has written, "is a snippet of a conversation, a quick glimpse through a crack in the door. If we do not focus all of our attention on how to get that snippet and get that glimpse, we will miss them."[3]

Bernadette Brooten assumed her position at Brandeis in 1993, after eight years at the Harvard Divinity School. Before that she had taught for several years at the Claremont Graduate University and the University of Tübingen. She pursued her doctoral work mostly at Harvard and completed it in 1982, but an important part of her academic training also took place in Germany. She remembers the German academic environment for women in much the same way that Elisabeth Schüssler Fiorenza does. "German theologians," she told me once, "will just say outright that they don't want women involved in theological work. I remember hearing one theologian at the breakfast table at a conference saying quite simply that women shouldn't be allowed to become full professors. 'Why is that?' I asked. And he said, 'Because they have a different style. They have a different way of looking at scholarship. We can't have that.'"

Oddly, though, the University of Tübingen is where Brooten encountered her first women's studies course: Leonard Swidler, on leave from Temple University, happened to be a visiting professor there during one of her sojourns, and he was offering a seminar on women and the Church. Brooten, it turned out, was one of only two students who signed up for it. "In the university as a whole," she recalls, "there was no interest in such things at all." That was in 1972. Times have changed, somewhat. Returning to Tübingen in the 1980s, when her doctoral work was done, Brooten found that at least in certain quarters, gender issues were eliciting more than a little attention. She had to restrict the enrollment in a class she taught on women and sexuality in early Christianity to seventy.

Brooten's earliest scholarly writing involved women and religious leadership — in synagogues of the Roman era and in the first Christian communities as reflected in the writings of Paul. Her most recent work, on same-sex love among women in early Christian times, may seem like a narrow or tightly focused subject. One of her academic mentors at Tübingen, Hans Küng, who has long maintained an interest in women's issues and the Catholic Church, forbade her to pursue the subject as she envisioned it while she was involved in a research project at his Institute for Ecumenical Research — an ironic development, given that Küng at the time had just been censured and penalized by the Vatican for insistently expressing his own views.

The subject of same-sex love among women, compelling in its own right, also offers a surprisingly direct means of access to an issue that eventually confronts any scholar who contemplates women and religion in antiquity. That issue can be framed as follows. Jews and Christians in the Greco-Roman world inhabited relatively small, marginal religious cultures that existed for centuries within a powerful and dominant civilization. Those religious cultures cherished certain distinctive values and outlooks. At the same time, they were hardly insulated from the values and outlooks of the larger civilization — values and outlooks that, with respect to women, scholars roll up into the encapsulating phrase "the Greco-Roman gender system." This refers (simplifying radically) to a deeply pervasive ideology of gender difference, a philosophical presupposition, a pattern of thinking that powerfully reinforced gender stratification and inequality. Over the centuries, inevitably, this commonly held pattern of thought left its stamp on matters both of specific religious belief and of ordinary religious practice. From the vantage point of our own time, it is not always easy to tell these entangled elements apart. Yet we know that by the time "antiquity" reached its end, certain disdainful stances toward women had become fixed in aspects of Western religion. Those who harbor hope that the Western religious traditions are not at their essential core irretrievably anti-women must therefore ask themselves where such stances came from. They must ask themselves, for instance, if Jesus *was* a feminist, then how do we account for some of the traditions that evolved in his name?

These are among the questions on Brooten's mind. One body of New Testament texts that cannot fail to raise the issue of Christianity and women is, of course, the writings of Paul. Paul, a onetime Pharisee and an indefatigable persecutor of the followers of Jesus, who eventually became a follower of Jesus himself and the Jesus movement's most important evangelist, emerges from his epistles as a man not only of piercing vision but also of passion, will, energy, organization, and pragmatism, with streaks of peremptoriness and, strangely, self-doubt. Paul's authentic writings (for example, the epistles known as Galatians, Romans, 1 and 2 Corinthians) and to an even greater degree the writings attributed to his authority but not actually written by him (for example, 1 and 2 Timothy and Titus, known as the pastoral epistles) offer strong but not always consistent opinions on the proper role of women in the religious and social order. As we have seen, Paul affirms the right of women to prophesy in public, and he offers public gratitude to women in the young Christian movement, whom he mentions by name and regards as his equals or as superior. In the epistle to the Galatians, he not only embraces an egalitarian formula but grounds it in the very essence of Christianity: "There is neither Jew nor Greek, there is neither slave nor free, there is neither male nor female, for you are all one in Christ Jesus." At the same time he tells women to be subordinate to their husbands, to learn in silence, and to refrain from teaching men or having authority over men. Do his opinions in these passages reflect a distinctively Christian message, and if so, do they reflect an aspect of the message that goes to Christianity's very heart? Or do they sometimes, perhaps, reflect nothing more than Greco-Roman society's ordinary social and gender conventions and its underlying state of mind?

One clue may lie in Paul's condemnations of same-sex love. The relevant verses are at Romans 1:26–27, where Paul, writing about the behavior of human beings who have fallen away from God, states, "Their women exchanged natural relations for unnatural, and the men likewise gave up natural relations with women and were consumed with passion for one another." What was Paul's understanding of "natural" and "unnatural" in this context? What differences, if any, existed among Christians and Jews and pagans in their understanding of femaleness and maleness and of the symmetries or asymmetries involved in sexual relationships of any kind?

"My overarching interest," Brooten explains, "is in the origin of our moral values — understanding historically how specific values came to be." As she argued in the course of one of our conversations and discusses at length in *Love Between Women*, Paul's views of same-sex love and the template of gender that underlies them make him a more or less typical product of the cultural world in which he was formed, one that viewed women as "inferior, unfit to rule, passive, and weak."[4] Whatever the exceptions in practice, in the typical Roman view, some behavior is inherently masculine and some inherently feminine, and these categories of behavior are not supposed to be confused. In sexual relations between members of the same sex, the categories are indeed confused. In male-male relations, one man becomes "like a woman," the ancient commentators argue, because that man is penetrated; conversely, in female-female relations, one woman becomes "like a man." Underlying all this is a worldview that, Brooten contends, saw the distinction between "active" and "passive" as more fundamental even than distinctions of gender. It was the basis of social order and hierarchy, a conceptual framework that defined the categories of superior and inferior. To erase or ignore this distinction was an act of "insubordination."[5]

"What this helps us to understand," Brooten says, "is how people in the Roman world as a whole, including Christians, understood the bounds of what it is to be male and female. We define the territory by the boundaries, so if you say a woman who does *this* has overstepped the boundaries and is no longer feminine but is trying to be masculine, or if you say a man who does *this* has overstepped the boundaries of what it means to be masculine and has become feminine, then you see something about what constitutes allowed behavior for all women and all men, even aside from sexual matters."

This view of gender seems to be as taken for granted by Paul as it was by the broader Greco-Roman civilization of which he was a part. Thus he matter-of-factly refers to a woman as being "under" a man. The fact that he does take it for granted is, in Brooten's view, one element of the palpable tension in his writings on issues involving women. Standing apart from his time though he did in many ways, Paul could not fully escape aspects of its more conventional outlook. "On the one hand, Paul was happy to work with women as colleagues, and encouraged them," Brooten said. "So, for example, he mentioned Junia, and he acknowledged Prisca and Tryphaena and Tryphosa and Persis and other women. He taught with them, and he recognized their prophecy, and he worked with them as missionaries in the Roman world. On the other hand, while he was very willing to make a religious and societal break with Jewish tradition on points that were considered very central to Judaism, such as the issues of dietary laws and the circumcision of men, in order to permit Jew and Gentile alike to come together to accept Jesus as the Christ, with some customs concerning women he was *not* willing to make that kind of break — for example, on the issue of the hairstyling and the veiling of women. And indeed, at that very point in the text he describes Christ as the head of man, and man as the head of woman, which goes beyond tolerating a custom and gives a theological underpinning to gender differentiation. I see Paul's position as essentially ambivalent. On certain issues — gender, slavery, Roman power — he is very much interested in maintaining social order. But what's fascinating about Paul is that he *experiments*."

And his experimention, his ambivalence expressed out loud, has consequences, for his is among the most authoritative voices of the early Christian world.

In the course of a conversation one day in her home town of Philadelphia, Ross S. Kraemer was ranging rather freely around the Greco-

Roman world, and around the question of how we can be confident that we know very much about it, when she asked, "Do you know what a squeeze is?" Under other circumstances I might have confidently ventured a reply, but after several hours of listening to Kraemer, who at the time was a fellow at the University of Pennsylvania's Center for Judaic Studies and who now teaches in the university's department of religion, I had the feeling that the answer would be out of the ordinary.

We had met for lunch, and the conversation continued afterward during a drive through town, interrupted by Kraemer's attempted calls (dialing; busy) to a housekeeper on the car phone. Kraemer dresses with striking but easy stylishness and seems slightly too young to have a daughter halfway through college. She is an accomplished discussion partner. Her familiarity with the relevant scholarly literature extends deep into fields tangential to her own. Among her current projects, she is assisting Carol Meyers with the biblical *Dictionary of Women in Scripture* (and is writing the entries for female historical figures mentioned in the New Testament). Even when she is not overtly expressing an opinion on a subject, she will at least position it for analysis, as you might fix a specimen on a slide. Kraemer can hold up not only her end of the conversation but also, if necessary, yours. She spoke about the Greek cult of Dionysus, which, though little attention had been paid to the fact, was in its ecstatic rites the province of women. (A study of the cult of Dionysus formed the nucleus of Kraemer's doctoral dissertation at Princeton.) She spoke about Mary Magdalene and the process that led to Mary's being commonly, if wrongly, identified as a prostitute. She spoke about women writers in the Greco-Roman world and the methodological problems facing those who investigate questions of gender and authorship in antiquity. She spoke about Lydia of Thyatira, the "dealer in purple cloth" mentioned in the Acts of the Apostles, as an example of the kind of independent woman of means who seems to have played an especially active role in early Christianity.

The conversation gravitated naturally from there to the work of Elisabeth Schüssler Fiorenza. Kraemer acknowledged the enormous debt that everyone owes to Schüssler Fiorenza, acknowledged that her work had been groundbreaking in providing a new but comprehensive and coherent way of viewing the Jesus movement and its context. But she added that she herself was less, well, *optimistic* than Schüssler Fiorenza about a number of things.

"I'm not as optimistic, not so much in terms of her recovery of what she thinks women in early Christianity *did*, what roles they played — I think she's likely to be right about a lot of that. Where I would part company is with her argument that the earliest theology of Christianity is *intentionally* egalitarian and feminist. I'm really not persuaded of that. Elisabeth wants to locate the intent in Jesus himself. It's not so much that I think she's wrong as that I'm simply not convinced we can know she's right. It's very hard to argue that we know anything about what Jesus really thought. The few things that any scholar would be willing to attribute to Jesus himself with any confidence don't address this particular issue" — the issue, that is to say, of the place of women in the social order.

And then it was on to the subject of squeezes. A squeeze is a mold of an ancient inscription carved in marble or other stone, obtained by coating the hard surface with a pliable substance (latex has supplanted papier-mâché as the medium most commonly used) and then peeling it off. Epigraphers, as those who study inscriptions are called, frequently have a selection of squeezes in their possession, along with files of photographs and transcriptions. Squeezes had come up when Kraemer began describing the types of sources auxiliary to the Bible on which scholars can rely in the study of Jewish and Christian women in ancient times. As chronology rolls forward from distant epochs, the sources of information become increasingly plentiful, including works of art, history, and literature; a diverse array of documents involving women (letters, tax receipts, wills, lawsuits, wet-nurse contracts); and large numbers of inscriptions and fragments of inscriptions from buildings and monuments. Kraemer naturally pointed to the work of Bernadette Brooten, whose analysis of Greek and Latin epigraphical evidence led her to conclude that at least some Jewish women occupied prominent leadership roles in the ancient synagogue.

That the sources become more plentiful and their diversity more pronounced suggests a Mediterranean world in the process of becoming more complex, more cosmopolitan, more interconnected. In the millennium beginning with the return of the Israelites from Babylon, the biblical heartland was ruled by Persians, by Greeks, by Romans. The ancient world as a whole felt the influence of new economic and cultural systems. The religion of the Jewish people evolved out of one centered on sacrifice and the Temple into rabbinic Judaism — to modern eyes, a more familiar-seeming form of expression. Christianity, a new and sometimes discomfiting religious force, emerged into sometimes fierce social hostility on the part of official Rome, but within three centuries of the death of Jesus it was established, by the emperor Constantine, as the Roman Empire's state religion.

Kraemer's book *Her Share of the Blessings* is a wide-ranging exploration of the role of women in Greco-Roman religions — pagan, Jewish, Christian — from about the fourth century B.C. through the end of the Roman era. The comparative approach that Kraemer takes, across cultures and belief systems, has great advantages, allowing her to see how structures in one realm may have influenced those in another. If she believes that, for whatever reason, Christianity was as a practical matter more egalitarian in terms of gender in the early days than it became later on — and she does — it is not only because of the interpretation she accepts of early Christian writings. She knows also, from looking at gender in other religious contexts, that it was not unusual for women to hold cultic office in (for instance) pagan religion, not unusual for them to play the role of patron. In light of the social mores of the time, the emphasis in much of early Christianity on sexual asceticism, on nonmarriage and celibacy, would, she understands, also have served to enhance female independence. Asceticism offered free women a radical new option, a path to follow other than the traditional one of marriage, childbearing, and domesticity. Another force conducive to egalitarianism was the expectation among many early Christians that the present earthly order would soon pass — that the Lord was about to return in glory. In such a climate, with its focus on the transience of human institutions, attachment to social structures that were plainly "of the world" was considerably lessened. Did women serve as priests? The formal establishment of a priesthood in Christianity came very late, Kraemer writes, but a diverse body of evidence shows that women in early Christianity held the title *presbytera* and that people who held this title performed all priestly functions: they taught, they baptized, they blessed the Eucharist.

There is, of course, also evidence of profound unease. As noted, you cannot read very far into the writings of Paul without becoming aware of his inner conflict when it came to questions of gender and sexuality. George Bernard Shaw once characterized Paul as the "eternal enemy of woman."[6] Paul may have expressed sentiments in Galatians that an egalitarian would hail — and perhaps those sentiments are the most important ones for women in the Pauline corpus — but in 1 Corinthians he showed himself to be clearly disturbed by the powerful and independent women in the Christian community at Corinth. He did not forbid the Corinthian women to prophesy, but he demanded that they cover their heads when they prayed in public, and in 1 Corinthians 11:8–9 he added a statement — "For man was not made from woman, but woman from man. Neither was man created for woman, but woman for man" — that uses Genesis, a sacred text, to define women as subordinate to men. Later, in 1 Corinthians 14, he employed a reprise of the same argument to single out women and insist that they should keep silent in church. Is this last statement (along with some other passages that characterize proper female behavior) the product of a hand other than Paul's? Is it a later interpolation in the text, as many scholars now believe? Perhaps. But tensions exist nonetheless, Kraemer writes, and they become deeper and more intractable as Christianity moves further away in time and place from its specific origins and closer to the heart of the contemporaneous Greco-Roman social establishment.

The conflicting perspectives on women so evident in Paul become explosively apparent in later writings. Kraemer cites the argument of Dennis MacDonald, a New Testament scholar at the Iliff School of Theology in Denver, who discerns what amounts to a duel between sensibilities in several divergent Christian texts. One of these texts is called the *Acts of Paul*, also known as the *Acts of Paul and Thecla*. In direct opposition to this work stand Paul's pastoral epistles. MacDonald's contention, as set out in his book *The Legend and the Apostle*, is that the camps embodied in *Acts*, on the one hand, and the pastoral epistles, on the other, represent developed, evolved versions of the conflicting strands in Paul's original thinking.

The apocryphal *Acts of Paul and Thecla*, probably written in the second century, would be the evolved version of the egalitarian impulse. This work celebrates the life of an ascetic female missionary supposedly sent out by Paul to teach and spread the word of the Lord. Thecla is an upper-class woman, a pagan, who is converted to faith in Jesus by Paul's preaching. She breaks off her engagement, embraces a life of sexual asceticism, and takes up the work of evangelization. Many bizarre and picaresque adventures ensue, with miraculous interventions from time to time foiling murderous and persecutorial intent. At one point in the story Thecla performs a successful act of autobaptism by jumping into a pool of seals. In the end, she receives an explicit commission from Paul to go and preach the word of Jesus.

The *Acts of Paul and Thecla* enjoyed wide popularity in the ancient world; versions of it survive, MacDonald observes, in Greek, Coptic, Syriac, Slavic, and Arabic and in four different Latin versions. In Syria, he notes, the story of Thecla was added to the stories of Ruth, Esther, Judith, and Susanna to make up a text known as the *Book of Women*. Among some groups of Christians, the story was seen as giving legitimacy to preaching and baptizing by women.[7]

The other perspective is embodied in the epistles to Timothy, also written in the second century, which contain some of the most stringently restrictive passages about women in the New Testament. These represent, in MacDonald's view, the evolved version of the socially conventional Paul, the Paul who remained beholden to the larger society's norms and expectations. No celebration is to be found here of women's leadership or autonomy or the virtues of celibacy. Rather, "Let a woman learn in silence with all submissiveness. I permit no woman to teach or to have authority over men; she is to keep silent. For Adam was formed first, then Eve; and Adam was not deceived, but the woman was deceived and became a transgressor. Yet woman will be saved through bearing children, if she continues in faith and love and holiness, with modesty."

The author of 1 Timothy, MacDonald concludes from a raft of internal evidence, seems to have the *Acts of Thecla* explicitly in mind as he (and surely it *was* a he) advances his arguments. At one point he urges readers not to be swayed by "godless and silly myths" (1 Timothy 4:7). MacDonald explains, tellingly, that the Greek terminology that the Revised Standard Version translates as "silly myths" in fact literally means "tales told by old women." After reviewing the context in which the later, pastoral epistles came to be written, and after limning the byways along which a number of specific passages achieved *ex post facto* insertion into earlier epistles, MacDonald writes:

> In other words, the Pauline corpus [that is, the body of writings consid-
> ered in its entirety] has not come down to us with the accuracy and
> dispassion of a genderless Xerox machine. It has come down to us from
> the hands of pious, dedicated, and skilled men — males of a particular
> social position and world view, who in spite of their respect for the
> Pauline text put their own signatures to his letters, and thereby to some
> extent helped him write them. The Pauline corpus is mostly his, but
> also unmistakably theirs.[8]

And theirs, in essence, is the (male) perspective on the nature, role, and function of women that hardened when Christianity became the religion of the Roman state, embraced by the secular powers, absorbed socially into the establishment.

To a considerable degree indeed, Kraemer suggests, religious thinking and rituals that reflect an elevated status for women came to be condemned as heretical on those grounds alone — that is, on the grounds that they elevated women's status. Church authorities denounced many groups in which women numbered heavily among the leadership. Ancient jeremiads are strewn with their names: the Valentinians and Montanists, the Quintillians and Cataphyrigians and others. As Kraemer writes, "Most movements we know to have been characterized by the prominence of women were ultimately judged heretical." One chapter title sums up the argument succinctly: "Heresy as Women's Religion: Women's Religion as Heresy."[9]

Understanding what such women-influenced movements (which appear in various manifestations throughout antiquity) looked like from the inside, as it were, has been significantly enhanced at least for the

Christian world by the discovery of the cache of ancient documents at Nag Hammadi. In their own way, though, these documents also illustrate what a history of women in early Christianity is actually up against. They remain in some respects impenetrable, because it is not clear whose materials they are. "With very few exceptions," Kraemer observes, "we don't know who wrote them. We don't know where they were written. We don't know who read them. There is no question that there are some interesting things going on in those texts, *whoever* wrote them, *wherever* they came from. Female figures for the divine are all over the place, sometimes in a positive way, sometimes in ways that, if you look closely, are not so positive. The question of the correlation between those documents and real women — women in communities, women as authors, women's view of the universe — is both incredibly tantalizing and incredibly frustrating.

"Even Elaine, I think, would now concede that we probably know less than we thought we would about the world from which this material came."

Yes, Elaine Pagels probably would concede as much, and has. But it is also the case, as she once described the situation to me, that before the Nag Hammadi discoveries in 1945, scholars had only the most indirect form of access to a whole world of early Christian thought. They could make contact with it only through what is known as "mirror reading." In other words, certain suppressed points of view — in a word, what commentators down the ages have labeled heresies — have survived mainly as references in works intended as denunciations of them. To a certain extent, we can deduce the opposing argument from the polemic itself, but the process can be taken only so far. The results, though, may be highly tentative, and the context elusive. "Imagine," says Pagels, "reading tracts on anticommunism but never having read Karl Marx." And then imagine the task of trying faithfully to reconstruct the ideas of Marx, or even a few of those ideas, on the basis of what you found in, say, J. Edgar Hoover's *On Communism*.

Elaine Pagels is the person who was largely responsible for bringing the Nag Hammadi texts to the attention of a wider public in the first place, through her 1979 book, *The Gnostic Gospels*. Today she is the Harrington Spear Paine Professor of Religion at Princeton University. When I first met her, a number of years ago, she was working primarily at the Institute for Advanced Study, which is also in Princeton but is not connected with the university. The institute offers distinguished scholars a chance to pursue research without the distraction of teaching — far away, as the institute's founder, Abraham Flexner, once put it, from "the maelstrom of the immediate."[10] Waiting for Pagels, I watched as scholars there gathered for afternoon tea (daily, at 3:00 P.M.) in the common room of Fuld Hall.

They were a subdued group, these historians and physicists, mathematicians and anthropologists. Gazing upon the assembly, I could not help but recall the evocation by J. Robert Oppenheimer, the institute's director during the 1950s, of his colleagues as "solipsistic luminaries" working in "helpless isolation." I also could not help but think, though, what a diverse and valuable trove these men and women would produce — a strange new Nag Hammadi library for the future — if, in the face of an impending catastrophe, someone asked them to run back to their offices, grab a copy of whatever they were working on at the time, and, heeding Jeremiah's ancient counsel, stuff it all for safekeeping into an earthenware jar. If Elaine Pagels had grabbed what she was working on that day, it would have been the beginnings of the manuscript of her book *The Origins of Satan*. If she grabbed instead the work she had most recently published, it would have been a copy of *Adam, Eve, and the Serpent*.

Pagels was a doctoral student in religion at Harvard University during the late 1960s, when mimeographed transcriptions of the Nag Hammadi library began circulating among American and European scholars. Her area of interest was the history of early Christianity. There were no women then on the faculty of Harvard's program in religion, and the dean who accepted Pagels as a doctoral candidate had turned her down the first time she applied. In this field, he explained in a letter, women didn't last ("Unless nobody would marry them," Pagels says, supplying the presumptive gloss). But now, after applying again, there she was at Harvard. The Nag Hammadi mimeographs caught her attention.

"I discovered," Pagels said, thinking back to her initial encounter with the new materials, "as did other graduate students, that our professors had file folders full of Gnostic texts of secret 'Gospels' that many of them told us were absurd and blasphemous and heretical — but interesting. And I *did* find these texts interesting. And exciting. They did not look to me like the gobbledygook that I was told they were. I think that perhaps my empathy for them had something to do with being a woman in an environment that was almost exclusively male. I found things among the heretics that were startlingly congenial." Pagels became part of the team that was to translate the texts into English and provide a critical apparatus for them.

Not until 1975, five years after completing a doctoral dissertation on certain aspects of the Nag Hammadi library, did Pagels have an opportunity to inspect the documents firsthand. At various times during a stay in Egypt, she visited the small, unprepossessing room in the Coptic Museum in Cairo where the materials are kept, one day perhaps to examine *The Interpretation of Knowledge*, another to examine *A Valentinian Exposition* or the bizarrely compelling *Thunder, Perfect Mind*. The documents looked like tobacco leaves, she remembers thinking, each fragment flattened between sheets of hard plastic, the black lettering stark against a mottled golden background. The Coptic Museum was a place of columns and courtyards and quiet. The only interruption was caused by the cleaning woman. Pagels and other scholars would continue working at their desks when she came in, lifting their legs as soapy water was spilled and spread beneath them over the stone floors.

In *The Gnostic Gospels*, which received considerable notice when it was published and occasioned a sometimes bitter scholarly debate, Pagels took some of those fragments that lie flat between plastic and sought to give them dimension, set them in history, bring ancient sensibilities to life. Many of the texts offered images of women in some early Christian communities and of the place of women and of feminine ideology in religious thought that are radically at odds with images that the dominant Christian tradition has transmitted. The texts were full of feminine imagery for God. There was a substantial amount of sexual imagery as well — very surprising, from an orthodox point of view. All of this found resonance with a substantial segment of the public, which rightly saw a precedent for feminist stirrings in present-day religion.

The book also offered a reminder, or perhaps a warning, about what has happened historically to sources of knowledge about women. "The paucity of information doesn't necessarily correspond with what was actually happening — doesn't necessarily reflect the whole social reality," Pagels says. "Many things don't survive. The documents that do survive will reflect the point of view of the people writing them and the groups they represent. Generally women weren't a part of those groups." Bernadette Brooten, musing about how much of women's history has in all likelihood gone up in smoke, literally, once suggested that women might want to think about reintroducing the practice of chiseling their words into stone.

Some of the Gnostic communities gave particular attention to the Creation stories in the Book of Genesis. Pagels too became intrigued, and in 1988 she published *Adam, Eve, and the Serpent,* a more ambitious work than *The Gnostic Gospels.* The Bible's Creation stories (or, more precisely, the particular interpretation of the Creation stories that came to be accepted) form the basis for the view that humanity exists in a fallen state, that woman led humanity astray, that man is ordained to be the master of woman, and that sexuality is a corrupting aspect of human nature.

Yet as Pagels shows, this is not how the Creation stories were read and heard by many Jews and early Christians. Indeed, it is sometimes difficult to see how such conclusions came to be drawn — or, once drawn, widely accepted. Pagels points to more hopeful traditions in Jewish and Christian thought, in which the Creation stories were parables of human equality, men and women both being formed in the image and likeness of God, and were evocations of God's gift of moral freedom. That is to say, the Creation stories justified a view of human will and human potential that can be simply stated: God gave to human beings dominion not only over the earth but also over themselves as individuals. The fourth-century theologian Gregory of Nyssa, reflecting a long tradition of both Jewish and Christian thinking, wrote: "Preeminent among all is the fact that we are free from any necessity, and not in bondage to any power, but have decision in our own power as we please; for virtue is a voluntary thing, subject to no dominion. Whatever is the result of compulsion and force cannot be virtue."[11]

Adam, Eve, and the Serpent traces the clashes of interpretation that eventually arose in the early church, culminating in the triumph of Augustine, whose harsh views on the subject of human will and sinfulness would become those of much of the Western world and helped to define Western consciousness for a millennium and a half. Augustine's *Confessions* are a landmark in Western literature for their searing personal analysis; his personality, in a modern understanding of that term, is perhaps the first historical one to which later ages have access. His frank admission of sexual excess in his youth and his inability to exert self-control has been endlessly psychologized. And, too, it has been theologized. Rather than seeing in the Creation stories an affirmation of human will, Augustine saw a demonstration of its powerlessness. And if the transgression in the Garden of Eden was, as Augustine believed, a sexual one, then the sexual will of woman was, in his view, more troublesome than that of man.

Transferring this individual template to the larger society, Augustine emphasized the need for external government, for stern control of the body politic. Where earlier Christians invoked moral freedom to justify resistance to state oppression, Augustine, inhabiting a world in which imperial and ecclesial power stood in alliance, invoked moral weakness to justify the necessity of a vigorous secular order. And as in society, so too in the household. "Although originally created equal with man in her rational soul," Pagels writes, "woman's bodily nature made her the 'weaker part of the human couple.'" In consequence, she goes on, summarizing Augustine's argument, "God himself reinforced the husband's authority over his wife, placing divine sanction upon the social, legal, and economic machinery of male domination."[12] As Pagels shows, Augustine's philosophy was not universally embraced; indeed, it was fiercely contested. But within a few centuries of his death, older views had been labeled as heresies or otherwise consigned to the margins.

Phyllis Trible and Tikva Frymer-Kensky have from time to time spoken about writing a book together called *Feminists Who Love the Bible*. I somehow doubt that there will ever be a book called *Feminists Who Love Augustine*. But any reader of Elaine Pagels will come away with an appreciation for the man. Pagels does not deal in caricatures. At the same time, she can give eloquent voice to skepticism about how far our own (including *her* own) version of enlightenment can penetrate. We may succeed in restoring certain women and ideas to a prominence they may once have had. We may succeed in discerning attitudes toward gender in religion that never joined the broadest or swiftest-flowing channel. But it is difficult, perhaps impossible, to escape completely the pull of our own preoccupations.

"The trouble with the history of Christianity, the early history of Christianity," Pagels says, "is that it has always been read as a *religious* history. Christianity, like Judaism, claims that its history is a sacred history. The assumption is that if you get back to the Golden Age, back to what Krister Stendahl used to call Play Bible Land, you would find something very right and true and transcendent. When people set out to rewrite the history of Christianity, they have to write themselves into it. Every reformer in the history of the Church has done this. Saint Francis of Assisi thought he was recovering the early Church. Martin Luther thought so. And the same goes for many people working today. If they have an agenda, they tend to insist that the early Church was like whatever that agenda is.

"I always think of Kierkegaard saying that life is lived forward and understood backward. I myself was, like many other people, looking for the *real* Christianity. And you can read anything you want into so much. What my work has taught me is that you must be as self-aware as possible. That is the only way to avoid reading theological dreams into what you find historically."

To some extent, though, the theological dreams are inevitable, and unavoidable. So are the caricatures. The New Testament scholar Paula Fredriksen, of Boston University, once lampooned the glib, shorthand, all-purpose feminist version of religion's evolution in the West as follows: "The Judaeo-Christian tradition is Bad, though Jesus was Good. Paul was Bad. The Gnostics were Good. Augustine was Very Very Bad."[13] Of course, the caricature would hardly be recognizable if there were nothing to it at all — if there were nothing familiar about, say, the set of the jaw, the cast of the eye.

Below the level of caricature, or abstraction of any kind, are the actual lives of women in antiquity, whose daily preoccupations, including whatever room was left for religious activities, private or communal, remain dimly apprehended. Most people do not pass their days, at least consciously, in the realm of caroming ideas and cross-fertilizing philosophies. They adapt their worldviews as the circumstances of their existence may warrant. Understanding just what those circumstances might be for typical women of various classes in various eras is, obviously, one aim of social history, an aim that many feminist biblical scholars strive to pursue. This quest is precisely what Vanderbilt's Amy-Jill Levine has in mind when thinking about the question she would pose to the sisters Martha and Mary, about why they had become followers of Jesus in the first place: "What was in it for *you?*"

It is much easier, Ross Kraemer once observed, to move from knowledge about a community to accurate speculations about the nature of that community's philosophical and religious ideas than it is to move in the opposite direction — that is, from an awareness of certain philosophical and religious ideas to accurate speculations about the nature of the communities that produced them. What were those Gnostic gatherings or societies actually like? How did their adherents spend most of their time? What roles did the women play outside those religious associations? No one can really say — we have so far been granted only Brooten's momentary glimpse through the door.

For all we know, it may likewise prove difficult, a millennium hence, to infer lineaments of our own society from surviving fragments of *Her Share of the Blessings* and *Love Between Women* and *Adam, Eve, and the Serpent,* tantalizing as the fragments would surely be. Were they produced by a society that was waning or waxing in religiosity, waning or waxing in terms of women's economic or social power? Was it a period that witnessed a sudden bloom of Montanists with car phones? One element that no one would be able to miss, though, is how for women, the issues and the biblical texts under discussion had remained in many cases constant after the passage of fifteen or twenty centuries. That realization, in the present time, has been both bitter and welcome.

"What this meant," Elaine Pagels recalls, sorting out her reaction to the rediscovery of these ancient debates, "was that the issues women were raising were not just invented in the twentieth century. Women were not bringing up alien issues and trying to impose them on a religious tradition that had a very firm structure. Rather, the structure we now see represents the narrowing of a much wider river."

Epilogue

....

THE WORD
ACCORDING TO
EVE

SAN FRANCISCO: on a Saturday evening in November, the Society of
Biblical Literature prepares to assemble once more in solemn conclave.
The Committee on the Status of Women in the Profession has already
convened and dispersed. So have the panel discussions on "Jobs and
Gender" and "Mentoring Networks" and "Enhancement and Development for Women in Religious Studies." A meeting of a new group called
the Feminist Liberation Theologians' Network has by now taken place.

The annual presidential address, delivered promptly at 8:00 P.M.,
serves as a symbolic starter's flag. It is also the traditional occasion for
poring over the meeting program (366 pages long this year) in an at-
tempt to concoct a schedule. In the course of the next few days, Karen L.
King will be speaking about the *Gospel of Mary*, Elisabeth Schüssler
Fiorenza about Revelation 17–18, Karen Jo Torjesen about "A Quarter
Century of Women's Studies in Religion." Sessions will be devoted to
"Corinthian Women Prophets and Paul's Argumentation in 1 Corin-
thians" and to "A Fresh Look at Jephthah's Daughter" and to "A Korean
Feminist Reading of Matthew 15:21–28."

This meeting marks the fiftieth anniversary of the discovery of the
Dead Sea Scrolls. On this subject too there will be discussions with a
feminist orientation. Taken as a whole, the Dead Sea Scrolls offer a
deeply misogynistic (or perhaps gynephobic) view of gender. What sort
of community produced or preserved these texts? What connection did
it have to the community whose remains (a significant archaeological
site) lie close to the caves at Qumran where most of the scrolls were
found? Was the community all male? Was it celibate? "What about all
those graves of women and children?" someone will ask.

At the meeting on "A Quarter Century of Women's Studies in Religion," one participant thinks back to the early days: "We were told not to write anything about women's issues until after tenure." Another participant, looking around at the scores of unfamiliar faces, remarks, "When I first came here, I knew the names of all the women." A woman who teaches at Barnard, which is now a unit within Columbia University, recounts a conversation she has overheard between a Barnard professor and someone else: "So what's it like, being part of Columbia?" "It's like being the wife." "What kind of husband is he?" "Well, it's not like he's abusive, but he's definitely more interested in his own career." At a session convened to discuss a new anthology, *A Feminist Companion to Reading the Bible*, one of the commentators, the poet Alicia Ostriker, concludes a manifesto of complaint against the Bible with the frank affirmation that "the religion of the Bible is also the source of every value I hold precious." She asks the audience of several hundred women and about twelve men, "What is it that people in this room don't want to let go of?"

Another commentator, the young anthropologist Miriam Peskowitz, half seriously compares feminist biblical studies to a game of cat and mouse: "It all looks like a game, until you realize that the ultimate aim is to maim or kill." When the laughter has subsided, the next commentator, Carole Fontaine, who coedited the anthology under discussion, takes the podium and quietly adds this gloss: "No one is more surprised than my cat when the mouse dies."

There are some who hope, some who fear, and some who merely predict that the modern engagement of women and the Bible through scholarship will turn out to be a short-lived phenomenon, remembered as at best an efflorescence, at worst an irrelevance, but at any rate as a blip. Given the natural life cycle of past social movements, which has often paralleled the turning of the generations, such a view is certainly understandable. It is also, in my view, mistaken.

To be sure, academic work on women and the Bible faces certain inherent problems, certain inherent risks. In my talks with people in the field, one scholar after another voiced the same worries. One concern is the sometimes facile comparisons made between Christianity and Judaism, the playing off of one against the other. Another has to do with the distinction between deriving an interpretation from a text and reading an interpretation into a text. It is one thing if a personal agenda — a desire, say, to see women enjoy a position of full equality in religious institutions — helps to focus a scholar's research. Agendas of one sort or another almost always drive scholarship. But agendas can also get out of hand.

Still, a number of factors will ensure the vitality and longevity of feminist biblical studies. First, intellectual curiosity simply has not come close to reaching its natural limit: there is more to learn, and more that is learnable, about women and the world of the Bible. Some fields of study dry out or go barren as specialists pick over the same small, tired patch with tools of increasingly sophisticated irrelevance. But archaeology, linguistics, and the study of societies parallel to or contemporaneous with those depicted in the Bible continue to sprout new material. The perspectives of social history, especially as they apply to gender, remain fresh.

The Bible, moreover, is no longer banished to the fringes of mainstream academic life, as it was for more than a hundred years after its dethronement in the nineteenth century as an authoritative document for a modern mind. To be sure, the foundation of Bible study continues to rest on departments of religion and theology, as it always will, but approaches to the subject matter have moved closer to the center of modern academic sensibilities. The Bible has gained new attention from literature departments, history departments, anthropology departments, and sociology departments. This is owing in some measure to the protection afforded by the interest of women. Feminist concerns were not acknowledged in academe without resistance, to say the least, but once acknowledged, they have tended to confer a form of immunity on whatever they come in contact with. Academe's hostility toward religion and spirituality has at times been justifiable, as Richard Hofstadter showed in *Anti-Intellectualism in American Life*; that hostility closed off certain avenues of inquiry. Those avenues are open once again.

The deep involvement of women in the work of organized religion has always sustained it, but their involvement now extends to unprecedented levels of institutional authority. The influence of women will only grow, both in conventional channels and in unconventional ones.

Something similar to the impetus that produced the house-church in early Christianity is operating once again in gatherings of Christian and Jewish women. The significance of women's influence in religion in America may be ignored or dismissed by some, who wrongly see it as a phenomenon of the margin. In truth, of course, the United States is the most pervasively religious nation in the developed world, and people who have something to say about religion can draw, if they must, on resources that have little or nothing to do with traditional denominations.

Finally, there is that matter of the wider world, which of course shapes religion in our own time as much as it ever did in times past. Some feminists cram an impressive amount of scorn into a term like "the Greco-Roman gender system," but that system and its byproducts and successors have been deeply undermined in the present century. Technology has given women control over their reproductive behavior. The workforce is open to women as never before. We may hear these developments bemoaned for various reasons on all sides, by those who say they go too far and those who say they do not go far enough. But they are facts, and they represent a sharp and irreversible turn.

What has been accomplished thus far? One achievement has been simply the staking out of ground. Several decades ago no one was particularly concerned — indeed, the thought rarely occurred to anyone — that what was known about the biblical world was based on what was known about men's lives and generalized from men to humanity. Those days are gone. Leaving aside the specific details, scholars have traveled a long way toward bringing women into sharper relief in biblical and early Christian times. They have also shown how meaning has been clouded by the lacquer of interpretation.

Another achievement has been a new emphasis on the sheer variety of thought and practice that sometimes existed within ancient religious groups. Scholars who perhaps went searching after some lost Golden Age, driven by the "earlier is better" bias that seems to be a familiar tendency in human thought, have stumbled into worlds that were more confused and complex than scholars anticipated, worlds that are in that sense not unlike our own.

Perhaps the most important lesson offered by the work of feminist biblical scholars comes in the form of a reminder: that in religion, as in other spheres, circumstances have not always been as we see them now. Evolution occurs. Some things, it turns out, are not sacred. This point may be obvious, but with respect to religion especially it is frequently overlooked, and in fact sometimes hotly debated. Whatever we believe about the circumstances of their origin, the handful of immutable principles at any religion's core are embedded in a vast pulp of tradition, interpretation, and practice. And that pulp bears an all-too-human character. It is variously diminished, augmented, scarred, sculpted, and otherwise shaped by powerful human forces in every society and every time period through which it passes. Sometimes the change occurs slowly and almost invisibly. Sometimes it happens quickly and right before our eyes, as I believe it is happening now — the proliferation of feminist scholarship on the Bible being both consequence and cause.

That scholarship is assessed by some as meaningless and by others as a persuasive argument for shunting the Bible back to the margins. To my mind, the Bible's powerfully troublesome qualities are part of its value. At a symposium held at the Smithsonian Institution a few years ago, a member of the audience rose and remarked that after listening to all the things that feminist scholars had to say about women and the Bible, she wondered if she had any choice but to throw up her hands and forget about the whole thing. One of the panelists replied, in effect, "I'm afraid you have no other choice." But Tikva Frymer-Kensky was also a panelist, and she sharply disagreed. "The Bible," she said, "is an extremely complex document that revels in a multiplicity of voices, that is filled with gapped texts, that demands that the interpreter complete the text, that raises all kinds of significant issues, that critiques its own society and confesses its divided opinion about everything. The Bible is a document of struggle, of God-wrestling. It is a record of a society and the response of individuals who constantly go back over their history and think about these things."[1]

What is it, Alicia Ostriker asked the audience, "that people in this room don't want to let go of?" That question may in a sense be the wrong one: it is the Bible itself that does not let go. Its stories and characterizations, its taut renderings of circumstance and motivation, of belief and assumption, are an inexhaustible source of moral reflection. They demand from any reader a response, whether the response comes in a spirit of anger or of uplift, of religious faith or of devout skepticism.

Think of it as we will — as "wandering rock," perhaps, or as "night visitor," or as "pilgrim" — the Bible remains an ageless provocation. That is why feminist scholars were drawn to the Bible in the first place. Their own biblical provocations in turn have caused discomfort and uncertainty, and a cacophony of agendas, and a sometimes acrimonious rethinking of yesterday and today. This hardly represents an upsetting of tradition. It represents, rather, a revitalizing of one.

And is not provocation Eve's true vocation? In the Bible, the last of the very few words given to Eve are those that follow an act of creativity, which is to say of provocation: the birth of a child. Creativity, curiosity, understanding: these are the provocative attributes for which Eve is remembered. They might not be needed in Paradise. They are made, as are we, for a world that falls short of Eden.

NOTES

BIBLIOGRAPHY

ACKNOWLEDGMENTS

INDEX

NOTES

Many of the quotations in this book derive from interviews, some conducted over the course of several years. Those quotations are identified as such in context, and receive no further citation below.

FOREWORD

1. We can debate endlessly about what to call the Bible and its parts so as to avoid both imprecision and offense. New terminology of various kinds ("First Testament," "Second Testament") has been proposed. I generally use the term "Hebrew Bible" to refer to the Jewish canon, though I am aware that some of the Hebrew Bible was written in Aramaic and that "Hebrew Bible" is not synonymous with the Christian term "Old Testament" (which is arranged differently and may include additional books). The term "New Testament" is accepted by almost everyone. Distinctions and clarifications will be noted as necessary. For the record, I also use the notation B.C.; the alternative, B.C.E., meaning "before the common era," raises more questions than it resolves. (For a concise review of these terminology issues, see William Safire, "The New Old Testament," *New York Times Magazine*, May 25, 1997, and "B.C./A.D. or B.C.E./C.E.?" *New York Times Magazine*, Aug. 17, 1997.) The Bible translation used unless otherwise noted, is the Revised Standard Version.
2. Trible, *Texts of Terror*, p. 4.
3. Cullen Murphy, "Women and the Bible," *Atlantic Monthly*, Aug. 1993, p. 64.

1. JOINING THE PROCESSION

1. Society of Biblical Literature. See also Bass, "Women's Studies," pp. 6–12.
2. Gimbutas, *Language of the Goddess*, p. xxi; see also Gimbutas, *Gods and Goddesses*.
3. Marketing department, HarperSanFrancisco; marketing department, Ballantine Books, New York. See also Lavonne Neff, "A Celebration of Women's Spirituality," *Publishers Weekly*, Jan. 8, 1996; Judith Weinraub, "The New Theology — Sheology," *Washington Post*, Apr. 28, 1991.
4. Sonia L. Nazario, "Is Goddess Worship Finally Going to Put Men in Their Place?" *Wall Street Journal*, June 7, 1990.
5. Peter Steinfels, "Female Concept of God Is Shaking Protestants," *New York Times*, May 14, 1994.
6. Gustav Niebuhr, "Pope Levels Criticism at Catholic Feminists," *Washington Post*, July 4, 1993.
7. Kenneth L. Woodward, "Feminism and the Churches," *Newsweek*, Feb. 13, 1989; *1995 Yearbook of American and Canadian Churches*, pp. 279–80. A useful survey of women in the ministry in mainline Protestantism is provided in Charlotte Allen, "Our Mother Who Art in Heaven," *Washington Post Magazine*, Dec. 10, 1995.
8. *Fact Book on Theological Education 1976–1977* and *1995–1996* (Pittsburgh, Pa.: Association of Theological Schools); Barbara Brown Zikmund, Adair T. Loomis, and Patricia Mei Yin Chang, *Clergy Women: An Uphill Calling* (Louisville, Ky.: Westminster/John Knox, 1998). For an introductory overview of the influx of women into divinity school, see Paul Wilkes, "The Hands That Would Shape Our Souls," *Atlantic Monthly*, Dec. 1990.
9. Morton, "Preaching the Word," p. 29.
10. Selvidge, *Notorious Voices*, pp. 23–37.
11. Trible, "Postscript," pp. 147–49.
12. Metzger and Coogan, *Oxford Companion to the Bible*, p. 760.
13. Lowell Weiss, "Language: Speaking in Tongues," *Atlantic Monthly*, June 1995, p. 36.

14. For a basic chronology of translation history, see Metzger and Coogan, *Oxford Companion to the Bible*. Useful introductions to certain translation issues include Gerald Hammond, "English Translations of the Bible," in Alter and Kermode, *Literary Guide to the Bible*; Robert Alter's introduction to his translation, *Genesis*; and Barry Hoberman, "Translating the Bible," *Atlantic Monthly*, Feb. 1985, pp. 43–58.
15. Taylor, *New Bible*, pp. 50–65, 69–70.
16. Worth, *Bible Translations*, p. 133.
17. Richard M. Harley, "New Testaments on Women and Religious History," *Christian Science Monitor*, Apr. 30, 1981.
18. Castelli, "Les Belles Infidèles," p. 28.
19. Bird, "Translating Sexist Language," p. 89.
20. Virginia Woolf, *Three Guineas* (San Diego: Harcourt Brace Jovanovich, 1938), pp. 60–62.
21. Carol L. Meyers, *Dictionary of Women*.
22. Pinnock, "Biblical Authority," p. 57.
23. Koester, *Ancient Christian Gospels*, p. xxxii.

2. THE SORCERER'S APPRENTICE

1. Margherita Arlina Hamm, "A Woman Suffragist Resolution to Be Presented," *Mail and Express* (New York), Jan. 25, 1896, in Susan B. Anthony, *Scrapbooks*, vol. 25, p. 23.
2. Griffith, *In Her Own Right*, pp. 212–13.
3. Stanton, *Woman's Bible*, vol. 1, p. 7.
4. Ibid., p. 36.
5. Ibid., p. 84.
6. Schüssler Fiorenza, *Bread Not Stone*, p. 54.
7. Stanton, *Eighty Years*, p. 453.
8. Hamm, "A Woman Suffragist."
9. Elizabeth Cady Stanton to Antoinette Brown Blackwell, Apr. 27, 1896, Blackwell Family Papers, Arthur and Elizabeth Schlesinger Library, Radcliffe College.
10. Stanton, *Woman's Bible*, vol. 2, p. 9.

11. Julian of Norwich, A *Shewing of Divine Love*, ed. Anna Maria Reynolds (London: Sheed and Ward, 1958), p. 17.
12. Selvidge, *Notorious Voices*, pp. 121–30.
13. Ibid., pp. 23–37.
14. Murray, "Equality of the Sexes," pp. 23–24.
15. Gifford, "American Women and the Bible"; Milne, "Feminist Interpretations."
16. Gifford, "American Women and the Bible," p. 15.
17. Rossi, *Feminist Papers*, p. 287.
18. Griffith, *In Her Own Right*, p. 37.
19. Stanton, *Eighty Years*, p. 80.
20. Gifford, "American Women and the Bible," p. 21.
21. Hardesty, *Women Called to Witness*, p. 104.
22. Cazden, *Antoinette Brown Blackwell*, p. 42; see also Rossi, *Feminist Papers*, pp. 323–77.
23. Douglas, *Feminization of American Culture*, p. 10.
24. Bass, "Their Prodigious Influence," p. 281.
25. Stanton, *Woman's Bible*, vol. 1, p. 11.
26. Gage, *Woman, Church, and State*, p. 13.
27. Stanton, *Woman's Bible*, vol. 1, p. 11.
28. Ibid., pp. 11–12.
29. Stanton, *Eighty Years*, p. 452.
30. Selvidge, *Notorious Voices*, pp. 214–24.
31. Stanton, *Woman's Bible*, vol. 1, p. 46.
32. Ibid., p. 64.
33. Ibid., p. 94.
34. Stanton, *Woman's Bible*, vol. 2, pp. 19–20.
35. Ibid., p. 30.
36. Ibid., p. 65.
37. Stanton, *Woman's Bible*, vol. 1, p. 112.
38. Stanton, *Woman's Bible*, vol. 2, p. 46.
39. Stanton, *Woman's Bible*, vol. 1, pp. 72–73.
40. Griffith, *In Her Own Right*, pp. 122–25, 134. See also Thistlethwaite, "The Bible and the Feminists," pp. 20–23.
41. Gifford, "American Women and the Bible," p. 16.

42. Stanton, *Woman's Bible*, vol. 1, p. 9.
43. Bass, "Women's Studies and Biblical Studies," pp. 6–12; Saunders, *Searching the Scriptures*.
44. Mary Wilhelmine Williams, "Elizabeth Cady Stanton,"in *Dictionary of American Biography*, vol. 17 (New York: Scribner's, 1943), p. 522.
45. Gifford, "Politicizing the Sacred Texts," p. 60.

3. BY THE HAND OF A WOMAN

1. Thomas P. Slavens, "The Librarianship of Charles Augustus Briggs," *Union Seminary Quarterly Review* 24 (Summer 1969): 357–63.
2. Union Theological Seminary, Office of Public Affairs.
3. John Updike, *Roger's Version* (New York: Knopf, 1986), p. 28.
4. Greenfield, "The Bible and Canaanite Literature," pp. 545–60; Gordon, *Ugarit and Minoan Crete*.
5. Craigie, "The Tablets from Ugarit."
6. Steven S. Tuell, "A Riddle Resolved by an Enigma," *Journal of Biblical Literature* 112, no. 1 (1993): 99–104.
7. Ralph W. Klein, *Textual Criticism of the Old Testament* (Philadelphia: Fortress, 1974), p. x.
8. Norman Perrin, *What Is Redaction Criticism?* (Philadelphia: Fortress, 1969), p. 1. Other surveys of critical method include Gene M. Tucker, *Form Criticism of the Old Testament* (Philadelphia: Fortress, 1971); William G. Doty, *Contemporary New Testament Interpretation* (Englewood Cliffs, N.J.: Prentice-Hall, 1972); and Edgar Krentz, *The Historical Critical Method* (Philadelphia: Fortress, 1975).
9. James Muilenburg, "Form Criticism and Beyond," *Journal of Biblical Literature* 88 (1969): 1–18.
10. Leach and Aycock, *Structuralist Interpretations*, p. 3.
11. Phyllis Trible's doctoral thesis has been recently published as part of a larger critical work, *Rhetorical Criticism: Context, Method, and the Book of Jonah* (Minneapolis: Fortress, 1994).
12. Hardwick, *Oh Thou Woman*, pp. 80, 104.
13. Friedan, *Feminine Mystique*, p. 351.

14. Crook, *Women and Religion*, p. 1.
15. Daly, *Church and the Second Sex*, pp. 74–75.
16. Ibid., p. 12.
17. Mary Daly, "Sin Big," *New Yorker*, Feb. 24 and Mar. 4, 1996, p. 81.
18. Daly, *Pure Lust*, p. xii. See also Daly, *Gyn/Ecology*.
19. Beauvoir, *Second Sex*, p. 159.
20. Trible, *God and the Rhetoric of Sexuality*, p. 102.
21. Quoted in Pamela J. Milne, "Eve and Adam: Is a Feminist Reading Possible?" *Bible Review* (June 1988): 16.
22. Quoted in Melton, *The Churches Speak*.
23. John Milton, *Paradise Lost*, Book 9, ll. 1067–69.
24. Pelikan, *Mary Through the Centuries*, p. 28.
25. Brooke, "A Long-Lost Song," p. 64. The Miriam story as a whole is discussed by Phyllis Trible in "Bringing Miriam Out of the Shadows," *Bible Review* (Feb. 1989): 14–34.
26. Pelikan, *Mary Through the Centuries*, p. 1.
27. Pardes, *Countertraditions*, p. 24.
28. Lanser, "(Feminist) Criticism in the Garden."
29. Jobling, *Biblical Narrative*, pp. 41–42.
30. Shanks, *Feminist Approaches*, p. 100.
31. Trible, *Texts of Terror*, p. 3.
32. Ibid., p. 28.
33. Ibid., p. 80.
34. Bird, "'Male and Female,'" p. 155.

4. THE MOTHERS OF ISRAEL

1. Netzer and Weiss, *Zippori*.
2. Meyers and Meyers, "Finders of a Real Lost Ark"; Victoria Everett, "Eric and Carol Meyers Didn't Dig the Ark in 'Raiders' — They Found the Real Thing," *People*, Sept. 14, 1981, p. 58.
3. Silberman, "Who Were the Israelites?" pp. 22–30.
4. Carl N. Degler, *Is There a History of Women?* (London: Oxford University Press, 1975), pp. 5–6.
5. Meyers, *Discovering Eve*, pp. 132–35.

6. Judith Romney Wegner, "Leviticus," in *The Woman's Bible Commentary* (Louisville, Ky.: Westminster/John Knox, 1992), p. 38.
7. Meyers, "Family in Early Israel," p. 34.
8. Meyers, *Discovering Eve*, pp. 149–54.
9. Plaskow, "Blaming Jews," p. 11; Heschel, "Anti-Judaism."
10. Meyers, *Discovering Eve*, pp. 95–109.
11. Ibid., pp. 112–13.
12. Rice, "The 'New' Archaeology," p. 127.
13. Kendrick, *Bible Teaching at Wellesley*, p. 6.
14. *Wellesley College 1875–1975: A Century of Women*, ed. Jean Glasscock (Wellesley, Mass.: Wellesley College, 1975), p. 401.
15. Romanowicz and Wright, "Gendered Perspectives," p. 200.
16. Halpern, "Erasing History."
17. Meyers, "Kinship and Kingship."
18. Ibid., p. 33.
19. Greenspahn, "Words That Occur Once," pp. 28–30.
20. Freedman, *Anchor Bible Dictionary*, vol. 1, p. 256.
21. Meyers, *Discovering Eve*, pp. 179–80.

5. WORDS OF WISDOM

1. Frymer-Kensky, *In the Wake of the Goddess*, p. 1.
2. Frymer-Kensky, *Motherprayer*, p. 221.
3. Brenner and van Dijk-Hemmes, *On Gendering Texts*, p. 18.
4. Stern, "How Bad Was Ahab?"
5. Salway, *History of Roman Britain*, p. 346.
6. Haines-Eitzen, "Female Scribes in Roman Antiquity."
7. Ibid.
8. Friedman, *Who Wrote the Bible?*, p. 15.
9. Friedman's *Who Wrote the Bible?* offers an accessible survey of all the issues discussed here; see also E. A. Speiser, introduction to *The Anchor Bible: Genesis*, pp. 27–52.
10. Bloom and Rosenberg, *Book of J*, p. 32.
11. Ibid., p. 10.
12. Alter, *World of Biblical Literature*, p. 166.

13. Friedman, *Who Wrote the Bible?*, p. 86.
14. Meyers, "Text Without Context," p. 65.
15. Martin, *I Flew Them Home*.
16. Goitein, "Women as Creators," p. 2.
17. Ibid., p. 5.
18. Brenner and van Dijk-Hemmes, *Gendering Texts*, p. 7.
19. Ibid., pp. 97–103.
20. Savina J. Teubal, "Naming Is Creating: Biblical Women Hold the Power," *Bible Review* (Aug. 1995): 40–41.
21. Goitein, "Women as Creators," p. 10.
22. Meyers, *Discovering Eve*, p. 152.
23. For a fuller exposition of this point, see Camp, *Wisdom and the Feminine*.
24. Frymer-Kensky, *In the Wake of the Goddesses*, p. 107.
25. For discussions of Kuntillet Arjûd, see, for instance, Patrick Miller, Paul Hanson, and S. Dean McBride, eds., *Ancient Israelite Religion* (Philadelphia: Fortress, 1987); Hadley, "Some Drawings and Inscriptions"; Dever, "Asherah, Consort of Yahweh?"
26. Frymer-Kensky, *In the Wake of the Goddesses*, p. vii.
27. Ibid., p. 80.
28. Ibid., p. 99.
29. *New York Post*, June 17, 1991.
30. Marci McDonald, "Is God a Woman?" *Maclean's*, Apr. 8, 1996.
31. Frymer-Kensky, *In the Wake of the Goddesses*, p. 188.
32. Ibid., p. 141.
33. Charles Barsotti, *New Yorker*, July 28, 1997, p. 28.
34. Frymer-Kensky, *In the Wake of the Goddesses*, pp. 179–83.

6. THE WANDERING ROCK

1. Levine, "Sacrifice and Salvation," p. 322.
2. Fuchs, "Who Is Hiding the Truth?" p. 137. See also Fuchs, "'For I Have the Way of Women.'"
3. Esther Fuchs, "The Literary Character of Mothers and Sexual Politics in the Hebrew Bible," in Collins, *Feminist Perspectives*, p. 130.

4. Fuchs, "Who Is Hiding the Truth?" p. 143.
5. Craven, "Women Who Lied for Faith," pp. 46, 48.
6. Susan Niditch, "Esther: Folklore, Wisdom, Feminism, and Authority," in Brenner, *Feminist Companion*, p. 41.
7. Mieke Bal, "Afterword: Looking Back," in *Looking In: The Art of Viewing*, ed. Norman Bryson (Amsterdam: G & B Art International, forthcoming).
8. Bal, *Lethal Love*, p. 94.
9. Bach, "Throw Them to the Lions," p. 1.
10. Bal, *Lethal Love*, pp. 1, 132, 3.
11. Ibid., p. 50.
12. Bal, *Murder and Difference*, pp. 2–3.
13. Bal, *Death and Dissymmetry*, p. 1.
14. Ibid., p. 5.
15. Mieke Bal, "Between Altar and Wandering Rock: Toward a Feminist Philology," in Bal, *Anti-Covenant*, pp. 211–32.
16. Ibid., pp. 218–19.

7. WAS JESUS A FEMINIST?

1. Survey histories of this region and period are numerous. Readers might wish to consult Koester, *Introduction to the New Testament*; Sanders, *Judaism*; and Rousseau and Arav, *Jesus and His World*.
2. Funk, Hoover, and Jesus Seminar, *Five Gospels*, pp. 36–37.
3. Journalistic accounts of the Jesus Seminar include Charlotte Allen, "Away With the Manger," *Lingua Franca*, Jan.–Feb. 1995; Jeffrey L. Sheler, "In Search of Jesus," *U.S. News & World Report*, Apr. 8, 1996; "Bob Funk's Radical Reformation Roadshow," *U.S. News & World Report*, Aug. 4, 1997; and David Van Biema, "The Gospel Truth?" *Time*, Apr. 8, 1996.
4. Schüssler Fiorenza, "Feminist Theology and New Testament Interpretation," p. 32.
5. Schüssler Fiorenza, *Bread Not Stone*, pp. 58, 95.
6. Schüssler Fiorenza, *Discipleship of Equals*, p. 53.
7. Elisabeth Schüssler Fiorenza's few published personal reminis-

cences include "Wartime as Formative Experience"; "Biblical Interpretation"; and "Changing the Paradigms."

8. Schüssler Fiorenza, *In Memory of Her*, pp. 102–3, 121.

9. Ibid., p. 131.

10. Ibid., p. 138.

11. Ibid., pp. 137–38.

12. Ibid., pp. xiii, 153.

13. Ibid., p. 139.

14. Ibid., p. 168.

15. Schüssler Fiorenza, "Quilting."

16. Schüssler Fiorenza, "Feminist Theology as a Theology of Liberation."

17. Swidler, "Jesus Was a Feminist," p. 177.

18. Swidler, *Women in Judaism*, p. 167.

19. Witherington, *Women in the Ministry*, pp. 125, 127.

20. Corley, "Feminist Myths," p. 52.

21. Corley, "Jesus, Women and Palestine."

22. Corley, "Feminist Myths," p. 59.

23. Judith Plaskow, "Anti-Judaism in Feminist Christian Interpretation," in Schüssler Fiorenza, *Searching the Scriptures*, vol. 1., pp. 117–29.

24. Corley, "Jesus, Women and Palestine."

25. Levine, "Matthew," in Newsom and Ringe, *Women's Bible Commentary*, p. 256.

26. Ross S. Kraemer, "Women's Authorship of Jewish and Christian Literature in the Greco-Roman Period," in Levine, *Women Like This*, p. 221.

8. BORN OF A WOMAN

1. Joliffe, *Letters from Palestine*, p. 26. See also Charland, *Madame saincte Anne*, pp. 451–84.

2. Schneemelcher, *New Testament Apocrypha*, p. 376.

3. The "Mary Page," the web site of the Marian Library and the International Marian Research Institute, can be found at http://www.udayton.edu/mary/index.html.

4. Adams, *Mont-Saint-Michel*, p. 196.
5. Erasmus, *Praise of Folly*, p. 57.
6. Kenneth L. Woodward, "Hail, Mary," *Newsweek*, Aug. 25, 1997, pp. 49–55; Richard N. Ostling, "Handmaid or Feminist?" *Time*, Dec. 30, 1991, pp. 62–66.
7. Hamington, *Hail Mary?*, p. 23.
8. Woodward, "Hail, Mary," p. 49.
9. Cunneen, *In Search of Mary*, p. 238.
10. Johnson, "Toward a Theology," p. 11.
11. Hamington, *Hail Mary?*, pp. 20–23.
12. Donnelly, "Mary: A Sign," pp. 126–27.
13. John Paul II, *On the Dignity*, p. 64.
14. Warner, *Alone of All Her Sex*, pp. 338–39.
15. Adams, *Mont-Saint-Michel*, p. 196.
16. Daly, *Gyn/Ecology*, p. 84.
17. Johnson, "Toward a Theology," p. 2.
18. Rahner, *Mary*, p. 83.
19. Meier, *Marginal Jew*, pp. 205–52.
20. Barrett, "Virgin Birth."
21. *The New Encyclopaedia Britannica*, vol. 7, 15th ed. (Chicago), s.v. "Mary."
22. Levine, *Social and Ethical Dimensions*, p. 87.
23. Schaberg, *Illegitimacy of Jesus*, pp. 33, 1.
24. Ibid., p. 157.
25. Ibid., pp. 165–70.
26. Meier, *Marginal Jew*, pp. 246–47.
27. "Readers Reply," *Bible Review* (Feb. 1989): 6–9, 34–37.
28. Schaberg, "Contribution of Feminist Scholarship."
29. Kogan, *Great EB*, pp. 173–78, 294.
30. Pelikan, *Mary*, p. 98.
31. Ibid., p. 87.
32. Ruether, *Sexism and God-Talk*, p. 153.
33. Ibid., p. 224.
34. Ibid., p. 25.
35. Ibid., p. 26.

9. PROMINENT AMONG THE APOSTLES?

1. Tolotti, *Cimitero di Priscilla*, pp. 258–82.
2. John Paul II, *Letter of the Holy Father to Women*, pp. 3–4.
3. Ibid., p. 13.
4. Declaration on the Question of the Admission of Women to the Ministerial Priesthood (Washington, D.C., United States Catholic Council, 1977).
5. Alan Cowell, "Pope Rules Out Debate on Making Women Priests," *New York Times*, May 31, 1994.
6. Mark I. Pinsky, "Women in the Pulpit Divide Baptists," *Orlando Sentinel*, Oct. 13, 1996; "Furor in Germany Over Female Rabbi," *New York Times*, Aug. 2, 1995; "Cleric Hard-Liners Crack Down on Revealing Women's Eyes," *St. Louis Post-Dispatch*, Apr. 20, 1997; "Mormon Woman Faces Discipline for Feminist Essay," *Boston Globe*, Oct. 11, 1994.
7. For a concise summary of the ordination issue as it has been faced by various denominations, see Melton, *The Churches Speak*.
8. Armstrong, *End of Silence*, p. 211.
9. Torjesen, *When Women Were Priests*, p. 199.
10. Pinnock, "Biblical Authority," p. 58.
11. Summaries of the arguments relevant to women's ordination have appeared in many places. See, for example, van der Meer, *Women Priests*, and Dulles et al., "Women's Ordination," pp. 10–13.
12. Peter Steinfels, "Women Wary About Aiming to Be Priests," *New York Times*, Nov. 14, 1996.
13. Daneliou, *Ministry of Women*.
14. Gryson, *Ministry of Women*, p. 109.
15. Mary Rose D'Angelo, "Women Partners in the New Testament," *Journal of Feminist Studies in Religion* 6, no. 1 (Spring 1990): 68.
16. Schüssler Fiorenza, "Quilting," p. 45.
17. The material about Junia is drawn from Brooten, "'Junia,'" pp. 141–44.
18. Fander, "Historical Critical Methods," p. 214.
19. Irvin, "Ministry of Women."

20. Mary Ann Rossi, "Priesthood, Precedent, and Prejudice: On Recovering the Women Priests of Early Christianity, Containing a Translation from the Italian of 'Notes on the Female Priesthood in Antiquity,' by Giorgio Otranto," *Journal of Feminist Studies in Religion* 7, no. 1 (Spring 1991): 73–93.
21. Ibid., pp. 90–91.
22. Torjesen, *When Women Were Priests*, pp. 34–46.
23. Ibid., p. 12.
24. Tsafrir, "Ancient Churches."
25. Reimer, *Women in the Acts of the Apostles*, pp. 71–149.
26. Steichen, *Ungodly Rage*, p. 12.
27. Brooten, *Women Leaders*, pp. 11–12, 57–58, 75, 73.
28. Ibid., pp. 5–7.
29. Brooten, "Iael."

10. VENUS IN SACKCLOTH

1. Mendel Nun, "Cast Your Net Upon the Waters," *Biblical Archaeology Review* (Nov.–Dec. 1993): 47–56,70.
2. Shelley Wachsmann, *The Sea of Galilee Boat* (New York: Plenum, 1995).
3. Josephus, *Life and Works*, p. 737.
4. Mark Twain, "Innocents Abroad," in Twain, *Complete Travel Books*, p. 332.
5. Matheson, *Dura Europos*; Goranson, "Battle Over the Holy Day."
6. Nikos Kazantzakis, *Last Temptation of Christ* (New York: Simon and Schuster, 1960), p. 147.
7. Quoted in Schaberg, "Fast Forwarding to Magdalene."
8. The story of this conflation is concisely rendered in Schaberg, "How Mary Magdalene Became a Whore." For a fuller account of this issue and other matters, see Haskins, *Mary Magdalene*.
9. Schaberg, "How Mary Magdalene Became a Whore," p. 34.
10. *New Catholic Encyclopaedia*, vol. 9, s.v. "St. Mary Magdalene."
11. Nolan, *Basilica of S. Clemente*, pp. 1–4, 85–95.
12. Haskins, *Mary Magdalene*, p. 96.

13. Karen L. King, "Prophetic Power and Women's Authority: The Case of the *Gospel of Mary* (Magdalene)," unpublished ms. (a version of this article appears under the same title in Kienzle and Walker, *Heritage of Magdalene*); Karen L. King, "The Jesus Tradition in the *Gospel of Mary*," unpublished ms.

14. The story of the discovery of the Nag Hammadi codices is well told by Elaine Pagels in *The Gnostic Gospels*; see also Robinson, *Nag Hammadi Library in English*, pp. 1–26.

15. Pagels, *Gnostic Gospels*, p. 50.

16. King, "Prophetic Power and Women's Authority."

17. Shawn Carruth and Albrecht Garsky, "Q 11:26–4," in Robinson, Hoffmann, and Kloppenborg, *Documenta Q*.

18. Pagels, *Gnostic Gospels*, p. xxviii.

19. Translation of the *Gospel of Mary*, courtesy of Karen L. King.

20. *Pistis Sophia*, in R. McL. Wilson, *The Coptic Gnostic Library*, vol. 9 (Leiden: E. J. Brill, 1978), pp. 325, 52.

21. King, "Prophetic Power and Women's Authority."

22. Malvern, *Venus in Sackcloth*, pp. 71–99.

23. Warner, *Alone of All Her Sex*, p. 225.

11. A GLIMPSE THROUGH THE DOOR

1. *The Connection*, WBUR, July 9, 1997.

2. Brooten, "Early Christian Women and Their Cultural Context: Issues of Method in Historical Reconstruction," in Collins, *Feminist Perspectives*, p. 67.

3. Ibid., p. 83.

4. Brooten, *Love Between Women*, p. 301.

5. Ibid., pp. 190–92.

6. George Bernard Shaw, "The Monstrous Imposition Upon Jesus," reprinted in W. A. Meeks, ed., *The Writings of St. Paul* (New York: Norton, 1972), p. 299.

7. Dennis Ronald MacDonald, *The Legend and the Apostle: The Battle for Paul in Story and Canon* (Philadelphia: Westminster, 1983), p. 90.

8. Ibid., p. 89.
9. Kraemer, *Her Share of the Blessings*, p. 157.
10. Adam Begley, "The Lonely Genius Club," New *York,* Jan. 30, 1995, p. 63.
11. Pagels, *Adam, Eve, and the Serpent*, pp. 98–99.
12. Ibid., p. 114.
13. Paula Fredriksen, "The Myth of the Goddess: Evolution of an Image," *National Review*, Mar. 1, 1993, p. 56.

EPILOGUE: THE WORD ACCORDING TO EVE

1. Shanks, *Feminist Approaches*, p. 98.

BIBLIOGRAPHY

Adams, Henry. *Letters to a Niece, and Prayer to the Virgin of Chartres.* 1920. Boston: Houghton Mifflin, 1970.

———. *Mont-Saint-Michel and Chartres.* Boston: Houghton Mifflin, 1933.

Alter, Robert, trans. *Genesis.* New York: Norton, 1996.

———. *The World of Biblical Literature.* New York: Basic, 1992.

———, and Frank Kermode, eds. *The Literary Guide to the Bible.* Cambridge, Mass.: Harvard University Press, 1987.

Armstrong, Karen. *The End of Silence: Women and the Priesthood.* London: Fourth Estate, 1993.

Armstrong, Virginia. "Priesthood, Precedent, and Prejudice: On Recovering the Women Priests of Early Christianity." *Journal of Feminist Studies in Religion* 7, no. 1 (Spring 1991).

Bach, Alice. "'Throw Them to the Lions, Sire': Transforming Biblical Narratives into Hollywood Spectacles." *Semeia* 74 (1996).

Bal, Mieke, ed. *Anti-Covenant.* Sheffield, Eng.: Almond, 1989.

———. *Death and Dissymmetry.* Chicago: University of Chicago Press, 1988.

———. *Lethal Love: Feminist Literary Readings of Biblical Love Stories.* Bloomington: Indiana University Press, 1987.

———. *Murder and Difference.* Bloomington: Indiana University Press, 1988.

———. *On Story-Telling: Essays in Narratology.* Sonoma, Calif.: Polebridge, 1991.

Barber, Elizabeth Wayland. *Women's Work: The First 20,000 Years:*

Women, Cloth, and Society in Early Times. New York: Norton, 1994.

Barrett, J. Edward. "Can Scholars Take the Virgin Birth Seriously?" *Bible Review* (Oct. 1988): 10–29.

Bartlett, Elizabeth Ann, ed. *Sarah Grimke's Letters on the Equality of the Sexes.* New Haven, Conn.: Yale University Press, 1988.

Baskin, Judith R., ed. *Jewish Women in Historical Perspective.* Detroit: Wayne State University Press, 1991.

Bass, Dorothy C. "Their Prodigious Influence." In *Women of Spirit,* ed. Rosemary Ruether and Eleanor McLaughlin. New York: Simon and Schuster, 1979.

———. "Women's Studies and Biblical Studies: An Historical Perspective." *Journal for the Study of the Old Testament* 22 (1982).

Beauvoir, Simone de. *The Second Sex.* 1952. Trans. H. M. Parshley. New York: Vintage, 1989.

Bellis, Alice Ogden. *Helpmates, Harlots, and Heroes.* Louisville, Ky.: Westminster/John Knox, 1994.

Bird, Phyllis A. "'Male and Female He Created Them': Gen. 1:27b in the Context of the Priestly Account of Creation." *Harvard Theological Review* 74, vol. 2 (1981).

———. "Translating Sexist Language as a Theological and Cultural Problem." *Union Seminary Quarterly Review* 42, no. 1–2 (1988).

Bloom, Harold, interpreter, and David Rosenberg, trans. *The Book of J.* New York: Grove Weidenfeld, 1990.

Borg, Marcus. *Jesus: A New Vision.* San Francisco: HarperCollins, 1987.

Brenner, Athalya, ed. *A Feminist Companion to Esther, Judith and Susanna.* Sheffield, Eng.: Sheffield Academic Press, 1995.

———, and Carole Fontaine, eds. *A Feminist Companion to Reading the Bible.* Sheffield, Eng.: Sheffield Academic Press, 1997.

———, and Fokkelien van Dijk-Hemmes. *On Gendering Texts: Female and Male Voices in the Hebrew Bible.* Leiden: E. J. Brill, 1993.

Brooke, George J. "A Long-Lost Song of Miriam." *Biblical Archaeology Review* (May–June 1994).

Brooten, Bernadette J. "Iael προστάτησ in the Jewish Donative Inscription from Aphrodisias." In *The Future of Early Christianity: Essays in Honor of Helmut Koester,* ed. Birger A. Pearson. Minneapolis: Fortress, 1991.

—. "'Junia . . . Outstanding Among the Apostles' (Romans 16:7)." In *Women Priests: A Catholic Commentary on the Vatican Declaration,* ed. Leonard Swidler and Arlene Swidler. New York: Paulist Press, 1977.

—. *Love Between Women: Early Christian Responses to Female Homoeroticism.* Chicago: University of Chicago Press, 1996.

—. *Women Leaders in the Ancient Synagogue: Inscriptional Evidence and Background Issues.* Chico, Calif.: Scholars Press, 1982.

Brown, Raymond E. *The Birth of the Messiah: A Commentary on the Infancy Narratives in Matthew and Luke.* New York: Doubleday, 1979.

—, Karl P. Donfried, Joseph A. Fitzmyer, and John Reumann, eds. *Mary in the New Testament.* Philadelphia: Fortress, 1978.

Buby, Bertrand. *Mary of Galilee.* Vol. 1, *Mary in the New Testament.* New York: Alba House, 1994. Vol. 2, *Woman of Israel — Daughter of Zion.* New York: Alba House, 1995.

Büchman, Christina, and Celina Spiegel, eds. *Out of the Garden: Women Writers on the Bible.* New York: Fawcett Columbine, 1995.

Camp, Claudia V. *Wisdom and the Feminine in the Book of Proverbs.* Sheffield, Eng.: Almond, 1985.

Castelli, Elizabeth A. "Les Belles Infidèles/Fidelity or Feminism?" *Journal of Feminist Studies in Religion* 6, no. 2 (1990).

Catholic Bible Association. "Women and Priestly Ministry: The New Testament Evidence." *Catholic Bible Quarterly* 41, no. 4 (Oct. 1979).

Cazden, Elizabeth. *Antoinette Brown Blackwell: A Biography.* Old Westbury, N.Y.: Feminist Press, 1983.

Charland, Paul V. *Madame saincte Anne et son culte au moyen âge.* Paris: Librairie Alphonse Picard et Fils, 1913.

Christ, Carol P. *Laughter of Aphrodite: Reflections on a Journey to the Goddess.* San Francisco: Harper & Row, 1987.

—, and Judith Plaskow, eds. *Womanspirit Rising: A Feminist Reader in Religion.* San Francisco: Harper & Row, 1979.

Collins, Adela Yarbro, ed. *Feminist Perspectives on Biblical Scholarship.* Chico, Calif.: Scholars Press, 1985.

Corley, Kathleen E. "Feminist Myths of Christian Origins." In *Rethinking Christian Origins: Essays in Honor of Burton L. Mack,* ed. Elizabeth Castelli and Hal Taussig. Philadelphia: Trinity Press International, 1996.

——. "Jesus, Women and the Religious and Social Environment of Palestine." Paper presented at the annual meeting of the Society of Biblical Literature, New Orleans, Nov. 23–26, 1996.

——. *Private Women, Public Meals: Social Conflict in the Synoptic Tradition.* Peabody, Mass.: Hendrickson, 1993.

Craigie, Peter C. "The Tablets from Ugarit and Their Importance for Biblical Studies." *Biblical Archaeology Review* (Sept.–Oct. 1983): 62–73.

Craven, Toni, ed. *Collegeville Bible Commentary.* Vol. 16, *Ezekiel and Daniel.* Collegeville, Minn.: Liturgical Press, 1986.

——. "Women Who Lied for Faith." In *Justice and the Holy: Essays in Honor of Walter Harrelson,* ed. Douglas A. Knight and Peter J. Paris. Atlanta: Scholars Press, 1989.

Crook, Margaret Brackenbury. *Women and Religion.* Boston: Beacon Press, 1964.

Crossan, John Dominic. *The Historical Jesus.* San Francisco: HarperCollins, 1991.

Cunneen, Sally. *In Search of Mary.* New York: Ballantine, 1996.

Daly, Mary. *Beyond God the Father: Toward a Philosophy of Women's Liberation.* Boston: Beacon Press, 1973.

——. *The Church and the Second Sex.* Boston: Beacon Press, 1968.

——. *Gyn/Ecology.* Boston: Beacon Press, 1978.

——. *Pure Lust.* Boston: Beacon Press, 1984.

Daneliou, Jean. *The Ministry of Women in the Early Church.* London: Faith Press, 1961.

Dever, William G. "Asherah, Consort of Yahweh?: New Evidence from Kuntillet Ajrûd." *Bulletin of the American Schools of Oriental Research* (Summer 1984): 21–37.

Donnelly, Doris K. "Mary: A Sign of Contradiction?" *In All Generations*

Shall Call Me Blessed, ed. Francis A. Eigo. Philadelphia: Villanova University Press, 1994.

———, ed. *Mary, Woman of Nazareth: Biblical and Theological Perspectives*. New York: Paulist Press, 1989.

Douglas, Ann. *The Feminization of American Culture*. New York: Knopf, 1977.

Dubois, Ellen Carol, ed. *The Elizabeth Cady Stanton–Susan B. Anthony Reader: Correspondence, Writings, Speeches*. Rev. ed. Boston: Northeastern University Press, 1992.

Dulles, Avery, et al. "Women's Ordination: Six Responses." *Commonweal* (July 15, 1994).

Eigo, Francis A., ed. *All Generations Shall Call Me Blessed*. Philadelphia: Villanova University Press, 1994.

Erasmus, Desiderius. *The Praise of Folly*. Princeton, N.J.: Princeton University Press, 1941.

Fander, Monika. "Historical Critical Methods." In *Searching the Scriptures*, ed. Elisabeth Schüssler Fiorenza. New York: Crossroad, 1994.

Fewell, Danna Nolan, and David M. Gunn. *Gender, Power, and Promise: The Subject of the Bible's First Story*. Nashville, Tenn.: Abingdon, 1993.

Flusser, David, Jaroslav Pelikan, and Justin Lang, eds. *Mary: Images of the Mother of Jesus in Jewish and Christian Perspective*. Philadelphia: Fortress, 1986.

Fox, Everett. *The Five Books of Moses: Genesis, Exodus, Leviticus, Numbers, and Deuteronomy*. New York: Schocken, 1995.

Freedman, David Noel, ed. *The Anchor Bible Dictionary*. 6 vols. New York: Doubleday, 1992.

Friedan, Betty. *The Feminine Mystique*. 1963. New York: Norton, 1983.

Friedman, Richard Elliott. *Who Wrote the Bible?* New York: Summit, 1987.

Frymer-Kensky, Tikva. *In the Wake of the Goddesses: Women, Culture and the Biblical Transformation of Pagan Myth*. New York: Ballantine, 1992.

———. *Motherprayer*. New York: Riverhead, 1995.

Fuchs, Esther. "'For I have the way of women': Deception, Gender, and Ideology in Biblical Narrative." *Semeia* 42 (1988).

———. "The Literary Character of Mothers and Sexual Politics in the Hebrew Bible." In *Feminist Perspectives on Biblical Scholarship*, ed. Adela Yarbro Collins. Chico, Calif.: Scholars Press, 1985.

———. "Who Is Hiding the Truth? Deceptive Women and Biblical Androcentricism." In *Feminist Perspectives on Biblical Scholarship*, ed. Adela Yarbro Collins. Chico, Calif.: Scholars Press, 1985.

Funk, Robert W., Roy W. Hoover, and the Jesus Seminar. *The Five Gospels*. New York: Macmillan, 1993.

Gage, Matilda Joslyn. *Woman, Church, and State*. 1893. Salem, N.H.: Ayer, 1992.

Gifford, Carolyn de Swarte. "American Women and the Bible: The Nature of Woman as a Hermeneutical Issue." In *Feminist Perspectives on Biblical Scholarship*, ed. Adela Yarbro Collins. Chico, Calif.: Scholars Press, 1985.

———. "Politicizing the Sacred Texts: Elizabeth Cady Stanton and *The Woman's Bible*." In *Searching the Scriptures*. Vol.1, A *Feminist Introduction*, ed. Elisabeth Schüssler Fiorenza. New York: Crossroad, 1993.

Gimbutas, Marija. *Gods and Goddesses*. Berkeley: University of California Press, 1974.

———. *The Language of the Goddess*. New York: Harper & Row, 1989.

Goitein, S. D. "Women as Creators of Biblical Genres." *Pretexts* 8 (1988).

Goranson, Stephen. "The Battle Over the Holy Day at Dura-Europos." *Bible Review* (Aug. 1996): 22–44.

Gordon, Cyrus H. *Ugarit and Minoan Crete*. New York: Norton, 1966.

Gottwald, Norman K. *The Tribes of Yahweh: A Sociology of the Religion of Liberated Israel, 1250–1050 B.C.E.* Maryknoll: Orbis, 1979.

Greenfield, Jonas C. "The Hebrew Bible and Canaanite Literature." In *The Literary Guide to the Bible*, ed. Robert Alter and Frank Kermode. Cambridge, Mass.: Harvard University Press, 1987.

Greenspahn, Frederick E. "Words That Occur in the Bible Only Once — How Hard Are They to Translate?" *Bible Review* (Feb. 1985).

Griffith, Elisabeth. *In Her Own Right: The Life of Elizabeth Cady Stanton*. New York: Oxford University Press, 1984.

Grimké, Sarah. *Letters on the Equality of the Sexes and Other Essays.* 1838. Ed. Elizabeth Ann Bartlett. New Haven: Yale University Press, 1984.

Gross, Rita M. *Feminism and Religion: An Introduction.* Boston: Beacon Press, 1996.

Gryson, Roger. *The Ministry of Women in the Early Church.* Trans. Jean Laporte and Mary Louise Hall. Collegeville, Minn.: Liturgical Press, 1976.

Haddad, Yvonne Yazbeck, and Ellison Banks Findly, eds. *Women, Religion, and Social Change.* Albany: State University of New York Press, 1985.

Hadley, Judith M. "Some Drawings and Inscriptions on Two Pithoi from Kuntillet Ajrûd." *Vetus Testamentum* 37, vol. 2 (1987): 181–211.

Haines-Eitzen, Kim. "Girls Trained in the Art of Beautiful Writing: Female Scribes in Roman Antiquity." Paper presented at the annual meeting of the Society of Biblical Literature, New Orleans, Nov. 23–26, 1996. Publication forthcoming in *Journal of Early Christian Studies.*

Halpern, Baruch. "Erasing History: The Minimalist Assault on Ancient Israel." *Bible Review* (Dec. 1995): 26–27.

Hamington, Maurice. *Hail Mary?: The Struggle for Ultimate Womanhood in Catholicism.* New York: Routledge, 1995.

Hardesty, Nancy. *Women Called to Witness: Evangelical Feminism in the Nineteenth Century.* Nashville: Abingdon, 1984.

Hardwick, Dana. *Oh Thou Woman That Bringest Good Things: The Life and Work of Katherine C. Bushnell.* Kearney, Neb.: Morris, 1995.

Haskins, Susan. *Mary Magdalene: Myth and Metaphor.* New York: Harcourt Brace, 1993.

Heschel, Susannah. "Anti-Judaism in Christian Feminist Theory." *Tikkun* 5, no. 3 (1990).

Horváth, Eugene. *The Banat: A Forgotten Chapter of European History.* Budapest: Sabkany, 1931.

Irvin, Dorothy. "The Ministry of Women in the Early Church: The Archaeological Evidence." *Duke Divinity School Review* 45, no. 2 (1980): 76–86.

Jobling, David. *The Sense of Biblical Narrative: Structural Analyses in the Hebrew Bible*. Sheffield, Eng.: JSOT Press, 1986.

John Paul II. *Letter of the Holy Father to Women*. Washington, D.C.: United States Catholic Conference, 1995.

———. *On the Dignity and Vocation of Women*, Mulieres Dignitatem. Washington, D.C.: United States Catholic Conference, 1988.

Johnson, Elizabeth A. *She Who Is: The Mystery of God in Feminist Theological Discourse*. New York: Crossroad, 1992.

———. "Toward a Theology of Mary: Past, Present, Future." In *All Generations Shall Call Me Blessed*, ed. Francis A. Eigo. Philadelphia: Villanova University Press, 1994.

Joliffe, T. R. *Letters from Palestine*. London: Black, Black, and Young, 1822.

Josephus, Flavius. *The Life and Works of Flavius Josephus*. Trans. William Whitson. Philadelphia: Universal Book and Bible House, 1949.

Kates, Judith A., and Gail Twersky Reimer, eds. *Reading Ruth: Contemporary Women Reclaim a Sacred Story*. New York: Ballantine, 1994.

Kendrick, Eliza Hall. *History of Bible Teaching at Wellesley College, 1875–1950*. Wellesley, Mass.: Wellesley College, 1932.

Kermode, Frank. Review of *The Book of J. New York Times Book Review*, Sept. 23, 1990.

Kienzle, Beverly, and Pamela Walker, eds. *The Heritage of Magdalene: Women Prophets and Preachers in the Christian Tradition*. Berkeley: University of California Press, forthcoming.

King, Karen L., ed. *Images of the Feminine in Gnosticism*. Philadelphia: Fortress, 1988.

———. "Introduction." In *The Gospel of Mary*, ed. Douglas M. Parrott. Leiden: E. J. Brill, 1988.

Kleiner, Diana E. E., and Susan B. Matheson, eds. *I, Claudia: Women in Ancient Rome*. New Haven, Conn.: Yale University Art Gallery, 1996.

Koester, Helmut. *Ancient Christian Gospels: Their History and Development*. London: Trinity/SCM, 1990.

————. *History and Literature of Early Christianity.* New York: Walter de Gruyter, 1980.

————. *Introduction to the New Testament.* New York: Walter de Gruyter, 1982.

Kogan, Herman. *The Great EB: The Story of the Encyclopaedia Britannica.* Chicago: University of Chicago Press, 1958.

Kraemer, Ross Shepard. *Her Share of the Blessings: Women's Religions Among Pagans, Jews, and Christians in the Greco-Roman World.* New York: Oxford University Press, 1992.

Kroeger, Catherine Clark, Mary Evans, and Elaine Storkey, eds. *Study Bible for Women: The New Testament.* Grand Rapids, Mich.: Baker, 1995.

Lanser, Susan S. "(Feminist) Criticism in the Garden: Inferring Genesis 2–3." *Semeia* 41 (1988): 67–84.

Leach, Edmund, and D. Alan Aycock. *Structuralist Interpretations of Biblical Myth.* Cambridge, Eng.: Cambridge University Press, 1983.

Lefkowitz, Mary. "Fruits of the Loom." *New York Review of Books,* June 26, 1997.

Lerner, Gerda. *Why History Matters: Life and Thought.* New York: Oxford University Press, 1997.

Levine, Amy-Jill. "Character Construction and Community Formation in the Book of Judith." Society of Biblical Literature Seminar Papers (1989).

————. "Sacrifice and Salvation: Otherness and Domestication in the Book of Judith." In *A Feminist Companion to Esther, Judith, and Susanna,* ed. Athalya Brenner. Sheffield, Eng.: Sheffield Academic Press, 1995.

————. *The Social and Ethnic Dimensions of Matthean Social History.* Lewiston, N.Y.: Edwin Mellen, 1988.

————. "Tobit." *Bible Review* 8 (Aug. 1992).

————. *"Women Like This": New Perspectives on Jewish Women in the Greco-Roman World.* Atlanta: Scholars Press, 1991.

Malvern, Marjorie M. *Venus in Sackcloth: The Magdalene's Origins and Metamorphoses.* Carbondale: Southern Illinois University Press, 1975.

Martin, Edward Trueblood. *I Flew Them Home: A Pilot's Story of the Yemenite Airlift.* New York: Herzl, 1958.

Matheson, Susan B. *Dura-Europos.* New Haven, Conn.: Yale University Art Gallery, 1982.

Meier, John P. *A Marginal Jew: Rethinking the Historical Jesus.* 2 vols. New York: Doubleday, 1991.

Melton, J. Gordon, ed. *The Churches Speak on Women's Ordination: Official Statements from Religious Bodies and Ecumenical Organizations.* Detroit: Gale Research Inc., 1991.

Metzger, Bruce M., and Michael D. Coogan, eds. *The Oxford Companion to the Bible.* Oxford: Oxford University Press, 1993.

Meyers, Carol L. *Discovering Eve: Ancient Israelite Women in Context.* New York: Oxford University Press, 1988.

————. "The Family in Early Israel." *In Families in Ancient Israel,* ed. Leo E. Perdue, Joseph Blenkinsopp, John J. Collins, and Carol L. Meyers. Louisville, Ky.: Westminster/John Knox, 1997.

————. "Kinship and Kingship: The Early Monarchy." In *The Oxford History of the Biblical World,* ed. M. D. Coogan. New York: Oxford University Press, 1998.

————. "Text Without Context: On Bloom's Misreading of J." *Iowa Review* 21, no. 3 (1991).

————, ed. A *Dictionary of Women in Scripture.* Boston: Houghton Mifflin, forthcoming.

Meyers, Eric, and Carol L. Meyers. "Finders of a Real Lost Ark." *Biblical Archaeology Review* (Nov.–Dec. 1981): 24–39.

Mickelsen, Alvera, ed. *Women, Authority, and the Bible.* Downers Grove, Ill.: InterVarsity, 1986.

Miles, Jack. *God: A Biography.* New York: Knopf, 1995.

Milne, Pamela J. "Feminist Interpretations of the Bible: Then and Now." *Bible Review* (Oct. 1992).

Morris, Joan. *The Lady Was a Bishop: The Hidden History of Women with Clerical Ordination and the Jurisdiction of Bishops.* New York: Macmillan, 1973.

Morton, Nelle. "Preaching the Word." In *Sexist Religion and Women in the Church: No More Silence!* ed. Alice L. Hageman. New York: Association Press, 1974.

"Ms. Moses: Did a Woman Write Scripture?" *Time*, Oct. 1, 1990.

Murray, Judith Sargent. "On the Equality of the Sexes." In *The Feminist Papers: From Adams to Beauvoir*, ed. Alice S. Rossi. New York: Bantam, 1973.

National Council of the Churches of Christ in the U.S.A. *An Inclusive-Language Lectionary*. Atlanta: John Knox, 1987.

Netzer, Ehud, and Zeev Weiss, eds. *Zippori*. Jerusalem: Israel Exploration Society, 1994.

Newsom, Carol A., and Sharon H. Ringe, eds. *The Women's Bible Commentary*. Louisville, Ky.: Westminster/John Knox, 1992.

Niditch, Susan. *Ancient Israelite Religion*. New York: Oxford University Press, 1997.

————. *Folklore and the Hebrew Bible*. Minneapolis: Fortress, 1993.

————. *Oral World and Written Word: Ancient Israelite Literature*. Louisville, Ky.: Westminster/John Knox, 1996.

————. *Underdogs and Tricksters: A Prelude to Folklore*. San Francisco: Harper & Row, 1987.

Nolan, Louis. *The Basilica of S. Clemente in Rome*. 3rd ed. Grottaferrata: Tipografia Italo-Orientale "S. Nilo," 1925.

Pagels, Elaine. *Adam, Eve, and the Serpent*. New York: Random House, 1988.

————. *The Gnostic Gospels*. 1979. New York: Vintage, 1989.

Pardes, Ilana. *Countertraditions in the Bible: A Feminist Approach*. Cambridge, Mass.: Harvard University Press, 1992.

Parrott, Douglas M., ed. "The Gospel of Mary (BG 8502,1)." Trans. George W. MacRae and R. McL. Wilson. In *The Nag Hammadi Library in English*, ed. James M. Robinson. Leiden: E. J. Brill, 1988.

Patai, Raphael. *The Hebrew Goddess*. 1967. Detroit: Wayne State University Press, 1990.

Pearson, Birger A., ed. *The Future of Christianity: Essays in Honor of Helmut Koester*. Minneapolis: Fortress, 1991.

Pelikan, Jaroslav. *Mary Through the Centuries: Her Place in the History of Culture*. New Haven, Conn.: Yale University Press, 1996.

Peskowitz, Miriam A. *Spinning Fantasies: Rabbis, Gender, and History*. Berkeley: University of California Press, 1997.

Pinnock, Clark H. "Biblical Authority and the Issues in Question." In *Women, Authority, and the Bible,* ed. Alvera Mickelsen. Downers Grove, Ill.: InterVarsity, 1986.

Plaskow, Judith. "Blaming Jews for Inventing Patriarchy." *Lilith* 7 (1980).

———. *Standing Again at Sinai: Judaism from a Feminist Perspective.* San Francisco: Harper & Row, 1990.

Rahner, Karl. *Mary, the Mother of the Lord.* New York: Herder and Herder, 1963.

Ranke-Heinemann, Uta. *Eunuchs for the Kingdom of Heaven.* Trans. Peter Heinegg. New York: Doubleday, 1990.

———. *Putting Away Childish Things: The Virgin Birth, the Empty Tomb, and Other Fairy Tales You Don't Need to Believe to Have a Living Faith.* Trans. Peter Heinegg. San Francisco: HarperCollins, 1992.

Rashkow, Ilona N. *The Phallacy of Genesis: A Feminist-Psychoanalytic Approach.* Louisville, Ky.: Westminster/John Knox, 1993.

Reimer, Ivoni Richter. *Women in the Acts of the Apostles.* Trans. Linda M. Maloney. Minneapolis: Fortress, 1995.

Rice, Donna S. "The 'New' Archaeology." *Wilson Quarterly* (Spring 1985).

Rich, Adrienne. *On Lies, Secrets, and Silence: Selected Prose, 1966–1978.* New York: Norton, 1979.

Robinson, James M., ed. *The Nag Hammadi Library in English.* Trans. and introduced by members of the Coptic Gnostic Library Project of the Institute for Antiquity and Christianity. Leiden: E. J. Brill, 1988.

———, Paul Hoffmann, and John S. Kloppenborg, eds. *Documenta Q.* Leuven: Peeters, 1996.

Romanowicz, Janet V., and Rita P. Wright. "Gendered Perspectives in the Classroom." In *Gender and Archaeology,* ed. Rita P. Wright. Philadelphia: University of Pennsylvania Press, 1996.

Rossi, Alice S., ed. *The Feminist Papers: From Adams to Beauvoir.* New York: Bantam, 1973.

Rousseau, John J., and Rami Arav. *Jesus and His World.* Minneapolis: Fortress, 1995.

Ruether, Rosemary Radford. *Sexism and God-Talk: Toward a Feminist Theology.* Boston: Beacon Press, 1983.

———, and Eleanor McLaughlin, ed. *Women of Spirit.* New York: Simon and Schuster, 1979.

Russell, Letty M., ed. *Feminist Interpretation of the Bible.* Philadelphia: Westminster, 1985.

Sacred Congregation for the Doctrine of Faith. "Declaration on the Question of the Admission of Women to the Ministerial Priesthood." *Origins* 6 (Feb. 3, 1977).

Salway, Peter. *The Illustrated History of Roman Britain.* Oxford: Oxford University Press, 1993.

Sanders, E. P. *Judaism: Practices and Beliefs, 63 BCE–66 CE.* Philadelphia: Fortress, 1992.

Saunders, Ernest W. *Searching the Scriptures: A History of the Society of Biblical Literature, 1880–1980.* Chico, Calif.: Scholars Press, 1982.

Schaberg, Jane. "The Contribution of Feminist Scholarship to Historical Jesus Research." Unpublished manuscript, June 1993. A version of this paper appears in *Continuum* 3 (1994).

———. "Fast Forwarding to Magdalene." *Semeia* 74 (1996): 33–45.

———. "How Mary Magdalene Became a Whore." *Bible Review* (Oct. 1992): 31–52.

———. *The Illegitimacy of Jesus: A Feminist Theological Interpretation of the Infancy Narratives.* San Francisco: Harper & Row, 1987.

———. "Thinking Back Through the Magdalene." *Continuum* 1, no. 2, (Winter–Spring 1991).

Schneemelcher, Wilhelm, ed. *New Testament Apocrypha.* Trans. J. B. Higgins and others. Philadelphia: Westminster, 1963–1966.

Schottroff, Luise. *Lydia's Impatient Sisters: A Feminist Social History of Early Christianity.* Trans. Barbara and Martin Rumscheidt. Louisville, Ky.: Westminster/John Knox, 1995.

Schüssler Fiorenza, Elisabeth. "Biblical Interpretation in the Context of Church and Ministry: A Perspective for Theology for Christian Ministry." *Word and World* 10, no. 4 (Fall 1990).

———. *Bread Not Stone: The Challenge of Feminist Biblical Interpretation.* Boston: Beacon Press, 1984.

———. "Changing the Paradigms." *Christian Century* (Sept. 5–12, 1990): 796–800.

———. *Der vergessene Partner*. Dusseldorf: Patmos Verlag, 1964.

———. *Discipleship of Equals: A Critical Feminist Ekklesia-logy of Liberation*. New York: Crossroad, 1993.

———. "Feminist Theology and New Testament Interpretation." *Journal of Studies in the Old Testament* 22 (1982).

———. "Feminist Theology as a Critical Theology of Liberation." *Theological Studies* 36 (1975): 606–26.

———. *In Memory of Her: A Feminist Theological Reconstruction of Christian Origins*. New York: Crossroad, 1983.

———. "The 'Quilting' of Women's History: Phoebe of Cenchreae." In *Embodied Love*, ed. Paula M. Cooey, Sharon A. Farmer, and Mary Ellen Ross. San Francisco: Harper & Row, 1987.

———. "Wartime as Formative Experience." *Christian Century* (Aug. 16–23, 1995): 778–79.

———, ed. *Searching the Scriptures*. Vol. 1, *A Feminist Introduction*. New York: Crossroad, 1993. Vol. 2, *A Feminist Commentary*. New York: Crossroad, 1997.

Selvidge, Marla J. *Notorious Voices: Feminist Biblical Interpretation, 1500–1920*. New York: Continuum, 1996.

Sered, Susan Starr. *Women as Ritual Experts*. New York: Oxford University Press, 1992.

Shanks, Hershel, ed. *Feminist Approaches to the Bible*. Washington, D.C.: Biblical Archaeology Society, 1995.

Silberman, Neil Asher. "Who Were the Israelites?" *Archaeology* 45 (Mar.–Apr. 1992).

Slavens, Thomas P. "The Librarianship of Charles Augustus Briggs." *Union Quarterly Review* 24 (Summer 1969).

Smith, Mark S. *The Early History of God*. San Francisco: HarperCollins, 1990.

Stanton, Elizabeth Cady. *Eighty Years and More: Reminiscences 1815–1897*. 1898. New York: Schocken, 1971.

———, ed. *The Woman's Bible*. 1895–98. 2 vols. New York: Arno, 1972.

Steichen, Donna. *Ungodly Rage: The Hidden Face of Catholic Feminism*. San Francisco: Ignatius, 1992.

Stern, Ephraim. "How Bad Was Ahab?" *Biblical Archaeology Review* (Mar.–Apr. 1993).

Suggs, M. Jack, Katharine Doob Sakenfeld, and James R. Mueller, eds. *The Oxford Study Bible*. New York: Oxford University Press, 1992.

Swidler, Leonard. *Biblical Affirmations of Woman*. Philadelphia: Westminster, 1979.

———. "Jesus Was a Feminist." *Catholic World* (January 1971): 177–83.

———. *Women in Judaism: The Status of Women in Formative Judaism*. Metuchen, N.J.: Scarecrow, 1976.

———. *Yeshua: A Model for Moderns*. Kansas City, Mo.: Sheed & Ward, 1988.

Taylor, William C. *The New Bible: Pro and Con*. New York: Vantage, 1955.

Thistlethwaite, Susan Brooks. "The Bible and the Feminists." *Christianity and Crisis* (Feb. 1, 1993).

Tolotti, Francesco. *Il Cimitero di Priscilla*. Vatican City: Pontifical Institute of Christian Archaeology, 1970.

Torjesen, Karen Jo. *When Women Were Priests*. San Francisco: HarperCollins, 1993.

Trible, Phyllis. "Depatriarchalizing in Biblical Interpretation." *Journal of the American Academy of Religion* 4, no. 1 (Mar. 1973).

———. *God and the Rhetoric of Sexuality*. Philadelphia: Fortress, 1978.

———. "Postscript: Jottings on the Journey." In *Feminist Interpretation of the Bible*, ed. Letty M. Russell. Philadelphia: Westminster, 1985.

———. *Rhetorical Criticism: Context, Method, and the Book of Jonah*. Minneapolis: Fortress, 1994.

———. *Texts of Terror: Literary-Feminist Readings of Biblical Narratives*. Philadelphia: Fortress, 1984.

Tsafrir, Yoram. "Ancient Churches in the Holy Land." *Biblical Archaeology Review* 9, no. 5 (Sept.–Oct. 1993): 26–39.

Twain, Mark. *The Complete Travel Books of Mark Twain*. Ed. Charles Neider. Garden City, N.Y.: Doubleday, 1966–.

Vanderkam, James C., ed. *"No One Spoke Ill of Her": Essays on Judith*. Atlanta: Scholars Press, 1992.

van der Meer, Haye. *Women Priests in a Catholic Church?: A Theologi-*

cal-Historical Investigation. Trans. Arlene and Leonard Swidler. Philadelphia: Temple University Press, 1973.

Warner, Marina. *Alone of All Her Sex: The Myth and Cult of the Virgin Mary.* New York: Knopf, 1976.

Wegner, Judith Romney. *Chattel or Person?: Women in the Mishnah.* New York: Oxford University Press, 1988.

Weems, Renita J. *Just a Sister Away: A Womanist Vision of Women's Relationships in the Bible.* San Diego: LuraMedia, 1988.

Wire, Antoinette Clark. *The Corinthian Women Prophets: A Reconstruction Through Paul's Rhetoric.* Minneapolis: Fortress, 1990.

Witherington, Ben. *Women in the Ministry of Jesus: A Study of Jesus' Attitudes to Women and Their Roles as Reflected in His Earthly Life.* Cambridge, Eng.: Cambridge University Press, 1984.

Woodward, Kenneth L., with Larry Wilson. "The Woman Who Invented God." *Newsweek*, Oct. 1, 1990.

Worth, Roland H., Jr. *The Bible Translations: A History Through Source Documents.* Jefferson, N.C.: McFarland, 1992.

Wright, Rita P., ed. *Gender and Archaeology.* Philadelphia: University of Pennsylvania Press, 1996.

Yadin, Yigael. *Masada: Herod's Fortress and the Zealots' Last Stand.* Trans. Moshe Pearlman. London: Weidenfeld and Nicolson, 1966.

Zornberg, Avivah Gottlieb. *Genesis: The Beginning of Desire.* Philadelphia: Jewish Publication Society, 1995.

ACKNOWLEDGMENTS

This book has been made possible by the willingness of many people in the field of biblical studies or with related interests and knowledge to offer their guidance — in some cases by providing unpublished papers and bibliographies, in many other cases by making time available for conversations. A few of the conversations began almost a decade ago. Those in and around the field who have been of assistance include Mieke Bal, Timothy K. Beal, Bernadette Brooten, Anne H. Carr, Michael D. Coogan, Kathleen E. Corley, Tikva Frymer-Kensky, Karen L. King, Ross S. Kraemer, Amy-Jill Levine, Carol L. Meyers, Elaine Pagels, Jaroslav Pelikan, Judith Plaskow, Jane Schaberg, Elisabeth Schüssler Fiorenza, Leonard Swidler, Karen Jo Torjesen, Phyllis Trible, and David Tracy. I am also grateful to Charlotte Allen, Helène Aylon, John Breslin, S. J., and Leo O'Donovan, S. J.; and to Missy Daniel of the Harvard Divinity School, and the producer and Interfaith minister Mary Byrne Hoffmann. Charles Trueheart, a dependable and insightful friend, has always been available to talk about anything.

The staff at *The Atlantic Monthly* has over the years offered invaluable help. William Whitworth, the editor-in-chief, has been ever generous with advice and support; his values and standards are in themselves an unspoken form of advice and support. *The Word According to Eve* had its genesis in an *Atlantic* article that Bill Whitworth encouraged and published (in 1993). In various ways Leslie Cauldwell, Avril Cornel, Jack Beatty, C. Michael Curtis, Gregg Easterbrook, Robert D. Kaplan, Corby Kummer, Toby Lester, Deborah McGill, Lucie Prinz, Allan Reeder, Mileta Roe, Yvonne Rolzhausen, Sue Parilla, Martha Spaulding, Scott

Stossel, Barbara Wallraff, and Lowell Weiss have all provided both practical help and necessary perspective. A number of capable research assistants have pursued aspects of this project. They include Lessie Arnold, Emily Baillargeon, Anastasia Bakolas, Christopher Berdik, Scott Brown, Alison Callahan, Alexandra Custis, Mai Fernando, Celeste Katz, Francie Lin, Julia Livshin, Ashley Malcolm, Ryan Nally, Andrew Sargent, Maura Shea, and Jennifer Silverman. Charley Davis, the last of this steadfast troop, deserves particular thanks.

Much of the work on this book was made possible by the Corporation of Yaddo, at whose retreat in Saratoga Springs, New York, I spent much of the spring of 1997. This proved to be an enormously productive and in many ways essential period. Michael Sundell and his staff at Yaddo have earned the gratitude of hundreds of writers and artists. I am privileged to be among that number.

I am also privileged to have had the guidance of Raphael Sagalyn, of the Sagalyn Agency, and Peter Davison, of Houghton Mifflin. As others have discovered, Peter brings to his editorial endeavors not only a wide knowledge, a distinctive sensibility, and a stylish taste, but also long experience in administering the balm of discipline and the lash of patience. Liz Duvall and Mindy Keskinen of Houghton Mifflin and Amy Pastan and Ethan Kline of the Sagalyn Agency were of great assistance at various stages of the process.

Anna Marie, my wife and longtime editor, has lived with this project for longer than she cares to remember and contributed more to it than she can realize, and more than anyone else. I owe a debt as well to my children, Jack, Anna, and Tim, for their patience and forbearance. On balance, however, they remain in arrears.

INDEX

Aaron, 55, 57

Abel-Beth-Maacah: wise woman from, 102

Abolitionist movement, 24–27, 29, 39

Abraham, 42, 61, 122

Acts of Paul and Thecla, 214, 225–26, 227

Acts of the Apostles, 158, 177, 186, 187, 222; women in, 188–89

Adam, 2, 106, 118; amount of text devoted to, 97; Christ and, 161; interpretations of role and status of, 13, 20–23, 24, 52–54, 58–59, 226; sexualization of, 53

Adam, Eve, and the Serpent (Pagels), 229, 231–32

Adams, Henry, 155, 157

'adham, 53, 58–59

Adonai, 8. *See also Yahweh*

African Methodist Episcopal Church, 175

agrarian society, 67–68, 83; sexual egalitarianism in, 71; women's multiple responsibilities in, 68, 71–72, 79–80

Ahab, King, 25, 63, 91–92

Ahasuerus, King, 92

Aholibamah, wife of Esau, 33

Akkadian language, 44, 76, 104

Alexander the Great, 126

Allenby, Edmund Henry Hynman, 63

almah, 160

Alone of All Her Sex: The Myth and Cult of the Virgin Mary (Warner), 157

Alter, Robert, 97

Ambrose, Saint, 54

American Academy of Religion: annual meeting of, 1–3

American Baptists: on women in the ministry, 7

American Schools of Oriental Research, 205–6

American Standard Version, 9

Amnon: rape of his sister, 42, 60

Anchor Bible Dictionary, 84

cism, 46–47; work on Book of Jonah, 48

Truth, Sojourner, 39, 157

Tryphaena, 177, 178, 221

Tryphosa, 177, 178, 221

Tubman, Harriet, 39

Turner, John D., 206

Twain, Mark, 195

Tychinos, 179

Tyndale, William, 9

Ugaritic language, 44–46

Ugaritic tablets, 45

Ungodly Rage (Steichen), 190

Union Theological Seminary, New York, 7, 38–40, 43–44, 133

United Methodists: on women in the ministry, 7

unpointed languages, 45

Updike, John, 39

urban society: growth of ancient, 82–83; at time of Jesus, 126

Uriah, 114, 161, 162

Uttu, goddess, 106

Valentinians, 213, 227

Vanderbilt University Divinity School, 7

Vatican. *See also* Catholic Church: and cult of Mary, 155–56, 157; on translations of the Bible, 9, 10; and women in the ministry, 7, 140, 173–75

veiling of women, 105

Verhoeven, Paul, 128

Veturia Paulla, 191, 192

Via Salaria catacombs, 172–73

victory songs: by women, 101

violence: against women in the Bible, 121–22; by women in the Bible, 109–21

virgin: translations of term, 160

virgin birth, 122, 156, 160–61, 164; feminists and, 157

Visotzky, Rabbi Burton, 41

Vulgate, 9

Walker, Barbara, 6

Wall Street Journal, 6

"wandering rock" image, 123

Warner, Marina, 157, 214

weavers, female, 68, 79, 104–5

wedding ceremonies: in ancient Israel, 90; Yemeni, 102

Wegner, Judith Romney, 69

Wellesley College, 36, 75–76

When Women Were Priests (Torjesen), 185–86, 187, 207

Whittier, John Greenleaf, 25

"Who Is Hiding the Truth?" (Fuchs), 114

Wicca, 6

widows: status of Israelite, 64

Wilkerson, Ralph, 184

Willard, Frances, 35, 49

Wire, Antoinette Clark, 186

Wisdom, Lady, 87, 101–3, 107; Jesus and, 136–37; Mary as, 170

wise women, 87, 101–3, 108; Yemeni, 102

Witherington, Ben, III, 142–43